EXECUCOMP

EXECUCOMP

Maximum Management
with the New Computers

F. WARREN BENTON

JOHN WILEY & SONS

New York   Chichester   Brisbane   Toronto   Singapore

Library of Congress Cataloging in Publication Data:

Benton, F. Warren, 1948–
    Execucomp: maximum management with the new computers.

    Bibliography: p.
    Includes index.
    1. Management—Data processing. I. Title.

HD30.2.B46 1983   658'.054   83–17028
ISBN 0–471–89828–7

Printed in the United States of America

10 9 8 7 6 5 4 3 2 1

To Judy, Nicky, and Elizabeth

PREFACE

The ability to use computers effectively is critical to the achievement of organizational objectives and many individual career goals. However, most of the books and much of the available training emphasize the operation and programming of computers, or cater to very specific end-user groups. Yet the most basic decisions regarding computer systems, decisions as to their ultimate use within an organization, are usually made by managers who lack both familiarity with computer terminology and operations, and the proper perspective of their capabilities and limitations. As the pace of innovation accelerates, this deficiency becomes more significant, especially for the small business or individual computer user, or the user of a large system anticipating an upgrade of the system's terminals. Even larger management-oriented computer systems can be expected to become more flexible and versatile for users, challenging the managers using such systems.

This book is a comprehensive review of the uses of computers for the planning, organizing, and controlling of large and small business and governmental organizations. It is intended for managers in businesses and governmental agencies for professional reading and in-service training and career development, for individuals using computers for small businesses, as well as for upper undergraduate and MBA/MPA students. Focusing on the potential of the more recent computer technologies, including microcomputers, intelligent terminals of larger computer systems, and advanced office-oriented technologies, the book covers current approaches to management as well as such topical issues as productivity improvement, impacts of computers on employees, and effects of computers on organizations. Computer applications are examined to illustrate their possible contributions to these approaches and problems, and procedures for the planning and implementation of computer systems are presented.

The book includes sixteen "software profiles" which explain in a brief format a particular type of computer use in management, such as word processing, data base management, or graphics. The profiles occur as parts of chapters, but they are also identified separately for the following two reasons:

1. Separate identification allows readers to focus attention upon specific types of applications, when this is their immediate interest. The profile discussions then direct the reader to appropriate chapters for more detailed discussions of specific approaches to management problems.

2. Because management goals and problems are not usually perceived by managers in categories that directly correspond with specific types of computer programs, this approach allows a book organization that is recognizable to managers, while avoiding duplicative and repetitive discussions of software.

Each chapter begins with a short fictional quote, to introduce the chapter topic. The realistic situations portrayed in these quotes are drawn from my own experience (and the experiences of those working with me) as the Director of the Oklahoma Department of Corrections, as a management consultant, as an associate director of a productivity center, and as a professor.

Many people have helped in the development of the book. It is a pleasure to have the opportunity to thank them. Judy Silberstein contributed in many ways, as an understanding wife and as a creative and insightful critic. At the John Jay College of Criminal Justice, City University of New York, and at the National Center for Public Productivity (an institute within that College), my colleagues provided support, encouragement, and a wealth of information. At John Wiley & Sons, John Mahaney provided the initial editorial commitment for the development of the book, and provided creative support as it was developed. Balwan Singh supervised the editorial aspects of the book's production, including the generic coding process necessary for typesetting the book directly from microcomputer diskettes. Jane Bloom did the copy editing. The design was conceived and executed by Lee Davidson. Kirk Bomont was the production supervisor.

F. Warren Benton

New York, New York
August 1983

CONTENTS

PART I.   THE MANAGER AND THE MACHINE   1

1. **Computers and Management in the 1980s**   3

2. **Computer Technology and the Manager**   18
    Software Profile 1:   Operating Systems   49
    Software Profile 2:   Telecommunications Programs   50
    Software Profile 3:   General-Purpose Languages   51
    Software Profile 4:   Graphics Equipment and Software   52

PART II.   MANAGEMENT APPLICATIONS   55

3. **Computer-Aided Strategic Decision Making**   57
    Software Profile 5:   Spreadsheet Computation
                           Programs   61
    Software Profile 6:   Statistical Analysis Packages   63
    Software Profile 7:   Specialized Programs and Models   64

4. **Computer-Aided Operational Management**   91
    Software Profile 8:   Accounting Systems   103
    Software Profile 9:   Resource Management Systems   105
    Software Profile 10:   Small-Scale Filing Systems   106

5. **The Office of the Future**   110
        Software Profile 11:   Word Processing Systems   125
        Software Profile 12:   Executive Support Systems   127

6. **Computers for Small Businesses and Agencies**   137

7. **Improving Productivity with Computers**   152
        Software Profile 13:   Management Analysis with
                                Computers   166
        Software Profile 14:   Computer-Aided Document
                                Research   167
        Software Profile 15:   Networks   169
        Software Profile 16:   Computer-Aided Training   170

PART III.   IMPACTS ON THE MANAGEMENT
            ENVIRONMENT   173

 8. **Management Problems with Computers**   175

 9. **Organizational Design for Computers**   194

10. **Employees and Computers**   213

11. **Implementing Computer Systems**   230

12. **Crime, Security, and Computers**   247

BIBLIOGRAPHY   265

INDEX   267

EXECUCOMP

PART

I

THE MANAGER AND
THE MACHINE

CHAPTER 1
COMPUTERS
AND MANAGEMENT
IN THE 1980s

I saw it coming. The secretaries had been issued word processing computers, several managers at work were using portable computers which they brought home periodically, and the company's big computer system was expanding every year, taking over accounting, then inventory, then some of our personnel records, and so forth. However, when my son and daughter came home from school with a listing of the computer programs they developed at school, I finally saw the light. I needed to develop my skills in this new technology. I bought a personal computer through a program at the company, which covers part of the cost. After some formal training as well as some effort on my own, I found the computer to be very useful. I also understood more fully the company's big computer system. Recently, the effort paid off. I was promoted past several other managers, to manage the development of a company-wide office automation program, primarily because of my experience with the computer.

Business and government organizations are turning to computers to maintain records, process documents, facilitate communication, and provide management with information upon which to base planning and operational decisions. Today, practically all businesses and government agencies, along with many individuals and small businesses, use computers for some aspect of their operations, and expanded use is inevitable.

During the 1960s and 1970s the greatest growth in computer use was in large organizations. With the advent of smaller personal and desktop systems, the 1980s will see greater expansion of use in small businesses and individual applications. The large-scale computer systems will not be unaffected by this change, as the traditional terminals—the work stations connected to the main computer—will be upgraded to offer the benefits of desktop computers. Thus, a terminal that was used during the 1970s only for information retrieval from the main computer, in the 1980s can be capable of many desktop computer operations as well. Use of the small computers and enhanced terminals offers important opportunities:

Small businesses can benefit from the economies of computer-based record systems, accounting and inventory systems, and management analysis services.

Computers can aid managers in making decisions, allowing them to consider a wide range of important but complex factors in planning overall business strategy.

Management employees at all levels can be freed from day-to-day paperwork to focus on more important problems and opportunities.

The office systems of the future can be a reality not only for large corporations and government agencies but for small businesses and individuals as well.

Great opportunities for improved productivity and profit do not come without challenge and risk. The decisions made by computer professionals about large computer systems during the 1960s and 1970s will be made in the 1980s by individual managers with respect to their desktop computers and enhanced terminals.

A new dimension of executive competence is required to select and implement computer systems successfully. Along with traditional skills in organization planning and control, budgeting and finance, and personnel management, executives will need to become skilled in the application of computers to their work. Not only must managers, small business operators and owners, and individuals understand the technology, operations, and potentials of desktop computers and enhanced terminals; they should also take advantage of the insights developed through success and failure of large-scale management computer systems over the last two decades. This experience will help managers achieve the greatest benefits and avoid common but expensive mistakes.

We will look closely at the new computers and their programs and potentials. We will also examine the experiences of larger businesses and organizations with large-scale systems, in order to apply lessons learned from past successes and failures to future systems, both large and small.

RECENT COMPUTER TECHNOLOGIES IN MANAGEMENT

Since their earliest development, computers have been applied to management problems. However, because of the cost of both the acquisition and operation of such systems, initial applications have had to be large and highly structured in operation. People who operated such systems were passive extensions of the technology.

Several technological developments of the 1970s and 1980s are changing that early pattern, making possible active participation and control of computing by managers. Most important have been the technological advances in many of the components of computers, including the chips that process the information, the memory devices that store the information, and the peripheral devices that put the information on paper, send it to other computers, and perform many other functions as well. These advances are lowering the price, size, and operating cost of computers. Systems can thus be developed expressly for individual users or smaller organizations, enabling control to shift to the local user.

Improvements in software (the instructions that tell the computers what to do) have enabled computers to serve users in a more flexible, friendly, and responsive manner. This has also increased the control of the local user over the computer.

Improvements in software technology have enabled many widely used application programs to be operated on many different brands and models of computers. This has led to greater competition among software developers, and a greater volume of sales, permitting a combination of high performance and individual specification that would have been beyond the budget of the typical user a decade ago.

Developments in the technology of office applications—including electronic networks interconnecting several computer work stations with such peripheral devices as printers, as well as with other computer systems and networks outside the office through telephone lines—enable management-oriented computer systems to do much more than was possible a decade ago.

These innovations immediately affect the individual owner-user of a computer system, whether in a small business, professional practice, or home application. The innovations will also affect users of large-scale computer systems. The expression "dumb terminal," while usually used to refer to a very minimal type of computer terminal, actually describes the condition of many terminals attached to larger systems. The terminal, consisting of a screen, keyboard, and perhaps a printer, is dependent on the mainframe. The people using the terminal therefore become dependent on the mainframe and its programs as well.

New technology will permit the terminal to become a more flexible, diversified, and responsive device. At times it will function under the control of the mainframe in the traditional manner. At other times it will function under the direct control of the local user, as a word processor or general office systems device. Sometimes it will function as a personal computer, providing services of professional and personal benefit. Sometimes, through telecommunications, it will tie up with other terminals or with other mainframe computer systems or networks, enabling access to functional services, data libraries, and other systems of general use. The new terminal will have a greater range of peripheral devices available, although many will be shared with other users throughout an office.

High quality printing devices will provide multi-colored graphic presentations of materials.

Office copiers will accept documents directly from a terminal, producing collated and bound copies from the electronic signal.

Telecommunications devices will permit rapid communication of messages to large numbers of persons.

Records storage systems will permit rapid storage and retrieval of letters, documents, and data.

While the new computer technologies will enable systems to become more responsive and flexible, this will place new responsibilities on the users. Managers will have opportunities to make the same mistakes on their many small computer terminals and systems that the large-scale operators have made on their large systems over the last several decades. In the past, major losses of productivity occurred because of a relatively few very expensive mistakes. In the 1980s, even greater levels of productivity may be lost because of a great number of less expensive mistakes. While the cost of each error or problem will be lower, the cost resulting from such an error may be an economic disaster to a small business. Avoiding such mistakes will require a new competence on the part of the user-manager of the management-oriented computer system, whether served by a single computer or a large scale system.

MANAGEMENT COMPETENCE

Competence in the many aspects of computers is already an important element of the corporate manager's preparation for a successful career. It is fast becoming a necessity for the successful small business operator or individual professional as well. There are many interpretations as to what such a competence should consist of. One approach is to develop a familiarity with micro-computers and an ability to program in BASIC, which is a core element of some academic computer literacy programs. Other approaches include training in more traditional computer curricula, usually by students preparing to become computer programmers, designers, and engineers.

The problem with these and many other approaches to training and educating managers for a computerized work-world is that they are often incomplete. A skill development effort must confront the actual decisions and problems that managers, small business operators, and individuals face in dealing with computerization. Most often these involve:

Whether or not to use a computer for a particular activity or to continue to perform it manually.

Selecting and working with computer-related personnel and consultants, and computer stores and software sources.

Making or approving selection and purchasing decisions about hardware and software.

Developing or approving plans for implementation of a computer system.

Dealing with conflict and complaints about the performance of the computer system.

Diagnosing functional problems not due primarily to hardware or software error, but rather to manager or business ability to support and use the system.

Identifying, specifying, and implementing improvements in computer-generated reports and displays.

Training and motivating employees to use the system effectively.

These problems will not necessarily be managed more effectively merely because the manager or business owner can program a small computer at home to balance a checkbook. Nor will they be solved through insight into hardware operations, or knowledge of various programming languages. Rather, the manager must know how to use small- and large-scale computer systems *as management tools.*

TWELVE COMPUTER COMPETENCE STANDARDS FOR EXECUTIVES

The process of developing competence in management with computers should be guided by some basic goals and objectives. Competence standards are intended as guides that describe the general abilities needed by managers, not the methods or learning processes by which the abilities would be gained. Thus, a business organization might use such standards to guide selection of the content of a training program, while an individual manager might use them more as a self-evaluation checklist. The identification of a set of competence standards for executives must be grounded in some basic principles of management with computers.

A basic principle in the successful use of computers in management is that people manage organizations, businesses, and professional practices. Computers can only assist managers in this effort. Computers cannot be a substitute for competent managerial performance.

A second principle is that managers must be able to make informed decisions about the development of their computer systems, since they know the most about their businesses and professions. The ability to become competently involved in the ongoing development and operation of a computer system is itself a necessary management skill.

A third principle is that, while much of the programs and equipment associated with desktop computers and enhanced terminals is new, there is much to learn from the experiences of other users and operators, including those associated with large computer systems for big corporations and government agencies.

Based upon these principles, 12 computer competence standards for executives can be identified. These standards can guide an individual executive in career preparation and development decisions. They can guide trainers and academic professionals in the development of workshops, courses, and curricula in computer skills for executives. Finally, they can guide small and large organizations in the development of skills for their employees, to prepare them to use computers effectively in their daily work.

1. The executive should understand the basics of how large and small computers work, as well as the terminology used to describe those operations.

Managers must understand the basic operations of computers so that they can make informed decisions about equipment, software, and operations. While a technical knowledge of semiconductor operations or machine language is not required, an awareness of types of computer systems and peripherals, their capabilities, interfacing technologies, and application programs most certainly is. An important dimension is an understanding of the meaning of key terms and expressions used by computer professionals. Without this, plans and specifications cannot be read and interpreted, and problems cannot be diagnosed.

2. The executive should understand the evolving technologies of computer systems, especially as they apply to the full range of management applications.

Computers are evolving rapidly because of technological innovations that reduce costs, increase speeds, and expand the physical and functional capacities of computer systems. An executive should understand the technological innovations at a nontechnical level. In addition, the executive should be able to anticipate many of the changes in the management environment that technological innovation will bring about, so that plans and decisions can make the most of such opportunities. Maintaining such a level of awareness requires not only initial training but also continuing exposure to one or more magazines or newsletters that examine the evolving functions of computers in management.

3. The executive should be able to define the longer term organizational needs for computer support, so as to effectively participate with computer professionals in the development of new applications.

One characteristic of an effective computer system is the ability of the system to grow with the needs of the organization. Computer systems are becoming increasingly flexible and modular in their basic design. The most competitive strategic plans not only accommodate growth of existing computer-based functions but also incorporate new uses that provide a competitive edge in the marketplace. A critical factor in the design of such a plan is the ability of an executive to see opportunities in computer technology that can be applied to the goals and functions of the organization.

The initial planning, development, and acquisition of a desktop computer, enhanced terminal, or larger system, as well as the supervision of its ongoing operation, require the attention and support of management. Even if a system merely automates something that is already being done, the manager must first determine whether such a system is needed and whether the time, money, and effort involved in the project can be justified by the expected result. When a system provides for new information and new functions, computers can make even more complex demands upon the manager.

4. The executive should be able to evaluate requests and plans for computer hardware and operating software.

Many executives do not work directly with computers daily. Instead they see the work products of subordinates, developed through using computers. Nevertheless, as a result of their position in the chain of decision-making authority, these executives may be called upon to evaluate or decide about requests and plans for computer equipment and software. The development of plans and requests is usually delegated to trained subordinates or outside professionals, and their opinions carry great weight in the decision process. Nevertheless, it is not desirable for a manager to make a decision about a major expenditure without the ability to assess the fundamental factors that would determine the successful outcome of the decision.

As decisions are made regarding equipment and software purchases, and as the system is set up and operation begins, the manager will rely on skilled assistance from professionals at a local computer store or software outlet, or the manager will rely upon numerous technical manuals regarding the specific equipment and software in use. In developing larger systems, consultants and engineers may be employed. A manager who is informed about management with computers can use such resources with greater efficiency and effectiveness.

5.   The executive should be able to communicate effectively and coordinate with data processing professionals on a day-to-day basis.

The effective operation of a large and complex computer system requires coordination between those who directly operate the machine and those who use it in their work. Such coordination requires that the operators make a continuing effort to be flexible and responsive to user needs. It also requires that the users respect the complex limitations under which the operators function. In this way, the operators are not expected to accomplish tasks that are impractical, duplicative, or inefficient. This working relationship requires communication. The manager must understand what the data processing staff does, just as the data processing staff must understand what the manager does.

6.   The executive should be familiar with the range of uses of computer-generated information as a management tool, and should be able to define and assess the need for information, and the appropriate use of computers in developing and managing that information, in specific management contexts.

Computers manage information, which provides a factual basis for decision-making, supports the control of organizational efforts, serves as a basis for the allocation of incentives and rewards—sometimes as a reward in itself—and serves as a basis for interactions and relationships with external organizations.

Computers make two basic contributions to the effective and efficient management of information. Management-oriented systems aid in decision-making and planning and in the control and organization of a business or agency. Such systems might aid in planning a complex project or in forecasting demand for a new project. Operations-oriented systems perform routine management support functions with efficiency and accuracy. They might automate a previously manual function, such as processing payroll checks, including making all the necessary calculations and maintaining the records of such transactions. Without thorough consideration of the purpose of the computer for the organization, business, or person it is to serve, the chances for expensive failure increase. Some typical computer applications in support of basic management functions follow.

Function	Application
Planning	Statistical analysis
	Simulation
	Projection of trends
	Identifying resources
	Cost estimation
	Tax planning and analysis
Decision-making	Decision modeling programs
	Expenditure analysis programs
	Investment analysis programs
Organizing	Time management systems
	Communications systems
	Organizational evaluation packages
	Project scheduling
	Time accounting and billing for professionals
	Employee shift scheduling
Leading	Performance evaluation systems
	Job enrichment through computers
Controlling	Information management
	Performance monitoring systems
	Inventory control and materials management
	Energy management

A competent manager should be aware of these and many other uses of computers for management.

7.   The executive should be familiar with automated office systems, so that (with the assistance of professionals) the need for such systems can be evaluated and implementation can be planned.

The office of the future will rely heavily upon computer technology for most of its functions. While a manager should not attempt to become an expert in such technologies, since they are constantly changing, the manager should be familiar with the basic features of such systems, so as to participate effectively in decisions and plans.

8.   The executive should be capable of working effectively within an automated professional working environment. Such competence includes awareness of the changing roles of office workers when these systems are operational.

The executive should be able to participate in the evaluation and planning of an automated office and to work within one once it is operational. This requires the ability to use the equipment intended for executives, as well as the awareness of changes in the functions and roles of other workers in the office so that obsolete and inefficient expectations are not transferred from the old to the new working environment.

9.   The executive should be able to use a desktop work station both for administrative support and decision support functions.

Administrative support functions include small record systems, schedules, word processing, and related tasks. Decision support functions include projecting alternative courses of action, modeling management situations, and evaluating operations and expenditures.

10.   The executive should understand the potential impacts of the introduction of computers on employees and organizations.

Computers must ultimately be operated by people for people. A well-prepared manager must anticipate how an organization and its employees will react to a computer system. For a business or organization employing several persons or more, some basic issues must be anticipated: the management of conflict over power, authority, and "turf"; and the reshaping and reorganizing of the business or agency in response to new patterns of work and communication.

The manager must be prepared for the resistance and fear of individual employees, and must motivate such workers to use the new system effectively. New opportunities for job enrichment and career development must be structured, both to motivate employees and to make best use of human resources. Changing patterns of work, both within the large conventional organization as well as for individual employees, must be anticipated.

11. The manager should be able to diagnose the sources of dysfunction of computer systems, when such failures are due to problems other than hardware and software defects.

Past use of computer systems in the management of businesses and other organizations provides examples of errors and problems to learn from, and models of successful systems to emulate. A manager with such experience is aware of early warning signs of future problems. Through a study of the failures of others, a manager new to the computer field can benefit from the experience of others.

An inexperienced person might assume that the most common problem would be a breakdown or malfunction of computer equipment. However, a physical breakdown of a computer is often a relatively easy problem to solve. More important and difficult problems often result from software. But probably the most basic and critical problems result from a poor match of the computer and software to the needs of the business or organization they serve. Thus, when computer systems prove unsatisfactory to their users, it is usually because of application failures, not hardware or software problems.

With application failures, the problem may lie in the relation between the system and the organization it serves. The computer may not be large enough to accommodate the growth of the organization. Those who planned the system may have underestimated the employee time required to put information into the computer. Or employees may never have resolved internal conflict as to the major purpose of the system, so that a struggle ensues over access to the system, resulting in dissatisfaction with the computer because it cannot serve all who expected to be served.

Responsibility for an application failure may vary from case to case. A safe generalization, however, is that with a large system the blame must be shared between the computer professionals–the programmers and hardware experts–and the general managers. At the heart of the problem is usually a pattern of miscommunication, where both parties listened only to what they wanted to hear, or worse, did not seek advice at all. With a personal computer or a desktop system for a small business or practice, programmers and hardware experts are not directly involved, and so usually the responsibility must rest with the person who owns or operates the computer.

12.   The executive should be able to work effectively with external sources of professional expertise.

External expertise is often useful and cost-efficient because the manager does not need such assistance on an ongoing and routine basis. Sources of external help include consultants and sales personnel, but they can also be acquired as final products. For example, it is often more practical to purchase prewritten software packages than to develop them internally. The executive should be able to assess the trade-offs among the various approaches to solving a problem.

CLOSING OBSERVATIONS

As managers become increasingly competent in the use of computers in their work, computers will also change management in significant ways, placing new demands upon small business operators and professionals. Toan (1968, p.112) expects computers to change management in some important ways:

Reducing the cost and increasing the accuracy of information available.

Increasing the speed with which information becomes available for use.

Assisting in the coordination of interdepartmental activities.

Facilitating the extension and supervision of delegated authority.

Increasing the opportunity to centralize or decentralize operations.

Increasing the accessibility of information to the decision-maker.

Increasing the risks involved in developing information systems.

To these, the author adds a couple:

Increasing the complexity and interdependence of information systems.

Increasing the skills and competencies necessary for effective management.

These advantages have been routinely achieved, and the problems and challenges overcome, in large-scale computer systems. For the individual, the owner of a small business, or the manager working with an enhanced terminal, the same benefits are possible and the same problems must be overcome.

Effective managers must be able to plan, decide, organize, lead, and control. Accomplishing these functions in a business or agency cannot be done by the top administrator alone. They must be delegated to others, and accomplished through the development of appropriate procedures and systems. Computers can directly perform some of these functions, and they can support employees who are delegated these functions. The ultimate performance of the computer will depend, however, upon the executive's skill in planning and managing its use.

____ CHAPTER 2 ____
COMPUTER TECHNOLOGY
AND THE MANAGER

I was the third project manager for the department store's computing system to quit this year. Top management was not aware of this, but the key problem was with the vice president assigned to oversee the project. He was interested and enthusiastic, but he had no grasp of the complexity of computers. The final straw was his most recent list of management report requests. These reports called upon the computer to develop almost magical insights into the store's operations, beyond what was possible with the information stored in the system.

An automobile owner who understands the basics of auto mechanics can usually be expected to make better judgments about the auto's use and maintenance. Similarly, a manager who understands how computers work usually can put them to more effective use. While a manager cannot be expected to learn the details of microelectronics or semiconductor technology, it is not difficult to learn about the basic operations of most computer systems. Provided with such information, a manager should be able to work more effectively with the computer, as well as with the supporting professionals, such as salespersons, software programmers, system designers and planners.

This chapter will describe how computers work and explain several trends in patterns of computer use brought about by improvements in technology. Of all the topics covered in this book, computer technology may be the most likely to induce "computer anxiety" among managers. However, a basic grasp of this subject is the foundation for executive computer competence.

THE CHANGING RELATIONSHIP BETWEEN MANAGERS AND COMPUTERS

In many fields, the development of new technologies has not affected users very much. For example, the technology of telephone systems has developed greatly during the last two decades, but these improvements have largely affected the methods the telephone companies use to provide services, not the way an individual consumer uses a phone—the telephone still rings, sounds a dial tone and busy signal, and requires a phone number. Granted, there have been changes in cost patterns, direct dialing systems, and telephone styles, but the basic way a person uses a telephone remains largely unchanged.

In contrast, the changes in computer technology are directly affecting the user today, both expanding and modifying the purposes for which computers can be used. Because of the high cost of early computer systems, the earliest computers served relatively large numbers of users at once. This large-scale operation made the expensive systems economically feasible. These early systems generally carried out a small number of repetitive operations, such as updating bank account records, processing payrolls, or managing mailing lists. However, this type of system and application split the people operating and using the computer systems into two groups.

The operators and programmers had to be relatively closely involved and informed about the work the computer was doing. They were writing programs to enable the computer to do the work, and in the process of writing the programs, these people actually determined how the work was to be done.

The users—the people feeding information into the system through terminals or keypunch machines, and the managers ultimately responsible for the work processes themselves—had little control over the system. In many ways, the computer controlled them, by requiring that work be done in specific ways, by specific deadlines. Most users had very passive relationships with early management computers. They fed them information and awaited results, always following the precise rules of the computer system.

The purposes of the early computers were determined by the limitations and potentials of the technology available. The relationship between managers and computers was also structured by the technology. As the technology of computers continues to evolve, new relationships become possible, and insightful, creative, and informed managers will be able to use computers in increasingly productive ways if they understand the technology.

COMPUTER SYSTEMS: HOW THE KEY COMPONENTS WORK

Since there is almost a limitless amount of information about how computers work, any attempt to explain the basics of computer technology has to begin by setting some priorities. What information does a manager most need to know about computers and how they work? A reasonable answer is that the manager should know about those aspects of technology that affect his or her work: the equipment that he or she will work with, or that employees will operate under the supervision of the manager; the

equipment and technologies that increase or limit computer performance as it affects the manager; and the types of programs that
will enhance a manager's work performance.

It is equally important that a manager develop a sense of the
basic directions toward which the technology is moving, since
these trends in the evolution of computer technology will affect
the practical uses of computers, and the benefits to the people
and organizations using them.

Computer systems used in the management and operations of
organizations can be described in terms of distinct groups of devices that make up the system, and in terms of the overall organization of the groups (see Figure 2.1). Each group has a special
function, process or operation, and potential for technological improvement.

System configuration refers to the overall design of the computer system, including the number of terminals and users, the
approach to processing information, and the size and range of
the system's functions.

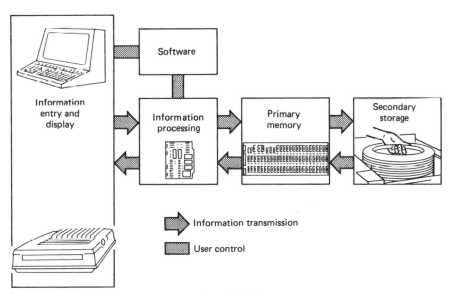

Figure 2.1.   A General Model of a Computer System.

Information processing refers to those parts of the computer that evaluate, locate, and transform information. In a general sense, these constitute the "brain" of the system.

Primary memory refers to those parts of the system that retain information for immediate processing.

Secondary storage refers to devices that provide for longer term retention of information, such as magnetic tapes or disks.

Information transmission refers to the parts of the system that send and retrieve information, over short distances between parts of the system itself or over long distances between a computer and a remote terminal, perhaps thousands of miles away.

Information entry and display refers to the devices that allow people to enter information into the computer system and that transform information within the computer into forms that can be used by people, such as terminal screen displays or paper reports.

Software refers to the instructions that tell the computer system what to do or that translate users' instructions into commands that the computer can understand and execute.

The operation of a post office illustrates the functions and relationships of these parts of computer systems.

System configuration corresponds to the overall organization and arrangement of the post office. Some are large and complex, able to handle large numbers of many types of materials. There may be many or few sorters, trucks, and delivery workers, and a great deal or only a little space for storage.

Information processing corresponds to the mail sorters, who evaluate each piece of mail and route it to a destination.

Primary memory corresponds to storage areas immediately adjacent to the sorters used to hold mail just before and after sorting.

Secondary storage corresponds to other larger holding areas and warehouses for mail storage.

Information transmission is like the process of moving mail from the originating post office to other post offices or final destinations.

Information entry and display is like mailboxes, where people can receive or send out their mail.

Finally, software corresponds to all the procedures and regulations that guide the operation of the post office.

Each of these features of a computer system must work together to create an effective result. We will examine each one in order to develop a picture of how computers work, as well as to identify technological trends that will result in vast changes in management approaches in the immediate future.

System Configurations

Today's computers range from massive machines supporting thousands of terminals deployed across the nation, to a single microcomputer owned and used by one person. The diversity of feasible configurations has increased as a result of lower costs and smaller sizes of computer parts as well as greater performance of each part. The earliest business computers were very large and supported many uses at once; the resulting volumes of use could justify the great expense. During the 1970s, minicomputer and microcomputer systems were developed, which cost less to purchase and operate, making smaller scale configurations feasible. Currently, there are a variety of types of configurations available, each responding to different functions and work situations.

The most simple configuration is the *individual terminal,* capable of independent operation (see Figure 2.2). It may include various devices to store or present information, but the system generally operates by itself. "Lap computers" are smaller versions of the independent terminal. They are small enough to rest on the user's lap, and usually include a keyboard, small display screen, modem for telephone communication, and memory.

The next level of configuration is the *multi-user microcomputer*

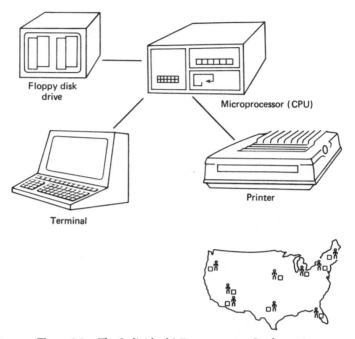

Figure 2.2. The Individual Microcomputer Configuration.

system, where several terminals are operated together (see Figure 2.3). There are several ways this is accomplished by different manufacturers. In some systems, all the terminals share one processor that performs operations for each terminal on a one-by-one basis. The processor works so quickly that users generally are not aware of the microsecond delays involved. In other systems, all the terminals share an information storage device called a disk, so that each terminal has access to information stored by another. In most cases, the result is practically identical performance. There are a several matters to consider, however, in comparing different systems.

The shared-processor systems can sometimes be less expensive per user terminal, because the terminals are less complex and costly than the fully developed microcomputers required in the shared-disk approach. This is not always the case, however, because of the added cost of the complexity and expense of the multi-user processing system.

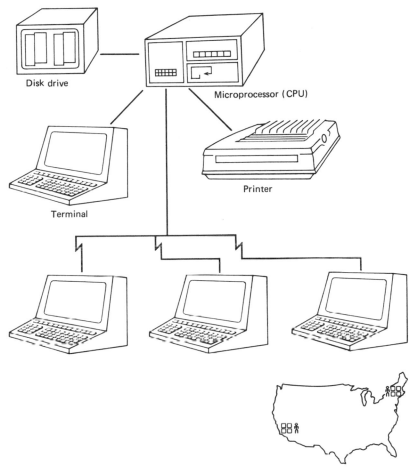

Disk drive

Microprocessor (CPU)

Printer

Terminal

Figure 2.3.   The Multi-User Microcomputer Configuration.

As the number of terminals and intensity of use is increased, the performance of the shared-processor systems may begin to deteriorate. In the shared-disk systems, each microcomputer terminal processes information at normal speed regardless of numbers of terminals because it does not depend on a shared processor. However, the performance of the shared-disk system can also deteriorate as more and more terminals demand disk access. The degree of deterioration varies depending upon the system and the application, but generally the shared-disk microcomputer systems support many more terminals than do shared-microprocessor systems.

The next level of configuration is the *multi-user minicomputer system* (see Figure 2.4). Generally, these systems share a central processing system, but processing is much more powerful than in the microcomputer systems, so that 50–100 or more terminals can be operational simultaneously without a loss of performance efficiency.

A *distributed minicomputer system* is the next level (see Figure 2.5). Under this approach, two or more multi-user systems are combined. For example, a retail store chain, with minicomputer systems at each store for the cash register terminals, might operate a central administrative computer system that would receive updates every night from the computer systems at the stores.

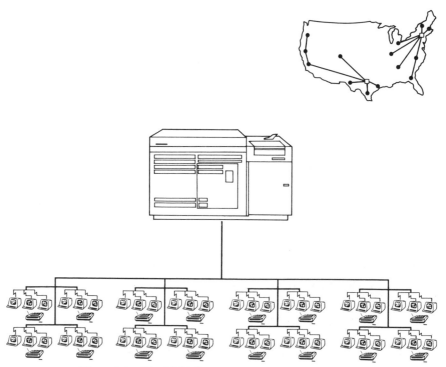

Figure 2.4. The Multi-User Minicomputer Configuration.

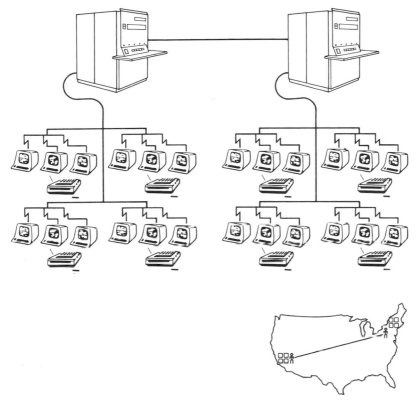

Figure 2.5. The Distributed Minicomputer Configuration.

The largest type of configuration is the *megacomputer system* (see Figure 2.6). Such systems support many terminals that all share a very powerful central processing system. Some of these systems are devoted to a few types of high-volume operations, such as airline reservations. Others support a wide range of operations, such as university computer systems that support data analysis for research along with many university record-keeping functions (e.g. student grades, class scheduling, accounting, and library operations).

Several trends in the performance of system configurations are becoming apparent in management computing. Probably most important is the increase in local control over the terminals and systems themselves. In early computer systems, all operations were

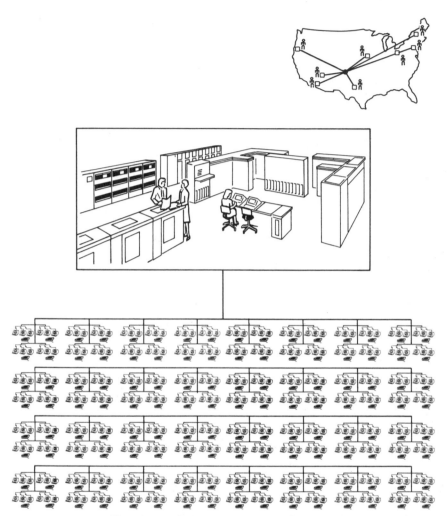

Figure 2.6.   The Megacomputer Configuration.

controlled by the professionals who operated the systems. While top management determined the basic uses of the system and established priorities for its growth and development, the users of the terminals could not influence day-to-day operations. Currently, a microcomputer is completely under the control of the user, who is free to determine its use within the limitations of available software. The multi-user microcomputer and minicomputer systems allow smaller organizations to develop and operate their own computer systems. In addition, configurations have evolved to permit more user control and decision making.

A second trend arises in response to competition among the manufacturers of the various types of systems. A generalization is that each type of configuration is evolving to include the capabilities of the other types. Large-scale systems are evolving to permit more options for users, so that a terminal can act like a microcomputer when it is not needed for its major function. The microcomputer manufacturers are developing configurations that permit hundreds of microcomputers to share a single disk, providing many of the performance features of larger systems for certain smaller types of applications. As a result, the management challenges and opportunities presented by computers will not be limited to one type of system only. Generally, whatever one type offers will gradually become available from the other types as well.

However, some important differences between configurations are not likely to change quickly, and these should be considered as one evaluates existing or proposed systems.

Systems that share a processor may be less expensive per terminal to purchase and to operate, depending on the number of terminals involved. Sharing a processor will be less costly as long as the added cost of the multi-user processing system is less than the combined savings of less expensive terminals.

A major benefit of the minicomputer and megacomputer configurations is that they can handle larger tasks more rapidly than can microcomputer processors. However, as processing capabilities of microcomputers increase, this advantage may also be eliminated.

The ongoing telecommunications cost of a multi-user system that has many distant terminals can be very expensive. If there is no need for each terminal to continually update a central file and if the tasks performed can be accomplished by smaller processors, then sometimes a system with processors at each location can be more economical. Sending and receiving information from a central file is done periodically (such as every night) rather than continuously.

Decentralized processing also offers flexibility and reduced exposure to maintenance problems. It is easy for terminals to take on new uses, and if one terminal has a breakdown, the rest of the system is not affected.

The selection of a system configuration depends primarily on the nature of the work to be done. Certain task characteristics demand large centralized computers with constant access by the terminals to the main system. However, as a general rule, smaller decentralized computers are to be preferred when they can perform the necessary work. Although they bring the risk of disorganization and future undercapacity, they also bring economy and flexibility.

Information Processing

Information processing refers to the devices in computer systems that locate, evaluate, and transform information. These devices are called central processors, and every computer has at least one. A processor is, in a sense, the "brain" of the computer, because nothing is done that is not controlled directly or indirectly by the processor, and all the operations of the computer that involve transformations of information are done by the processor. Larger computers will have many processors that either perform a set of specific processing tasks or provide for most of the processing for one or a few terminals. A microcomputer will have one central processor, and perhaps a few more if certain operational functions, such as managing information flow to long-term storage devices, are microprocessor controlled.

Central processors perform three operations: They store and retrieve information from memory; they calculate (add, subtract, etc.); and they compare sets of information. Everything that is done by any computer ultimately must be broken down into a series of such operations. Processors have *instruction sets* which are preset combinations of operations to carry out specified tasks. Such tasks include arithmetic operations; tasks that get, transfer, and save data on storage devices; operations involving logical comparisons; and "interrupt" operations that stop a program either temporarily or permanently. Every brand or model of processor has a unique instruction set, consisting of 50 to several hundred commands. More powerful processors have instructions that accomplish in one step what would take several steps with another device. A computer equipped with the more powerful device can therefore work faster and do more. Generally, a computer user does not control a computer by literally using the instruction set of its processor. Instead, the user deals with a specially written program or general programming language that translates into the processor instruction set the information and commands entered by the user.

The scope of the instruction set is one factor that determines the relative computing power of a processing device. A second factor is the size of the computer's memory that can be managed and effectively used by the processor. A processor must be able to send information to and from each position in the computer's memory. Some common microcomputer processors can effectively use memory that can contain more than 500,000 pieces of information, although others are limited to less than 65,000 pieces. (The nature of these pieces of information is discussed below.) Some more recent microcomputer processors, and the processors for most minicomputers and megacomputers, can manage substantially larger memories. For many operations, the size of available memory is not a limitation. However, when a job is too big, it must be divided into manageable parts by loading and saving information to storage devices, a process that increases the time required to complete the program.

A third factor that determines the computing power of a processor is the size of the pieces of information that the processor can handle. The processor evaluates and transforms information in small chunks called "bytes". If a processor can handle information in chunks that are twice as large as those of another processor, then under ideal conditions it can complete a task twice as quickly. Most processors deal with bytes which are either 8, 16, or 32 bits long. A bit is a binary digit, expressed in an electronic circuit as "on" or "off", or "high" or "low". Combinations of these bits form bytes that represent letters and numbers. Thus, computers use the binary code arrangements of "ons" and "offs" in much the same way that the Morse code uses dots and dashes.

The development of faster and more powerful processors has been one of the factors that has enabled computers to improve in cost and performance in recent decades. The advancements result from several innovations in the design and manufacture of processing chips in particular, and semiconductor devices in general.

A major innovation has been the development of increasingly larger scale integrated circuits. In essence, this means that larger and larger amounts of circuitry are fit into smaller and smaller spaces on semiconductor devices. The major advantage of this technology is that it reduces the number and size of the interconnections in computer hardware. Such interconnections have a cost: They create delays in processing information because of the time required for the information to move from one location to another; they create the need for more power to the hardware because of the energy loss as information moves over the lines; and they create electronic signals that can cause unreliability in the equipment. To reduce the signal interference between transmission lines, the circuits must be made larger, thereby compounding the other problems. The integrated circuit solves these problems by reducing interconnections as much as possible.

How this is done constitutes the second major innovation. The integrated circuits are applied to a silicon chip through a lithographic and photographic process. Many chips are produced much like printing a sheet of postage stamps. The magnitude of the circuitry that can be fit on a silicon chip is determined by several factors.

The width of the lines of conductive material on the chip are reduced, decreasing the size of the circuitry and the overall size of the chip.

The percentage of defective chips produced has been reduced. This allows larger and more complex circuitry to be applied to the chips without increasing the percentage of defective chips to an uneconomic level.

The designs of the circuits have been made as efficient as possible, so that larger and larger circuits can be applied to each chip. One way to create a more efficient design is to develop more specialized processors, so that unnecessary instruction sets are eliminated, enabling the necessary ones to be organized most efficiently.

Major innovations in these three areas have permitted, and will continue to permit for the foreseeable future, great improvements in computer price and performance.

Primary Memory

Primary memory consists of the parts of a computer that retain information before and after processing, so that it can be directly fetched, evaluated, and transmitted by the central processor. Generally, this memory is in the form of silicon chip electronic circuits. Secondary storage, which will be discussed later, is used to retain information, usually on magnetic tape or disks, when it is not needed in primary memory. Primary memory costs more per unit of information stored than secondary storage. However, information stored in primary memory must be more directly and quickly available to the processor, to avoid delays in computing. The amount of primary memory in a computer is generally limited to that amount which can be directly managed by the central processor. Most computers have both primary and secondary storage capabilities.

To the manager, the exact type of memory technology in a computer is usually unimportant, as long as the machine performs well. Yet computer advertisements and specifications often tout chip characteristics. A manager should understand what the terms mean, if only to avoid misleading, high-pressure sales promotions.

There are several types of primary memory commonly found in computers. *Random access memory* (RAM) is called "random" because the processor can directly get information stored at any location within it without having to move through another location. In random access memory, information is stored as bytes of data which are sequences of eight bits, the most basic form of information in a computer. Random access memory capacity is measured in terms of the number of bytes that can be stored within it. For example, a 16K chip can hold approximately 16,000 bytes of information.

Read-only memory (ROM) is exactly like random access memory with two exceptions. First, the information stored in the chip can only be read from it, no new or additional information can be stored within the chip. Second, the information is not lost when the computer's power supply is turned off. Sometimes ROM chips are used for programs that are routinely needed by the computer, such as a word processing program. ROM is also used sometimes for initial instructions to the computer when it is first turned on when there are no previous instructions within the machine about what to do.

Several other types of memory chips are commonly used in computers: *Programmable read-only memory* (PROM) is like read-only memory, except that it is possible to encode it with information once, under specific conditions. After that, PROM functions like ROM. *Erasable programmable read-only memory* (EPROM) can be erased under certain conditions (exposure to ultraviolet light) and reprogrammed. *Electronically alterable read-only memory* (EAROM) can be modified using electronic signals, usually from the computer. *Bubble memory* works like random access memory but has the advantage that it retains information after power is turned off. This is a distinct advantage for portable or lap computers.

Secondary Storage

Secondary storage refers to devices that retain information for longer periods of time and, unlike random access memory, do not require continuous power to do this. The two most commonly used media for such storage are magnetic tape and magnetic disk (see Figure 2.7). Other less frequently used media include "charge-coupled devices" and bubble memory, as well as increasingly obsolete media such as punched paper tape and paper cards. Bubble memory can work as both primary memory and secondary storage.

The secondary storage devices are used before, during, and

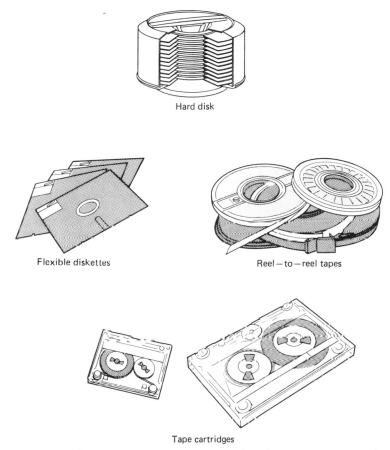

Hard disk

Flexible diskettes

Reel — to — reel tapes

Tape cartridges

Figure 2.7. Secondary Storage Media: Hard and Soft Disks, Cartridge and Reel-to-Reel Tapes.

after information is processed. Before a computer is turned off, a copy of the information in primary memory may be saved on a tape or disk so that the computer can start up again where it left off. The programs that tell the computer what to do may be saved on such devices. While a computer is operational, it may juggle information between primary and secondary memory to create room for additional information to be processed. The informational contents of a large record system may be kept permanently on tape or disk, and individual case records may be fetched by the processor from secondary storage into primary memory only when needed.

Random access memory chips are sometimes used for temporary secondary storage. This technique permits a processor with limited capacity to interchange primary memory and secondary storage quickly, to approximate the performance of larger-capacity processors by minimizing time lost in saving and getting information that could not fit in primary memory.

Each information storage technology has particular advantages and disadvantages in terms of speed, volume, and cost. Each is changing and improving, and new approaches are under development.

Magnetic tape is essentially the same material used for recording and playback of sound in acoustical recording systems. However, the format for recording the information onto the tape is digital, which means that the magnetic trail on the tape represents numbers. In a sound recording system, the magnetic trail is analog, which means that the signal directly corresponds to the patterns of the recorded sounds. In some simpler microcomputer systems, information to be saved on cassette tapes is converted into analog (sound) signals, but in more sophisticated systems, the digital format is used because it is more compact, rapid, and accurate.

The major advantage of tapes over other methods of secondary storage is their relative economy, and their capacity for storing large amounts of information. A major disadvantage is the time expended in reeling and unreeling the tape to get to the stored information.

Disks are made of the same material as tapes, and the information is recorded on the surface of the disk in the same digital format. However, the flat shape of a disk (somewhat like a phonograph record or stack of records) permits direct movements of the recording head to the exact place where a particular piece of information has been recorded. This enables disks to have much faster access times than tapes.

Disk storage media come in a variety of sizes, shapes, and technologies. The simplest disk is the flexible or floppy diskette which is used in many microcomputer systems. They come in several sizes, the most common of which are 5¼ inches and 8 inches square. Smaller disks measuring about 3 inches square are also increasingly available. The diskettes consist of a circular sheet of magnetic material, covered by a envelope of plastic with a window through which the read/write head can directly contact the diskette's magnetic surface. The disk drive unit spins the round diskette and positions the head that reads and writes the magnetic traces that contain the information. The drive is designed to write this information in a specified pattern onto the surface of the disk. The patterns vary from device to device so that a disk written on by one type of drive may not be understood by another drive.

A more advanced type of disk is the "hard" disk, which has been used in large computer systems for many years and in recent years has also become commonly available in smaller systems. These disks are made of the same type of material as the flexible disks, except that it is thicker and thus rigid. In most devices, the disks are like platters or phonograph records stacked one on top of the other, with about a half-inch of space between them. There are multiple heads to read and write onto the magnetic surface, one for each side of each platter. The multiple platters create a large surface, and any point on the surface can be reached very quickly. In addition, since the surface is rigid, information can be packed more densely and more rapidly onto the device.

The performance of disks has improved remarkably over the last 15 years. They have become faster, more dense, more accurate, and less expensive. A number of factors have contributed to this progress and will stimulate further advancements:

The heads that read and write the magnetic traces of information have been positioned closer to the surface of the disk, reducing the access time and improving the accuracy and consistency of the traces of information.

Disks are spun more and more rapidly, which reduces access time and also implements faster reading and writing by he disk heads.

Disk controllers, the electronic components that manage the process of storage and retrieval of information by the disk, have been made more intelligent to permit better error checking and recovery if something unexpected occurs, and to permit more efficient operational processes for the devices.

The layouts of tracks on the disk or diskette have been made more efficient and dense, so that more information can be written more quickly.

The general designs and technologies of disk drives have improved, so as to tolerate faster speeds and more densely packed information. New techniques are emerging that pack information in a very dense vertical pattern, so that magnetic particles are stacked on their ends rather than laid on their sides. This can radically increase storage capacities.

Several emerging technologies in secondary storage may result in great future advancements in performance and cost. One such technology is bubble memory, which is capable of storing very large amounts of information in very small chips, such as 256,000 characters in a device which can fit on a fingertip. The access time is much faster than with a disk, but somewhat slower than with a conventional RAM chip. The technology does not require continuous power, so it can be used as a long-term storage system. When and if this technology improves in cost and performance so as to be competitive with the prevailing disk technologies, computers will become even smaller, simpler, and more powerful.

Information Transmission

Information transmission concerns the devices and processes associated with the movement and transformation of information from one device to another, or one location to another. For example, information inside a computer must be transmitted to a printer before it can be printed on paper. Two computers that are in separate locations must transmit information over telephone lines to achieve communication.

Generally, there are three ways that computer devices can be connected so that information can be transmitted between them: equipment-specific connections, which vary from device to device, parallel connections, in which several lines are used to carry the signal; and serial connections, in which most of the information is carried on one line.

Serial communication is the only practical and generally available approach for devices that communicate over phone lines, because the information is transformed into a series of signals that can then be transmitted over one line. Because communication between computer devices still requires other signals to coordinate the sending and receiving devices, more wires are often used. However, the efficiency of this approach for communicating written information generally reduces the number of cables needed and the complexity of the interface specifications. Because of this efficiency, many computers, printers, telecommunication devices, and other supporting equipment for computers use serial communication.

There are several approaches to serial communication, but by far the most common follows a standard called RS-232-C. This standard was developed by the Electronic Industries Association, and it describes what a signal should look like as it leaves or enters a communicating device, so that a variety of brands and types of equipment can communicate. A serial signal that meets the RS-232-C standard consists of a series of positive and negative volt transmissions, denoting ones and zeros. These are interpreted through another standard called ASCII, or the American Standard Code for Information Interchange. This code transforms a seven-signal sequence of ones and zeros into letters of the alphabet, single numbers (0–9), written symbols (such as #,&,*,#,@), and control characters that instruct devices to take specific actions such as clearing a screen, feeding a new sheet of paper, or ending transmission of information.

The speed of communication can vary according to the design of the device. Speed is usually expressed in terms of a baud rate, which measures the velocity by which information is transmitted over a communications line. Generally speaking, two lines of information in this book transmitted at the rate of 300 baud (a common speed) would take about 4 seconds. At 1200 baud they would take about 1 second, and at 9600 baud they would take about ⅛ of a second. These times may seem fast, but keep in mind that a two-page memo of about 55 lines per page would take almost 4 minutes to communicate at 300 baud, and a little less than 1 minute at 1200 baud.

When the devices are more than approximately 50 feet away, RS-232-C interfacing through a cable may become unreliable. The feasible transmission distance can be increased with use of very efficient cables or electronic devices that enhance the signal strength. However, for distances over 300–1000 feet, the common alternative is to use telephone lines. To communicate in this manner, a device called a modem is necessary. This converts a computer signal into a series of sounds that can be carried over a conventional telephone line. The receiving device must also have a modem to translate the sounds back into signals that can be understood by the computer.

Some modems can communicate only in one direction, but it is common for users to need communication in two directions, just as people talking over the telephone need to be able to speak back and forth. Two-way communication is achieved either by complex protocols that enable the two modems to know when to stop speaking and start listening, or by using several distinct pitches of signals at once.

When a large computer must communicate with many terminals at once and a group of the terminals are at one location such as a district office of a business, then a device called a *multiplex modem* can be used. Such a device can provide for communication between many pairs of terminals (or terminals and computers) over one phone line, rather than requiring one line for every pair of modems. This supermodem takes the signals from each terminal, converts them into the appropriate sounds, and then splits them into short signals that are sent one-by-one over one phone line. The incoming signal on the other end is then split again and converted back into the individual messages.

The technologies that support transmission of information between computers have advanced markedly in the last 25 years, so that information can be transmitted more rapidly and accurately, at lower cost. Further innovation will occur in several areas.

A variety of communications technologies are being developed to provide interconnections between various types of office equipment. The general advantage provided by these systems over standard RS-232-C communication is that they can support a wider variety of communications at greater accuracy and speed. For example, these systems will support the transmission of images or pictures, sounds such as voices, and machine-specific types of communication such as might be required by a copier. The major disadvantage is that these systems are not sufficiently standardized at this point to assure compatibility between the products of different manufacturers. These communications technologies are discussed in greater detail in Chapter 5.

An important new communications technology is the use of light transmitted over flexible glass fibers, as a substitute for electricity over metal wires. There are several advantages in fiber-optic technology, as this is called, including lower costs of basic materials, savings in space because only very thin strands of fiber are needed, greater speed and accuracy of transmission, and a natural electrical insulation between communicating devices since electricity cannot travel over the glass fibers. This technology is already in use and will gradually replace the electric wire technology in new installations (and in some older ones) in coming years.

Unfortunately, present information transmission methods are often incompatible. Thus, office equipment made by one manufacturer may not readily communicate with equipment made by another manufacturer. From a management perspective, one can hope that all the progress and innovation will lead not only to greater communication speed and sophistication but also to simpler and more standardized interconnections.

Information Entry and Display

Information entry and display refers to devices and processes for entering information into a computer and for getting information back in usable forms. The most common examples are printers and video display terminals. Generally, information entry and display devices provide some means of entering information (such as a keyboard), of displaying information (such as a video screen or a printing capability), and of communicating with an external device (such as an RS-232-C port).

A wide variety of such devices are available, and they vary according to the purpose served and the degree of intelligence (or help to the user) built into the equipment. Video display terminals can consist of only a keyboard, a screen, and a communications port, with supporting electronics so that what is typed on the keyboard is sent out of the communications port, and information that goes out of or comes into the communications port is displayed on the screen. This is sometimes referred to as a "dumb" terminal. More sophisticated terminals offer a variety of features to help the user.

Some terminals offer printer ports so that what is displayed on the screen can be printed on paper. Usually, a printer port must be a separate direct connection to the computer itself. Such a capability can save communications costs, but on some devices, the printed material is merely a copy of what is on the screen. Since the screen is usually only 25 lines long, and a sheet of paper can contain more than 55 lines of text, reports generated as copies of screen displays can be severely limited.

Some terminals are equipped with temporary storage units called buffers, so that more than a full screen of information can be kept in the terminal at once. This allows the user to reexamine a previous page of information, after examining the most recent page of display.

Some terminals can send information by the line or page, rather than a character at a time. This may be faster for the computer on the other end, and it permits errors to be corrected at the terminal rather than in interaction with the computer after the wrong character has been sent. When terminals send information a line or page at a time, the cursor (which is a moving point on the screen at which characters are generated) can often be moved around the screen with great speed and flexibility.

Terminals vary as to the general quality of their screen displays. This quality can be observed in the character formations themselves, in the degree of resolution of the characters, and in the number of characters that can be fit onto a screen. In word processing, for example, it is very important that the screen be 80 columns wide, because most letters and papers are about 65 columns wide and most word processing programs locate important information in the margins as well. Some terminals offer what is called "reverse video," which means that the characters are black against a white background.

Terminals designed as office work stations sometimes also have built-in telephones and other common office devices. Some terminals have been upgraded by their manufacturers to include all the common capabilities of microcomputers. Also, some microcomputer manufacturers have designed their computers to fit into terminal enclosures. This gradual blending of these two important types of equipment will stimulate some major changes in management computing in coming years. All the advantages and capabilities of microcomputers will be available to people who, in the past, have had access only to "dumb" terminals.

Printers are available in an even greater range of styles and technologies. As entry and display devices, printers are much like video terminals, except that the screen is replaced by a printing mechanism. Printers can generally be classified according to the technologies used to perform various functions: character impression, paper handling, and general control technology.

Character impression refers to the technique used to form a letter, number, or symbol on the paper. A very common type of computer printing technology is the dot-matrix printer, which creates character impressions as combinations of dots. The dots are generated by thrusting pins or wires at the inking ribbon and paper surface, usually by changing electromagnetic fields, causing the pin to move rapidly up and down onto the paper as directed by the printer. The pins move extremely fast, often at rates of 600–1000 movements per second. The major advantage of dot-matrix printers is that they are relatively fast devices, able to print text onto a page at speeds of several lines per second. A disadvantage is the quality of the letters on the page. They are sometimes not fully formed, unless many dots are printed to create each character, which slows the transmission. Printers which create letter-quality impressions on a page generally use technology associated with the better office typewriters. Some typewriters feature an interchangeable round typing element that has been used in printers driven by computers. Other printers use a pinwheel element sometimes called a *daisy wheel* which also provides for interchangeable type styles and can perform at higher speeds. Several other comparable technologies are available as well.

Some older or more specialized printers use chains of letters that are spun into position and whacked against the page, sometimes with 80 or 160 chains together so that a whole line can be printed at once. Electrostatic printers use a special paper that changes color when a small voltage is passed through it. The characters are formed as dot matrices. High speed and volume printers used with large computer systems generally print a page or more at a time, by printing many lines of characters simultaneously.

Fabric or carbon ribbon, much like those used in typewriters, is commonly used as a source of ink. There are also electrostatic printers that activate chemicals embedded into special paper, which become visible or change color when voltage passes through the paper. An ink-jet printer squirts a small stream of ink at the paper to form the characters. The ink is magnetic, so that the direction and flow can be guided by electromagnetic charges.

The head movement technology of a printer can be a limitation on speed and other aspects of performance. In an old style typewriter, the head does not move at all—the paper is moved by the typewriter so that the head can print in the proper location. This very slow and mechanically complex system was necessary because traditional typewriters had very primitive character impression technologies. In a modern typewriter, the head moves from left to right and returns to the left when a line is completed; the paper stays still. Most computer printers use such a technique. Faster printers type the first line from left to right and then the next line from right to left (backward), but with the proper order of letters and words. This avoids the delay associated with the return to the left side of the paper.

The most common *paper handling* technique entails the use of continuous paper. This means that each sheet is connected to the sheet coming before and after it. The quality of the resulting reports depends upon the quality and style of the paper itself. For reports that do not require good appearance, a roll of paper can by used which is torn from the printer by the user periodically. The paper can be pressure fed by rollers, much like most office typewriters. Better appearance and greater reliability occurs when the paper is sprocket fed, with a device that guides the paper using holes punched along the side of the sheets. If the paper is precut so that the strips of sprocket holes can be removed and the sheets can be separated in a uniform manner, the final sheet will look much like conventional typing paper. Automatic sheet feeders load paper into the printer one sheet at a time and catch the sheets released by the printer. These devices are sometimes slower to use and somewhat more prone to jams than those that use continuous paper, but the appearance is exactly like standard office typing paper. Some devices can support several types of paper such as the first page of office stationary, and the later pages.

The *general control technology* of a printer affects its performance characteristics. Even with a very advanced character impression device, if the component that controls it does not make full use of the potential of the printing mechanism, the overall performance potential of the machine is limited. Printers, like terminals, can be "dumb" or "smart." Sometimes the electronics within a printer include a small microcomputer. An advanced electronic printer may have its own capability to perform in the following ways, regardless of the capabilities of the computer driving it:

It may justify margins, which means that the right margin as well as the left margin are both straight. This is accomplished by adding spaces between words, and sometimes between characters, to hold the length of each line to a standard dimension.

The printer may be able to select the fastest head movement pattern to print a series of lines. If printing a line backward is the fastest technique, then the printer will print the line in that manner.

The printer may have a large buffer, so that it can accept information from the computer in large chunks and store it until it can print it on the page. This frees the computer to perform other functions.

The printer may be able to change character styles and sizes when instructed either by hardware adjustments (switches) or by software instructions. This capability is prevalent in dot-matrix printers.

The printer may be able to generate graphics symbols as well as conventional letters, numbers, and associated symbols.

In the next two decades, printers may change radically by merging with copiers into much more flexible devices. Copiers can function at the rate of several copies per second. As these devices become more intelligent, they will be able to print letters and documents directly from the communications signals that would otherwise go to a printer. As a result, mechanical processes of character impression will not be as necessary. Also, the copiers can be simplified because mechanically complex tasks, such as collating documents, can be accomplished electronically, so that each document page is copied in proper order.

Software

Software refers to the instructions that tell the computer what to do. There are several types of software, distinguished by the level of. work performed.

Machine-level languages use the instruction set of the processor in a form that can be executed directly by the processor. Ultimately, every program must be translated into this type of code. This is done by "low-level languages," which translate more complex programs into machine-level instructions.

High-level languages are designed to be used by programmers, and sometimes by users if they are trained in a particular language. Examples include BASIC, COBOL, FORTRAN, ALGOL, and PASCAL. These languages represent standard shorthand instructions for series of machine-level instructions. An instruction in a high-level language can accomplish a given task with fewer commands than would be necessary in machine language.

Operating system programs coordinate the operation of the computer and perform housekeeping tasks, such as transferring a file from one disk to another or inspecting a disk to see how much of its capacity is used. They are usually written in machine language.

Source programs are written in a particular high-level language, such as BASIC, to do a particular job.

Application programs enable the computer to perform practical tasks, such as maintaining a record system, or word processing. These programs are sometimes written in a high-level language, but they are also sometimes written in machine languages to increase the speed of operation.

Most managers will use only a limited set of software packages directly: a word processing program for developing and printing reports, a spreadsheet calculation program for computations and mathematical models, and a telecommunications program for electronic mail and for connection with other computer systems. Indirectly, the manager will probably have to use an operating system. In addition, each manager will use any special programs associated with his or her organization, such as an accounting, inventory, or record system.

Managers can expect to have one other level of involvement with software, as a participant in the selection and purchasing decision. In evaluating software for a particular application, there are several general questions to consider.

Is the program easy to operate? Common operator errors should not lead to disasters, and recovery and correction should not be difficult. Help in problem solving should be available, either in a well-written manual, in the program itself through prompting on the screen, or through assistance in person or by phone.

Is the program flexible? You should be able to adapt the program to changing application needs and requirements in the future. The program should support expanded capabilities in your equipment, such as new peripheral devices.

Can the program be used on other computers? Software packages used to be limited primarily to one model of computer. A program written for a particular IBM computer would not work on a Digital Equipment Corporation computer. With the advent of many small computer systems, software companies developed operating systems, languages, and application programs that could run on many different models. This expanded the market for software vendors, encouraged price competition, and it increased the number of available products for the software consumer to choose from. Software portability (i.e. the ability to run on different computers) is not as available or practical for larger and more complicated computer systems. For small and large systems, portability is often limited for any one user by the terms of the license granted by the vendor when the package was originally acquired, which may restrict use of the software to one particular computer.

Whenever a computer system is to be acquired for a specific purpose that is known at the time of purchase, it is wise to focus decision making initially on software, not hardware. If you can find a software package that provides the capabilities needed, the vendor of the software usually can provide detailed specifications about computers and peripheral equipment necessary to support the software. Approaching the problem by choosing equipment first can sometimes lead to a dead end, when the computer cannot be made to support the application without expensive specialized software development.

GENERAL PURPOSE COMPUTER PROGRAMS

Throughout this book, different types of computer programs are introduced. Each type is discussed in the appropriate chapter, together with related technology and management problems. Since this chapter deals with general computer technology, we will introduce computer programs of general application: operating systems, telecommunications programs, general-purpose languages, and graphics software.

SOFTWARE PROFILE 1:   OPERATING SYSTEMS

An operating system supervises the entire operation of the computer, provides for some "housekeeping" functions, and matches the physical equipment in the computer to the elements of particular software languages.

Very large computer systems use operating systems that coordinate the processing of many programs at once, managing "waiting lists" of programs to be processed, keeping track of charges to various users, and managing the use of peripherals, such as printers. Some microcomputers have no separate operating system, they function automatically in one language, such as BASIC. A very common microcomputer operating system is CP/M, which means Control Program for Microcomputers. It was developed by and is a product of Digital Research, a California software company. Literally hundreds of microcomputers have the capability to run under this operating system, which means that many programs written on one brand of machine can be run on another brand without modification. There are some limitations on this transfer capability. The CP/M versions must be comparable, as some earlier versions do less than some more recent versions. Also, the machines must have the same basic equipment, because a program may require a specific peripheral such as a graphics printer. One additional limitation is that disks from one brand of computer are often not readable on another brand, because the approaches to recording information on a disk are not standardized. While these are significant limitations (and not really due to limitations of CP/M), they are not insurmountable and they permit a great deal of flexibility in software selection. There are other operating systems for microcomputers, including products for the IBM, Apple, and Radio Shack systems.

Operating systems for small computers are advancing in several important ways:

Multi-user operating systems will allow several people to share use of a small computer, and allow several small computers to share information.

Multi-task operating systems will allow several programs to run on the same computer at once. Word processing, accounting, and electronic mail could run simultaneously on an office computer. The operator could split the screen between programs.

The overall capacity of operating systems is increasing, allowing use of greater amounts of primary memory and secondary storage.

Graphics capabilities are increasingly supported by operating systems.

As operators of large computers recognize the important role of small computers in providing services, the operating systems of both the small and large computers will become increasingly compatible.

SOFTWARE PROFILE 2: TELECOMMUNICATIONS PROGRAMS

Telecommunications programs permit one computer to communicate with another computer. For example, two persons with desktop computers may need to send documents and reports back and forth, or someone with a desktop computer may need to communicate with a large computer system. The telecommunications program supervises the internal parts of the computer so that files or text typed at the keyboard can be sent and received through a communications port, usually over a telephone line, to and from the other computer.

A very simple program helps the computer to operate as if it were only a terminal, such as a cathode ray terminal or teletype printer. Whatever is typed on the keyboard is printed on the screen (or typed on paper) and sent out the communications port. Whatever is received through the communications port is printed on the screen or on paper. The computer seems just like a printer to the computer on the other end of the line. However, the telecommunications program has done two important jobs. First, it has coordinated computer operation so that the computer functions as a terminal. Second, it has processed the incoming and outgoing electronic signal for communication over a cable, and perhaps over a telephone line through a modem.

More sophisticated programs make full use of the capabilities of the desktop computer on which the program is operated. The only limits are the technology of the specific computer and modem, and the sophistication of the program. The user may be able to enter the telephone number of the other computer, so that the number is "dialed" by the computer. Some programs store the phone number as well, so that only a name for the other computer need be recalled. The rest is automatic. The material sent and received over the telephone may be stored on a disk. Subsequently, that material might be modified with a word processor for inclusion in a report, or it might be stored as backup documentation of the transmission content. The printer associated with the desktop computer might be turned on during the transmission to create a written copy.

In large computer systems, telecommunications programs are often built into the operating system or application program. This approach is common for applications requiring many distant terminals. Such telecommunications programs are much more complex, as they may assign terminals to communications ports as they are available and perform other housekeeping tasks for the computer system.

In large systems, another type of telecommunications program manages the transmission of information over the phone lines, to provide the lowest cost combination of phone lines. The programs and supporting equipment also can combine many transmissions into one very fast signal (reconstituting the individual signals at the other end), to reduce the number of phone lines needed to support each terminal.

SOFTWARE PROFILE 3:   GENERAL-PURPOSE LANGUAGES

There are three common ways to develop or acquire a computer program. It can be written in machine language, which would be very tedious and time consuming. A specialized program can be purchased, ready to run with perhaps a little modification. The third way is to write the program in a high-level language. There are many such languages, but several of the most common ones are BASIC (Basic All-purpose Symbolic Instruction Code), COBOL (COmmon Business-Oriented Language), FORTRAN (FORmula TRANslation), and PASCAL. Many books have been written on the various languages, and thus we do not explain them in depth here. However, there are some factors to consider in selecting a programming language to learn, use, or adopt for an organization.

BASIC is frequently used for small computers; FORTRAN and COBOL are often used in large systems. It is possible to use any of these languages on the opposite size machine, but you may find yourself relatively alone if you do.

BASIC has the advantage of being highly unstructured, so that it is easy to change a program in development, until you reach a point where the program becomes too complex and confusing to manage. The other languages require more precision as to the organization and location of program elements. This increases the speed and efficiency of the program as it runs, but it sometimes makes programming more complex.

A program written in BASIC sometimes can be understood by an untrained person more easily than one written in the other languages. The statements in BASIC resemble the English language, fewer codes and expressions are needed, and fewer instructions are implied by the locations of terms within the program. These features make BASIC less efficient, but easier to understand.

While not always true, BASIC usually runs more slowly than the other languages, especially if the program has not been *compiled* or translated into machine language before it is run. In most cases, BASIC is *interpreted,* which means that the instructions are not converted to machine language first, but instead this conversion occurs while the program is running.

Unless a manager plans to program a computer directly, it is usually more effective and practical to direct attention to what a program can do, rather than to what language it happens to be written in. If a manager desires to learn a programming language to use on a desktop computer, then BASIC is probably the best choice, because of its simplicity and extensive use on small computers.

SOFTWARE PROFILE 4: GRAPHICS EQUIPMENT AND SOFTWARE

A useful feature of many computer systems is the ability to describe information through illustrations and diagrams. This ability requires coordination between the computer itself, the software, and the device that creates the visual display. When the display is on the screen of the terminal, the process is less complicated than when a plotter or graphics printer is used.

While efforts are under way among equipment manufacturers and programmers to develop a common set of standards and definitions for graphics, a universal standard is still not fully developed and accepted. One such standard is NAPLPS (North American Presentation-Level-Protocol Syntax). It describes a standard set of instructions for drawing regular and irregular lines (such as in maps), defining new text or graphic characters (such as foreign language characters or graphic symbols), or describing the appearance of a field (such as the color and texture of a building drawing). A universal standard would permit computers with different graphics-handling approaches to share graphic information.

Until a standard is commonly used, building a graphics capability into a computer system cannot be done casually. The best results are often achieved when a package of equipment and software have been developed expressly for this capability. Some examples are the common game computers sold in stores. These systems offer excellent graphics capabilities for limited purposes.

There are also some other techniques. For example, some plotters and printers have a built-in graphics capability, so that all the computer has to do is send a control signal, and then a specific series of numbers and labels associated with the requested diagram, and the device produces the diagram without further instruction by the computer. This simplifies the process of matching the computer, software, and printer, but it limits the choices of diagrams available.

The most advanced systems are used for computer-aided design and computer-aided manufacture (CAD/CAM). These systems can manipulate a three-dimensional illustration so that it can be presented from several perspectives. They can measure characteristics of a design, such as weight or volume of metal, to aid in design decisions. They can also produce technical drawings used for construction or manufacture. This type of system is commonly used in manufacturing industries and in architectural and engineering firms.

FINAL OBSERVATIONS

What lessons might a manager recall from this discussion, beyond the information itself and the day-to-day benefits of an ability to understand and communicate about computers?

An important realization is that understanding how a computer system works has value for a manager only if the information is up to date. In a field that is changing quickly, this requires that a manager subscribe to one or several newspapers or magazines on the subject. Many periodicals are expressly developed for this purpose, and a good selection can usually be found in a library, computer store, or bookstore.

Another lesson concerns the pace of innovation. Any computer system can become obsolete in a matter of a few months or years. It will still perform as when purchased, but other systems will do the same tasks better. Such innovation will be a source of frustration from time to time, but often it will also be a stimulus for enthusiasm and creative insight as well.

PART
II

MANAGEMENT
APPLICATIONS

CHAPTER 3
COMPUTER-AIDED STRATEGIC DECISION MAKING

Sure, savings from the inventory system alone have paid for the computer already. It does the job more quickly and accurately, with lower staff costs. The big surprise to me, however, was the way that the computer helped me to make better decisions. Here's an example. Some recent tax law changes seemed to improve the outlook for some machinery investments I had been planning. I wrote a simple program that allowed me to identify the bottom line cost for each machine, using several different approaches to purchasing and leasing. After that, I figured the payback period given the most favorable and least favorable sales conditions for our products. The program gave me much more detailed information than I was used to, and provided it quickly. Today, I don't know how I'd get along without the computer.

D ecision making is one of the most important parts of a management job. When decisions are more accurate and timely, with credible backup documentation, then operational improvements, promotions, and other benefits are sure to follow. But problem analysis with a computer has a reputation for complexity and methodological difficulty. Large models and simulations deserve such an image, because the numbers of measures and the elaborate statistical relationships between the measures require powerful computers, complex programming, and insightful modeling design and methodological planning.

However, a manager with no experience in simpler and more direct applications forgoes a powerful and helpful administrative tool. An important insight into computer-aided decision making is that there is a range of complexity and precision in techniques and approaches, and that some can be applied very simply and easily by persons with little prior experience with computers. This chapter will review several groups of problem-solving methods, with an emphasis on simple and direct applications. Once a manager grasps the less complex approaches, it is then not difficult to visualize how decision analysis models can be made more sophisticated and powerful. A manager, faced with a real-world problem, can then attempt simpler approaches alone or obtain help in applying more complex strategies.

APPROACHES TO COMPUTER-AIDED DECISION MAKING

Computers are generally used either to support *operations* or to support *decision making.* In supporting operations, computers are most often used for data base management (record systems) or for process control (operating machines). Operational topics are covered in the next chapter. In aiding decision making, computers provide analysis of information used in making a choice.

There are several strategies in the use of computers to aid decision making. Sometimes the analysis programs are built into a larger scale records management system, providing continuous monitoring and guidance. Sometimes specialized programs are developed that are used periodically but are not built into a larger information system. Finally, outside organizations (usually consulting companies) maintain sophisticated and detailed programs for very special purposes. When a company purchases advice from an outside organization, part of what is bought is the use of the computer and the program.

During the 1960s and 1970s, most computer systems were large multi-user configurations. It followed, therefore, that most computer programs to aid in decision making were also large in scale and application. More recently, with the advent of smaller scale computers, a more individualized approach to such programs has emerged. The large and small systems differ in several important ways:

Large systems are usually operated for, not by, the executive. The operators are often the data processing specialists within the organization or consultants acquired from outside. The small systems are often operated directly by the executive, sometimes with assistance.

Large systems tend to force central control over decision making by the team of staff operating and using the programs. Smaller ones are more decentralized and are often not uniform in approach and application across an organization. This can represent both an advantage and a disadvantage.

Large systems tend to perform routine and repetitive analyses, because repeated use lowers the cost per use. Smaller systems are used for more unique problems.

Large systems tend to be highly structured, precise, and not amenable to change. Smaller systems are adaptive in nature, susceptible to evolution as definitions and circumstances of problems change.

Large systems tend to employ highly developed analytical methods. Smaller systems tend to mirror the executives own thought processes and questions in decision making, expanding the executives grasp of the problem instead of providing the answer to a highly defined question.

Large systems can be written in many languages in many ways. However, small systems, because they may not be used as

many times and because they are often developed directly by
the executive, must be easy to develop and revise.

How can a manager put a computer to work to improve decisions? The traditional approach is to call in an outside consultant,
or the corporate data processing or planning department, to apply
large and complex models. Because of the cost and time involved,
a request for such help often may be turned down. The alternative
is to consider smaller and simpler techniques.

One might write a program directly in a general-purpose language, such as BASIC. This requires that the executive either
learn the language or work with someone who knows it already.
Another approach is to purchase programs specially developed
to aid decision making, such as a scheduling or investment analysis program. For certain common problems, usually involving financial analysis, programs have been developed for use on
microcomputers that rival the large system offerings in terms of
precision and sophistication. A third approach is to use a general-purpose spreadsheet program that allows the executive to use
the computer both to develop and to revise the program with little
prior training and experience.

When should a manager attempt to model a decision making
problem with a small system? There are several points to consider in making the choice. One factor is the quality of the available descriptive information. Since the accuracy of the findings
and recommendations of a model is limited by the quality of the
information used as a basis for those findings and recommendations, it is pointless to apply a powerful, expensive, and complex
program using questionable source data. The old saying "garbage
in, garbage out" applies. Another factor is the value of a precise
answer. If, for example, the cost of a wrong decision might be
$300, it makes little sense to spend $5000 in formulating the decision. A final consideration is the nature of the problem itself.
Some problems are qualitative, not quantitative. Qualitative decisions often involve questions of values and goals, or judgments
about human nature and other unpredictables. A manager may
attempt to avoid basic judgments, hiding behind numbers and
computer printouts.

If the problem is quantitative, is the price of a wrong decision is high, and if good data are available, then use of a powerful and highly developed program might be worthwhile. If the problem can be quantified, if reasonably good data are available, and if there is moderate value in a precise answer, then use of a small system might be worthwhile.

SOME GENERAL TECHNIQUES IN COMPUTER-AIDED DECISION MAKING

Once a manager decides to apply a computer to the analysis of a decision or problem, the next step is to select an appropriate computer program. There are many specific programs to choose from, but it is possible to classify them in three groups: spread sheet computation programs, statistical packages, and specialized decision making programs. Each will be the subject of a software profile.

SOFTWARE PROFILE 5:   SPREADSHEET COMPUTATION PROGRAMS

For most executives, spreadsheet computation programs are the simplest and most effective approaches for help in decision making at a small scale. These programs are one of a set of commonly used executive computing tools. Many such programs are on the market, two of which are sold under the trade names VisiCalc and T-Maker. The concept behind these programs is relatively simple but very powerful as a computing tool. A spreadsheet program allows an executive to create an electronic two-dimensional table in the memory of the computer. Generally the rows correspond to cases, persons, district offices, or products, while the columns correspond to characteristics of each case, such as size, cost, success rate, level of production, or availability.

In creating an electronic table, the executive can either enter specific numbers or labels in columns, rows, or positions within the table, or the executive can define a column, row, or position in terms of one or more other columns, rows, or positions. Usually, the executive directly enters into the table information that is known at the start of the analysis. Then the program allows the executive to create additional rows and columns by defining these in computational or logical relationships to the existing rows and columns. For example:

A specific row/column position can be defined as a specific number: Let all the numbers in column 4 be 7.

A new row/column position can be a duplication of a specified existing one: Let the numbers in column 6 be a duplication of the numbers in column 2.

A new row/column position can be defined by adding, subtracting, multiplying, or dividing two or more existing ones: Let the numbers in column 7 be the result of adding the numbers in column 4 to the numbers in column 6.

A new row/column position can be given a specific value if a stated condition exists: If the number in column 7 is greater than 22, then make column 8 a 0; otherwise make column 8 a 1.

Consider the following illustration: a project budget in which the columns are labeled with letters and the rows are labeled with numbers. The four columns are (A) Item, (B) Unit Cost, (C) Number Purchased, and (D) Total Cost. The four rows are (1) Chairs, (2) Desks, (3) Tables, and (4) Project Budget. A table could be constructed using a spreadsheet program, and the program would require the following instructions:

LABEL the columns: A=Item, B=Unit Cost, C=Number Purchased, and D=Total Cost.

LABEL the rows: 1=Chairs, 2=Desks, 3=Tables, and 4=Project Budget.

ASSIGN the following values to positions in the table: B1=100, B2=200, B3=200, C1=10, C2=5, and C3=5. (Note that "B2" refers to "Column B, Row 2", "C1" refers to "Column C, Row 1", etc.)

MULTIPLY the numbers in column B by the numbers in column C for rows 1, 2, and 3, and ASSIGN the resulting values to column D.

ADD the values in positions D1, D2, and D3, and ASSIGN the sum to D4.

This series of instructions defines Table 3.1.

Each spreadsheet software package has its own exact language for defining tables and computations. Some programs have more developed instructions and capabilities for labeling rows and columns, as well as some sophisticated computational capabilities for projections of trends in the data. Each program allows the executive to construct tables from selected rows and columns to be printed out in report form.

A major advantage of some spreadsheet programs is that tables created and stored can be called up using another program and subjected to a different type of analysis or process. The reverse is also true, so that

Table 3.1. A Spreadsheet Illustration

	A Item	B Unit Cost	C Number Purchased	D Total Cost
1	Chairs	100	10	1000
2	Desks	200	5	1000
3	Tables	200	5	1000
4	Project Budget			3000

information stored in a record system, for example, can be analyzed using the spreadsheet program.

Many of the very complex approaches and methods to aid decision making can be applied in simple and somewhat preliminary ways using a spreadsheet program. For that reason, as specific decision analysis models and approaches are presented later in this chapter, some of the approaches will be illustrated using a small-scale spreadsheet approach.

SOFTWARE PROFILE 6: STATISTICAL ANALYSIS PACKAGES

When an accurate decision requires supporting information, a common use of computers is to analyze the source data and create tables that summarize the information and present the implications for the decision to be made. The role of the computer is to "number crunch," to apply a specific statistical procedure to data. The statistical procedures are relatively standard, since an average salary would be computed in the same manner as an average age.

Any introductory statistics book can provide a summary of the many commonly accepted computational procedures, and more specialized books can describe procedures that are applicable to more unique situations and applications. Some of the most common statistical procedures include the computation of means (averages), standard deviations (indicators of the variability of a given measure across a number of cases), frequencies (summaries of numbers and percentages of a measure—e.g., 60% male, 40% female), analysis of variance (comparison of the characteristics of two groups), correlation (measures of the degree of association of two measures), and regression (predicting the value, for a given person or case, of an unknown measure from other known measures).

Because standard statistical procedures can be applied to a wide range of types of data, provided that the basic assumptions and requirements of the procedure are complied with, a variety of statistical packages have been developed. Common examples of packages available on large computer systems are SPSS (Statistical Package for the Social Sciences), and SAS (Statistical Analysis System). Other packages are intended more explicitly for business, engineering, biomedical, and other specialized applications.

The common feature of such programs is that they consist of a library of programs to carry out standard computational procedures. The term *statistical package* is commonly used because the collection of programs is packed into a single overall system. Standard procedures apply for all the computations for common functions, such as entering data or defining and labeling tables. Each computational procedure provides for its own unique output tables and summaries. Usually the program requires the user to elect certain options in each computational procedure, to tailor the analysis to the specific type of information, research design, or application circumstance.

Most of these programs are available only on large computer systems, and sometimes on minicomputer systems. However, as the power and capacity of microcomputers increases, many of the major packages will be revised for the smaller machines. Also available are some lesser known statistical packages written specifically for the smaller systems. These packages usually perform a more limited number of computational procedures on smaller data bases.

SOFTWARE PROFILE 7:   SPECIALIZED PROGRAMS AND MODELS

Many management problems are unique, necessitating special computer programs for their analysis. Some management problems can be examined with greater precision if a special program is used that is fully developed to consider all the dimensions of the situation. Also, some problems are best considered in relation to past experiences, described in large data bases that include the characteristics and outcomes associated with similar previous cases. Much software has been developed for large and small computer systems in response to the need for special programs.

Where does a manager go to find the right program for the problem to be solved or the decision to be made? There are a variety of sources for special programs, and several factors limit how a manager should proceed with a search.

Some programs are available only as a service to be purchased from a consulting organization that owns and operates the program. What you buy is a report developed using the program, rather than the program itself. Usually this applies to programs that rely upon special data bases that must be constantly updated. If the program itself were purchased for independent operation, it would quickly become out of date and irrelevant.

Most programs run only on certain computers. Thus, one tactic is to contact the manufacturer or retailer of the computer that you intend to use. Such organizations usually maintain lists, manuals, handbooks, and summaries of available software, and often can provide the program itself.

Another approach is to search publications relevant to the problem to be solved, and especially those that deal with how computers can be used for such problems. The publications usually include articles and advertisements about software, as well as evaluations by experts and users.

One final approach is to identify and join a computer users' group. Some groups are organized around a specific type of equipment, while others focus upon computer solutions to particular problems. Often programs developed by other people dealing with comparable problems are swapped, shared, distributed free, or sold. While the reliability of such programs varies, some of the best and most expensive computer programs were initially developed this way or were creatively stimulated by user group efforts.

A description of the many special computer programs designed to aid in problem solving and decision making would fill a series of books that would be obsolete within months of publication. However, the next section of this chapter describes some of the common approaches used in many such programs.

SPECIFIC MODELS AND TECHNIQUES
FOR DECISION MAKING

Computer programs that aid managers in making or justifying decisions share one basic characteristic. They construct a model of the situation to be managed, using measures and characteristics of the situation. The models are usually dynamic, which means that relationships between key measures are specified, so that it is possible to change one measure and assess the possible impact of that change on or in comparison to other measures. The advantages of modeling a problem occur in several ways. First, a model can permit assessment of the possible effect of various decisions, so that an optimal decision can be identified in advance. Second, models can allow development of an optimal decision without the cost and risk of trial and error. Sometimes modeling is the only way to assess alternative decisions in advance because multiple trials (and errors) are not feasible.

The programs or models that aid decision making can be classified in a variety of ways, focusing upon the types of information used, the methods of analysis, and the scope of the recommendations generated. One approach is to examine the type of problem to be solved or question to be answered. On this basis, three groups emerge:

1.   The first group consists of models that predict future trends, events, or outcomes. Examples include the *financial statement* model, which predicts the future profit or cash flow of an organization; the *econometric* model, which predicts trends in the general economy and relates them to a specific organization's needs and goals; the *decision tree* model, which describes and predicts downstream impacts of upstream actions; the *queuing* model, which describes and predicts action and delay in complex processes; and finally, the *multiple regression* model, which permits the prediction of one characteristic of a case or event using other known characteristics of the case or event.

2.   The second group consists of models that compare and classify cases, persons, organizations, or assets, and prescribe alternative strategies to meet goals. Examples include the *comparison* model, which permits a comparison of two or more groups, persons, or events on a given measure; the *sampling* model, which permits description and comparison of large groups based upon a random selection of a subset of the members of the group; the *decision table* model, which permits the selection of courses of action based upon the systematic application of criteria; and the *market strategy* model, which identifies an optimal investment plan for a business with several operations competing for limited resources.

3.   The third group consists of models that aid in the selection or design of operational processes. Examples include the *linear* model, which aids in the determination of the best mix of alternative resources to achieve a goal; the *scheduling* model, which

aids in scheduling projects or in evaluating schedules once a project is under way; and the *inventory* model, which helps in determining the best time to order a given product and proper amount.

These categories overlap somewhat, but they do serve to orient a manager to the potential uses of the models. The discussion of each model below will focus upon the basic strategy and underlying logic of the model, especially as it might be used in an immediate application by an executive. Thus, the examples and explanations do not present in-depth methodological detail, which can be obtained from textbooks that focus explicitly upon each model. It is expected that, after initial exposure and experimentation, executives may need to make in-depth use of one or more models in a specific application. At such a point, the executive is encouraged to study the applicable model in greater detail than it is practical to present in this book.

Prediction Models

The first group of models attempts to describe future events on the basis of trends, relevant and comparable historical patterns, or relationships between the measure or event to be predicted and other measures and events that have already been predicted. There are many approaches to prediction, and the best one for a particular problem depends upon the degree of accuracy needed, the nature of the information available, and the scope of analysis desired.

A common approach is the *financial statement model,* a type of program that predicts the financial outlook for a project or organization on the basis of estimates of operational factors contributing to the financial outlook.

An executive might estimate the net income for a product line, for various levels of sales, using a formula that considers the fixed and variable costs.

A real estate investor, considering the purchase of a property, might estimate cash flow using formulas based upon past experience.

A spreadsheet program can be used for a basic example of this approach. Each row might represent information about separate product lines, investments, or activities, and the columns would represent performance, cost, and revenue measures. These measures could be combined to create additional columns predicting future costs and revenues. Table 3.2 provides an example of a simple cash flow spreadsheet that might be used by a real estate investor.

For this first example using a spreadsheet approach, let us examine in detail how the table was constructed.

1. The rows and columns were defined.
2. The cost and income for this year and last year for each property (in thousands) were entered directly by the executive. The "net" column was defined as income minus cost.
3. For "next year," the cost and income columns were defined by the growth rate between "this year" and "last year': The figure for "this year" is divided by the figure for "last year," and that ratio is multiplied by the figure for "this year," producing an estimate of "next year's" costs and income based upon an extension of past trends. The "net" column was defined as the difference between income and cost.
4. The row labeled "total" is the sum of each column.

The exact procedures to be entered into the computer to carry out these steps vary according to the specific spreadsheet program used. However, regardless of the program, the task described in each step must be done. An actual spreadsheet pro-

Table 3.2. Financial Statement Model

| Property | Last Year | | | This Year | | | Next Year | | |
	Cost	Income	Net	Cost	Income	Net	Cost	Income	Net
Green St.	10	15	5	12	15	3	15	15	0
Blue St.	6	8	2	6	10	4	6	12	6
Red St.	10	6	−4	10	8	−2	10	11	1
Total	26	29	3	28	33	5	31	38	7

gram would allow the creation of many more rows and columns, so that the electronic table within the computer would be much larger. A summary table including only some of the rows and columns might be developed to be printed on paper.

The model can be made more complex, reflecting real-world circumstances, by including, for example, components of costs and income, such as taxes, utilities, repairs, interest, and other costs, reaching back for more than one year, and predicting several years in advance. The formulas for predicting the growth of each cost and income element could be unique to each element, since interest costs might be fixed and taxes might grow at a slower rate than utility costs. Because such a small-scale model is adaptive, the executive might begin with a very simple and obvious model, and gradually build in complexity. Larger organizations often maintain very complex financial statement models for planning and budgeting that start with the simple type of model described here but define relationships in much more complex ways.

Major organizations have developed sophisticated financial statement models used in developing and evaluating financial plans and performance. Such models can include very complex relationships among variables.

Generally, financial statement models use information that is internal to the organization or project studied, such as costs, numbers of sales, and similar measures. Often, however, a good prediction must consider factors outside of the organization, such as future interest rates, unemployment rates, or tendencies of people to spend money. As these types of external measures are worked into the decision making model, it can become an econometric model.

Econometric models describe and predict measures of the economy on a local, regional, or national basis. A pure econometric model relates one economic measure to another—for example, to estimate the effect of high interest rates on unemployment. An applied econometric model relates economic measures to specific and immediate problems, such as the effect of interest rates on a company's sales. Such models are often used to estimate costs and opportunities for specific businesses and organizations, when the nature of the enterprise is tied to economic conditions. Many complex econometric models are maintained by consulting firms and are available to many organizations. In this way, the high costs of development and upkeep can be shared among the user organizations. Larger businesses sometimes maintain such models as well.

It is usually impractical for an individual manager or business owner to develop a pure econometric model. Simple applied models are easier to construct, but they usually rely upon published or generally available economic predictions for those parts of the model, rather than attempting to develop estimates independently. Such models might be used in the following examples:

In planning a new project, an executive might include estimates of future interest rates in a program, to compute estimated interest costs on a variable rate loan over future months.

For an employment agency where numbers of client contacts vary with the local unemployment rate, estimates of the unemployment rate for the next eight quarters might be used to estimate levels of client contacts.

The following spreadsheet in Table 3.3 illustrates how the executive in the first example might construct a table. The table is created by:

1. Defining the rows and columns.
2. Inserting the estimated interest rates in the first row.

Table 3.3. Econometric Model

Estimated Interest Rate	Principal	Quarterly Interest				Total Interest
		1st 3.0	2nd 3.6	3rd 3.9	4th 3.6	
Green St.	$10,000	300	360	390	360	1410
Blue St.	6,000	180	216	234	216	846
Red St.	10,000	300	360	390	360	1410
Total	26,000	780	936	1014	936	3666

3. Inserting the principals for the three loans in the second column.

4. Defining the interest columns as the principal for each row multiplied by the interest rate in the first row of each column.

5. Defining the total row as the sum of the columns except for the first row.

At this point, the table illustrates merely some interest costs for several loans. The executive can use the model to estimate interest costs over the next four quarters. However, by adjusting the model as estimates of interest rates are revised and when new loans are added and principals change, the model begins to relate the affairs of a local business to general economic statistics.

This example illustrates a very basic applied econometric model, and the factor that makes it econometric as opposed to merely a financial statement model is the reference to the external economic information to compute the answer. A pure econometric model, as explained earlier, would derive predictions of one economic measure from another, such as predicting future unemployment from a combination of such current measures as interest rates, growth in the money supply, government spending, and inflation. Governmental and consulting organizations and major corporations maintain complex econometric models for use in planning.

Another approach to prediction is the *decision tree* or *flow model,* which describes the breakdown of a group of people, cases, or asset units as they move through a process. They all may pass through point A, then split, with one-half going to point B and one-half to point C. Those at point C may further split, with one-third going to point H, and so forth. The model is useful in that it can illustrate the "downstream effects" of decisions or actions taken at earlier points. Such models might be used in the following types of situations:

In a retail business, the breakdown of consumer decision making can be described from the point of initial contact, through various stages of the sales process. The effects of changes in approach can also be estimated.

An insurance agency can track the processing of claims, describing the general intake of claims, the breakdown of types of claims, and the types of dispositions of claims once processed.

A spreadsheet program is not suited to complex decision tree modeling, because the models require the definition of complex relationships between sets of specific items, rather than general rows and columns. Generally, such models are developed using specialized software. For example, a package called GPSS (General Purpose Simulation Software) can be used to construct complex flow diagrams. Simpler models can also be constructed using general-purpose languages, such as BASIC, through a technique called *iteration.* Under this approach, a computational procedure is performed many times, and the ending values for key measures are used for each successive computation. The ending values of the key measures are also printed out at specific intervals, such as every 15 times the computation is performed. In large organizations, complex decision tree models are employed to predict downstream effects of changes in strategy and tactics. A classic use of such models is in criminal justice planning, where complex models estimate the downstream effects on prosecution, courts, and corrections of upstream law enforcement changes.

A spreadsheet approach is well suited to describing a particular path in a complex model. For example, an auto dealer might describe the marketing process from initial advertising contact to the ultimate sale, tracking only the path that leads to the sale itself. Table 3.4 shows what this might look like.

This table describes a particular pathway to purchasing a car. There are, of course, other pathways—for example, people might come in who did not see an advertisement. The table is constructed by:

1. Defining the rows and columns.
2. Entering the initial number, which in this example is the size of the total market.

Table 3.4.   Decision Tree or Flow Model

Step	Start Number	Success Percent	End Number
Total market	2,000,000	100	2,000,000
See advertisement	2,000,000	30	600,000
Come to dealership	600,000	1	6,000
Talk with salesperson	6,000	60	3,600
Negotiate price	3,600	30	1,080
Order car	1,080	40	432
Take possession	432	95	410

3. Entering the percentages of persons at each level who continue to the next level.

4. For each row except the first, defining the start number as the same as the end number for the previous level.

5. Defining the end number as the start number multiplied by the success percent.

A description of this particular pathway would allow the dealer to assess the possible impact upon sales of a change in advertising policy, an increase in sales force, or a change in sales tactics. A more complex model, using more sophisticated software, could take into consideration diminishing returns so that, when the percentage of people who talk with the salesperson is increased by 2%, the percentage of persons who discuss price might be reduced by 1%. The actual formula would have to be determined through examination of actual consumer behavior. Other variations would include the incorporation of additional pathways (such as people who do not see the advertisement), subpathways (such as a breakdown of people according to the specific advertisement seen), reverse flows (such as people who negotiate a price, leave for several months, and come back at an earlier level), and speed and duration factors (such as differentiating between people who buy in 1–2 days, as compared to those who take weeks to decide).

The advantage of the very limited spreadsheet approach is simplicity and ease in using existing information. However, should an executive achieve good results with such a limited approach, the next step would be to use some of the software packages developed specifically for decision tree modeling. While these packages are more complex and may require technical support in implementation, the benefits from increased computing power can be significant.

A *queuing simulation* is very much like a decision tree model, except that the flows from one point to another are not constant and exact proportions. Instead, they fluctuate unpredictably so that the average result over many trials corresponds to an exact proportion, but the breakdown in a specific trial varies above and below this average. This approach often requires that the computer run the model many times. An alternative source of uncertainty is to use actual information from the process being studied, such as orders placed over the last year. Queuing simulations might be used to answer the following types of questions.

A bank executive might want to estimate the size of waiting lines that would result from several approaches to staffing the teller windows.

A retail executive might want to identify the likely effects of stocking various levels of inventory of certain products, balancing the savings associated with reduced inventory costs against the risk of lost sales.

A spreadsheet queuing simulation would have to rely upon actual records as a source of uncertainty, as most of the spreadsheet programs usually do not have the capability to enter random information in designated rows or columns. In the case of the bank executive described above, a program could be constructed to assess typical lengths of waiting lines at the end of the noon hour given various numbers of tellers. Table 3.5 shows what a spreadsheet produced by such a program might look like.

The table is created by:

1. Defining the rows and columns.
2. Entering the number of customers served during the noon hour for each of the days.

Table 3.5.   Queuing Simulation

Day Number	Number of Customers	Waiting line length at 1:00 pm		
		3 Tellers	4 Tellers	5 Tellers
1	100	10	0	0
2	125	35	5	0
3	115	25	0	0
4	135	45	15	0
5	105	15	0	0
6	155	65	35	5
7	135	45	15	0
8	100	10	0	0
9	150	60	30	0
10	135	45	15	0
Number of days with a line		10	6	1
Percent of days with a line		100	60	10
Average line size		36	19	5

3. Defining the three teller columns as the number of customers minus 90, 120, and 150, respectively (assuming that each customer takes 2 minutes, and therefore that three tellers can service 90 people, four can service 120, etc.), changing any negative numbers to zero (since there cannot be a waiting line with fewer than 0 persons in it).

4. Defining the "number of days with a line" as 10 (the total number of days in the simulation) minus the sum of the number of zeros in each of the teller columns (which is the number of days when there was no line at 1:00 pm).

5. Defining the "percentage of days" as the figure in the previous row expressed as a percentage of 10.

6. Defining the "average line size" as the sum of the first 10 rows of each teller column, divided by the figure in the "number of days" row.

Using the program, the executive can estimate the number of days when there will be a waiting line, and how long the line will be. A more complex and realistic simulation would use many more days of information and could add the following dimensions to the program:

It could break down the lunch hour into quarter hours, and perhaps include the quarter hour before and after the lunch hour, to determine how often during the hour the line gets longer than it is at 1:00 pm.

It could break down customers according to the type of business they have to conduct, to estimate the number of times the lines might be lengthened because of the simultaneous arrival of an unusual number of people with large amounts of business.

Each of these additions would require more rows, for information about customer arrivals on a quarter-hour basis and for information about the number of customers arriving with large tasks to be accomplished.

Another model that uses prediction to prescribe approaches to the management of businesses or projects employs a statistical procedure called *multiple regression* to identify the recommended approach. This procedure generates a formula that can be used to predict the magnitude of one unknown characteristic of a case or process using known values of other characteristics of that case or process. A multiple regression equation incorporates several measures into the equation, to improve the accuracy of the estimate.

To perform a multiple regression analysis, it is generally most practical to use an existing program. Many programs are available for large computer systems, and microcomputer-based programs are increasingly available as well. The best use of the spreadsheet program occurs when a formula must be applied to a number of situations, as in the following cases:

In evaluating sites for a new franchised restaurant, a manager might develop a program to calculate the results of a standard formula predicting sales for each site under consideration.

In evaluating risks associated with various business loans, a bank might apply a formula derived through a multiple regression analysis of past performance of similar loans.

In the case of the franchised restaurant, the manager might obtain from the franchising organization a formula based upon past performance of restaurants in other locations, predicting unit sales volume from such site characteristics as vehicle traffic on the street, volume of traffic in adjacent stores, and combined capacity of adjacent restaurants. Computation of such a formula would require use of a special program because of the number of calculations to be made, and the size of the data base required. However, a spreadsheet program could be used to routinely apply the formula, once derived, to specific sites. For purposes of this example, a hypothetical formula might be as follows: The best estimate of the average unit sales per day is obtained by adding 2% of vehicle traffic plus 10% of the adjacent store traffic, and subtracting 30% of the capacity of the nearby restaurants. The result might look like Table 3.6.

The table is developed using a spreadsheet program by:

1. Defining the rows and columns.
2. Inserting in the second, third, and fourth columns the data for each site.
3. Defining the fourth column as the sum of 2% of column 2 plus 10% of column 3, minus 30% of column 4, as required by the formula.

The table shows that the Blue Street site is likely to have the best unit sales levels, even though it has the worst vehicle traffic and also a restaurant nearby. The model would permit the analysis of possible impacts on unit sales of changes in traffic patterns, adjacent store traffic, or new restaurants opening nearby. The

Table 3.6. Multiple Regression Model

Site	Vehicle Traffic	Pedestrian Traffic	Combined Capacity of Adjacent Restaurants	Predicted Unit Sales
Green St.	5000	1000	400	80
Blue St.	3000	1500	50	195
Red St.	8000	1000	800	20
Yellow St.	4000	500	0	130

new data would have to be entered into the model, and the program would be rerun.

Consulting organizations and some larger corporations maintain multiple regression models to support decisions and plans. For example, several models predict profit for a given business based on profit and performance measures of other comparable businesses.

Classification Models

Thus far, some examples of prediction models have been presented. Another very different purpose for decision support models is to prescribe management strategies for particular management circumstances. These methods do not predict the future; rather, they compare and classify cases or situations and recommend specific courses of action. Usually, the recommended course of action is based upon the policies or prior experience of the person or organization making the model, and the recommendations are therefore not intrinsic to the model.

The simplest classification model compares one case, person, or group to others. *Comparison models* compare groups, or the results achieved by a given group to what was expected, or actual results to the results achieved during another time period. Usually one or more groups, persons, or cases are identified (classified) as having accomplished more or as having a preferable method. For example:

A manager might compare the sales achieved in one district to the sales achieved in several others.

Sales of all sales personnel might be compared to the expected levels of sales proposed by management for each salesperson.

Sales achieved during the most recent year might be compared to previous years.

Much of the usefulness of comparisons depends upon the accuracy and relevance of the measures used as a basis for comparison and on the fairness of the purposes to which the comparisons are put. The use of a spreadsheet program for the computation of comparisons is a relatively simple process. Generally, each row of the table describes one case, employee, event, or location. The columns describe characteristics or performance measures applicable to each row. Table 3.7 is an example of a comparison spreadsheet in a sales organization.

Table 3.7. Comparison Model

1 Name	2 Actual Sales	3 Expected Sales	4 Percent
Smith	40	50	80
Jones	30	60	50
Murphy	50	40	125
Total	120	150	80

This simple example is constructed by:

1. Defining the columns and rows.
2. Filling in columns 1, 2, and 3, totaling columns 2 and 3; and letting column 4 be column 2 expressed as a percentage of column 3.

A simple and direct comparison approach is the most common method used in the development of many summary reports that are parts of management information systems. The complexity of such models arises when measures become more refined to adjust for differences in cases, so that comparisons may be more meaningful.

Most managers can recall many decisions based upon comparison information of this type. In the simple example above, the percentages of actual to expected might serve as justification for decisions about training, reward, promotion, and retention. In a larger organization, decisions about resource allocation might be based on such comparisons.

Another model, related to comparison, is *statistical sampling*. Statistical sampling allows one to estimate characteristics of a large group without having to measure directly each case or person in the group. The procedures used in estimation from samples are based on probability: A number of persons or cases are randomly selected from the entire group and measured, consistent with rules that indicate when a sample is large enough to be representative of the entire group. Actual procedures vary from situation to situation; many statistics books provide thorough explanations.

There are two roles that a computer can play in a sampling project: It can help in the analysis and summarization of the findings, and it can help in the interpretation of findings. There are many generally available statistical packages for the analysis of data, and thus it is usually unnecessary and impractical for an executive to write his or her own or to construct one using a spreadsheet program. One problem might be that the sizes of the data bases to be analyzed can get too large for small computer systems. But, both large and small computer systems can aid in the interpretation of sampling statistics and in their application to practical and specific situations. Routine and repetitive interpretations can be built into a program, enabling more explicit and efficient application of findings to work situations. In the case of an ongoing market research project, a spreadsheet might look like Table 3.8.

This table converts descriptive information about a group into information that can be used for administrative action. In this case, the red survey concerns the average income of potential customers for a product. The table indicates income ranges for four levels of customers: the bottom 25% in income, the top 25%, and the two middle groups. To reach only the top 25% of customers in income, those with incomes of $27,026 or more should be reached. The table uses a statistic called a standard deviation

Table 3.8. Statistical Sampling Model

Name	Size	Mean	SD	Cutoff Scores for Low to High Quarters			
				A(25%)	B(25%)	C(25%)	D(25%)
Red	2000	25,000	3000	< 22,975	22,975-25,000	25,001-27,025	27,026+
Green	100	1,000	300	< 798	798-1,000	1,001-1,202	1,203+
Blue	1000	100	10	< 93	93-100	101-107	108+

(the SD column in the table), which is described in practically any statistics text. It defines the extent to which scores in a random sample or group vary from the average score of the sample or group. For example, in a random sample, the highest quarter of a group of scores is always .675 standard deviations above the mean.

Developing the table with a spreadsheet program involves the following steps:

1. Define the row and column labels.
2. Enter the numbers for the size, mean, and standard deviation columns for each case.
3. Define the A column as the mean minus .675 of the standard deviation.
4. Define the range of the B column as the A column figure and the mean.
5. Define the range of the C column as the mean plus 1 and the mean plus .075 of the standard deviation.
6. Define the D column as the mean plus 1 plus .675 of the standard deviation.

A more complex and useful table might divide the groups into more parts, so that more precise decisions could be made. The executive might also modify the table to provide more specific information about actions to be taken, such as the expected levels of sales for each group based upon past experience. The table could be used frequently by an executive who must apply sampling statistics in support of actual decisions.

Generally, the use of small-scale computing in complex statistical studies requires the development or acquisition of special software designed to carry out the particular calculation desired. The same observation is generally true of formal research methodologies involving hypothesis testing and other procedures as well.

Another very different approach to classification is the *decision table,* which recommends a course of action depending upon specified conditions. It is generally applicable when there is a definite course of action that should be taken under particular combinations of circumstances, and these are known in advance. Thus, the table does not aid in the ultimate decisions about what ought to be done, but it does help in the efficient classification of specific cases to assure that decisions comply with the general policy. Decision tables might be used in the following situations:

A bank, in determining whether to make certain business loans, might define certain conditions as leading to a definite approval, certain conditions as requiring further consideration, and certain conditions as leading to a definite disapproval.

An agency having to make decisions about many clients might construct a decision guidance model that requires that key information be entered about a case under consideration, and then provides a preliminary recommendation for action.

For example, a prison system may be planning some changes in criteria for the assignments of prisoners to high, medium, and low security prisons. A simple decision model might consider the length of sentence, type of crime, and past behavior. If any of these is above a certain cutoff, then the prisoner is recommended for high security; if they are all low, then the recommendation is minimum. If neither condition is true, then the prisoner is designated for further consideration by staff. The table might look like Table 3.9.

The crime severity and behavior severity are ratings on a scale of 10, based upon assessment of each prisoner's record. The recommended action is as follows: a 3 implies high security, a 1 implies low security, and a 2 implies further consideration by staff. The development of the table requires the following steps:

Table 3.9. Decision Table Model

Prisoner Number	Sentence Length	Crime Severity	Behavior Severity	Recommended Action
1	25	10	8	3
2	3	2	2	1
3	8	4	3	2

1. Define the column labels.
2. Enter the data for each case for the first four columns.
3. As a starting point, define the action column as a 2.
4. Change the action column to 3 if sentence length is above 20 or if crime or behavior severity is above 7.
5. Change the action column to 1 if the sentence length is below 10 and the crime and behavior severity are both 3 or below.

A more complex and useful table would include additional columns with more precise information about each prisoner, and would incorporate more complex rules about assignments and recommendations for action. Summary tables might also be created to show the total number and distribution of cases by security level. Finally, an important advantage of the table is the potential to explore the impact of alternative rules, defined by changes in the logic or cutoff scores to recommend high, medium, or low security.

Decision tables are often used in organizations where abstract rules or conditions must be applied to numerous cases in a routine and repetitive manner. Usually the tables exist on paper as criteria for decisions and actions, and then are added to large computerized record systems to support case decisions.

A specific type of decision table model is the *market share and market growth models* used to evaluate businesses as to their potential for future growth. These models, employed in a variety of forms by many different organizations, classify businesses into groups according to two factors: the growth of the overall market for the product produced, and the growth of the share of the overall market served by the particular business under study. One model, the Boston Consulting Group market share-growth model, can be simply described as classifying a business into one of four groups, as shown in Table 3.10.

The model recommends that "cash cow" businesses be managed to develop cash for investment into new areas, that "dog" businesses be divested or closed down; that "problem child" businesses be carefully managed to modify their market position, and that "star" businesses be developed as fully as possible.

Table 3.10.   Market Share/Growth Model

Annual Market Growth	Market Share	Classification
10% or less	High	Cash cow
10% or less	Low	Dog
Greater than 10%	High	Star
Greater than 10%	Low	Problem child

There are other models, such as the Arthur D. Little Industry Maturity and Competitive Position Matrix or the McKinsey Screen, which are variations on the same theme. It is easy to see how a spreadsheet program could be used in the application of refinements in the criteria for classification of businesses.

Selection Models

A third general type of computer program for management decision making is used in operational decision making. One kind of program examines the use of resources in a production process, while another develops and evaluates schedules.

One approach is the *linear model,* which enables a manager to select the best combination of resources to accomplish a goal. Resources might be transportation mileage, raw materials, labor, machinery, or other components of a production process. For instance:

A company may evaluate the characteristics of many possible sites for a new factory to identify the site that would have the least cost to develop.

A manufacturer may evaluate combinations of materials and labor processes that to some extent can be substituted for one another, to identify the lowest cost manufacturing arrangement.

In the first example, a relatively simple analysis could be conducted using a spreadsheet program. An executive might need to know the cost to develop each site under consideration so that it is properly graded, has access by road, and has the necessary utilities, such as electric power, water, sewer, and a gas line. However, federal funding formulas might provide for 50% of the cost of all but land purchase costs. A spreadsheet could solve the problem through a process called *enumeration,* which means that all possible solutions would be calculated and the least-cost option explicitly identified. The table might look like Table 3.11.

The spreadsheet program to develop the table would include the following steps:

1. Define and label the rows and columns.
2. Enter the data in each row for the basic costs.
3. Define the "total cost" column as the sum of the four cost columns.
4. Define the "net cost" column as the sum of one-half of the utility, grading, and access cost, plus all of the site purchase cost.

A more sophisticated analysis could include more sites and more columns of additional factors contributing to a cost-effective site, such as transportation costs and costs of delay associated with developing the site. There are several mathematical techniques for solving problems such as these without enumeration—that is, without calculating all possible solutions. However, for relatively small-scale problems, the computer-time and technical competence required to do the more complex calculations may not save enough time to make the effort worthwhile.

Another type of operations-oriented decision support program focuses upon *scheduling,* either to develop a schedule or to evalu-

Table 3.11. Linear Model

Site	Land Cost	Utility Cost	Grading Cost	Access Cost	Total Cost	Net Cost
Green St.	150	50	25	150	375	263
Red St.	300	0	10	0	310	305
Blue St.	100	80	50	160	390	245

ate and manage one already in place. A linear scheduling method simply adds the time required for each step in a project and thereby computes the total time required to fulfill all tasks. However, when tasks overlap one another, or when tasks can be combined in more than one sequence, then the problem can become quite complex. Two roughly comparable methods to manage and evaluate complex schedules are the Critical Path Method (CPM) and the Program Evaluation and Review Technique (PERT). These methods also permit identification of those elements that determine the overall length of the project.

A construction company might use these techniques to schedule a large and complex construction project, to monitor progress, and to identify the particular tasks that, if delayed, could slow down the entire project.

A retail business might use these techniques to develop a schedule for opening a new store.

There are many programs available for both large and small computer systems that enable one to schedule projects. To apply CPM or PERT usually requires a specialized program. A spreadsheet program, however, could easily track a particular sequence of steps in a project, although it would be quite difficult and cumbersome to construct a program that would evaluate many possible combinations of task sequences. A linear scheduling problem for a retail business opening a new store might look like Table 3.12.

Table 3.12. Linear Scheduling Model

Task	Weeks to Complete	Staff Required	Starting Week	Ending Week	Required Staff-Weeks
Remodel store	8	2	1	8	16
Hire sales staff	3	2	9	11	6
Project summary	15	1	15	38	

The table is constructed using a spreadsheet program in the following way:

1. Define rows and columns.
2. Enter the weeks to complete and the staff required for each task.
3. Define the "starting week" column for the first row as a 1.
4. Define the "starting week" column for all the remaining rows except the last one as the value in the "ending week" column in the previous row plus 1.
5. Define the "ending week" column as the sum of the "starting week" column plus the "weeks to complete" column, minus 1.
6. Define the "required staff-weeks" column as the product of multiplying the "weeks to complete" column by the "staff required" column.
7. Define the first data column in the summary row as the sum of that column, the second as a blank, the third as a 1, the fourth as equal to the value in the column of the previous row in the column, and the fifth as a sum of that column.

A more complex program would have more tasks (and therefore more rows) and could define more complex descriptive measures of staff and resources expended. The project would probably require a specialized program. It would be possible, even with the spreadsheet approach, to identify overlapping task schedules by including, in a separate column, the week during the previous task after which a new task can begin.

Another method for evaluating or planning operational processes is one frequently used in planning inventory and purchasing systems. *Inventory models* determine the most efficient combinations of inventory and transportation deliveries to provide for needed materials on a timely basis. For example:

A store might determine the most profitable point at which to restock a product, given purchasing and carrying costs, as well as sales losses due to being out of stock.

A business might assess potential gains from an expanded warehouse, such as reduced costs of transportation achieved through elimination of frequent small lot purchases, and lower purchasing costs due to volume discounts.

Traditionally, tedious calculation has been required to solve such problems. However, with the increasing availability of computers and flexible calculation programs, it is possible to calculate reasonably satisfactory solutions to such problems through enumeration, where the costs of all possible solutions are calculated. With a computer, the calculations can be done rapidly without extra user effort.

An appliance store operator in a small town might consider the cost of purchasing portable television sets in larger lots at a lower cost per set, against bearing the added interest and warehousing costs until the sets are sold. Assume that the store sold 120 sets per year, at the rate of 10 per month, and that they could be purchased for $200 in a quantity of 120, $220 in lots of 60, $230 in lots of 30, and $240 in lots of 10. Because of lack of storage space and financing, the store had been buying them in lots of 10. A local warehouse will store the sets for $2 per set per month, and interest rates are at 20% per year. The spreadsheet might look like Table 3.13.

The table would be created by:

1. Defining the rows and columns.
2. Entering the alternative numbers of orders, number of sets per order, and total cost per order.

Table 3.13.   Inventory Model

Number of Orders	Number of Sets	Total Cost	Cost per Set	Total Interest	Interest per Set	Warehouse Rental	Total Cost
1	120	24,000	200	2400	20	12	232
2	60	13,200	220	320	11	6	237
4	30	6,900	230	690	6	3	239
12	10	2,400	240	240	2	1	243

3. Defining the "cost per set" column as the total cost divided by the number of sets.
4. Defining the total interest (at 20% per year) as 20% of one-half of the total cost. (Use of one-half assumes that half of the sets will be sold within one-half of the year, reducing the interest costs).
5. Defining the interest per set as the total interest divided by 120 (the number of sets).
6. Defining the warehouse rental as one-half of the number of sets per order, multiplied by $24 (the annual rent to store a set in the warehouse), divided by 120 (the number of sets altogether).
7. Defining the total cost per set as the cost per set, plus the interest per set, plus the warehouse rental per set.

From the analysis the operator of the store could conclude that it would be less costly to purchase the sets in large lots and pay the storage and carrying costs. The operator may also wish to know at what point it might be less costly to buy in smaller lots should volume discounts go down, or interest rates go up or down, or warehouse rates change. Using enumeration, the operator could merely change some of the entries in the various lines, or the interest rate calculation instruction, and alternative solutions would be calculated.

FINAL OBSERVATIONS

This chapter has illustrated various methods for using computers in decision making. All the methods presented share a basic characteristic: They construct a model of the problem to be solved, describing elements of the problem in terms that can be evaluated logically and mathematically. The models do not make decisions, although they can help managers to be better informed as they make decisions. The following are several observations that help place these methods in perspective and guide their use.

Solutions often develop through trial and error, and creative insight. A manager may initially approach a problem using one model and then switch to another as the nature of the problem becomes clearer. It is useful to keep in mind the creative dimension in problem solving and the human insight that is central to it.

A basic error in the use of problem-solving models is the "fallacy of misplaced precision." Managers may use computer-aided decision models that are basically not relevant in that the models may not focus on important aspects of their problems. When effort, resources, and attention are devoted to a decision support model, the developers may persist in its use, paying attention to methodological detail rather than the relevance of the model to the problem. This is more likely in larger organizations in which communication about the nature of a modeling exercise may be limited, and reputations and "turf" may be at stake.

Managers should bear in mind the expression "garbage in, garbage out." This refers to using bad input information in a perfectly good model, on an applicable and relevant problem. Obviously, in such a circumstance even the most advanced model can be of little value. The difficulty for a manager is to recognize when such a situation exists.

The value of time in decision making should not be forgotten. In many projects, costs increase as time passes. When the increases are great, the cost reduction due to more precise decisions can be less than the cost increase due to the time needed to construct, run, and interpret a model.

Finally, perhaps the most important perspective to retain in using computer-aided decision making models concerns the value of contingency planning. Most models in most situations are imprecise. They may be more accurate than guesswork, but still not perfectly on target. As a result, it is prudent to develop contingency plans to apply if things do not work out as expected. Computer-aided models can sometimes be used most effectively in this mode, since additional runs of a model with altered input data can provide useful information in contingency planning.

The use of computers as aids to decision making can reduce the uncertainty that managers often face. However, the manager must still have the judgment and experience to apply information effectively.

CHAPTER 4
COMPUTER-AIDED
OPERATIONAL
MANAGEMENT

For most of my career, which spans about 30 years, I have managed a group practice for several doctors. I started out as a secretary, and moved up as the practice expanded. Over the years, the greatest change has been in the amount and complexity of paperwork. When I started work, most people paid for services right after an appointment, or they paid for them when we mailed out a bill. Even insurance payments were relatively simple, and most often the paperwork was between the patient and the insurance company. During the 1960s and 1970s, paperwork problems exploded. The government and the insurance companies began to require complicated forms. Not only did we have to complete the forms, but we also had to keep detailed medical and financial records to support claims. Several years ago we finally got a computer. It stores much of the background information we need and produces most of the reimbursement forms and documents automatically. Without it, my job would have become impossible.

Even though the most exciting uses of computers in management most often involve strategic planning and decision making, the most common use of computers is in operational management. In this role, computers perform much of the ongoing work of businesses and other organizations. There are two ways in which computers can contribute. In *information or records management,* the computer manages a record system, including the storage and retrieval of information, and the development of summary reports and measures. In *process control,* the computer manages an ongoing activity, usually performed largely by machines.

MANAGEMENT OF INFORMATION AND RECORDS

The most common use of computers in operational management involves the operation of record systems. *Data base management* is a general term describing the diverse range of programs that store, retrieve, and summarize records. In management, these programs include accounting and inventory systems, case management systems, and numerous specialized record systems. While there are many purposes of such systems, they share some basic operational characteristics. Information is entered in repetitive records and retrieved individually and in groups. Records are identified sometimes by a record number and sometimes through searching for one or more characteristics. Summary reports describe individual records, groups of records, or all the records.

A computer program that manages records and other data usually contains certain basic functional elements: file building, data input, sorting, manipulation, retrieval, and reporting. These categories overlap somewhat, but they identify the common features of most systems. In a specialized software package, some of the functions may be tailored to the type of use, in order to simplify use of the system. For example, in a pharmacy record system, some product classifications and names might be built into the software, and certain reports would be automatically available without special programming. It is worthwhile to examine each function, however, because the tasks associated with each are practically always done, even though the user may not notice it because the process is done by the computer automatically.

File Building

File building describes the procedures and processes for building a specific data base. The term *data base* refers to a collection of records or statistics that a computer manages. Assuming that an organization has just acquired a general-purpose data base management system, the first step would be to define the record system according to the rules and procedures of the software package. Procedures vary among software packages, but there is a common set of typical steps.

Usually the first task is to define the items to be stored, and their arrangement. A data base is stored by a computer as a set of files, and each file consists of a set of records. Usually one record contains information pertaining to a single case, person, or object, depending upon the purpose of the system. Records, in turn, consist of specific data elements. Data elements are the pieces of information which are to be stored, such as wholesale cost or retail cost in an retail store inventory system. Each element is stored in a *field* which is a specific position in a record.

In an inventory system for a food store, all of the information might be stored in one file. A specific record might be devoted to each product, one for Campbell's pea soup, one for Heinz's chicken soup, one for Crest toothpaste, and so on. Within each record would be stored, in fields, the name of the product, its shelf location, the number on hand, the wholesale cost, the retail cost, and so on. Sometimes a large record system might be broken up into several files. In a large food store, for example, one file might include only meat items, one file only dry goods, and so on. Using several files can sometimes speed up processing of the information.

The information within records can be organized in several ways. Sequential access records store items as continuous sets of fields. Thus, to reach information in the middle of the record it is necessary to read from the beginning. This is much like what one would have to do to find a particular song in the middle of a reel-to-reel tape recording. Random access files store items at predesignated points on each record, so that a given piece of information can be found directly. This is more like finding the cut of a song on a phonograph record. One can find a particular item more quickly within a random access file, since the computer can go directly to the location of the item. Sequential files, however, often can store information more efficiently, especially if the information within each record varies from case to case.

In developing a record system to be managed by a computer, it is necessary to define the files, records, and fields for the computer. Otherwise, it would not know where to store information, or where to find it when needed. Definition of a data base usually involves a series of steps.

First, each data element must be named and identified as to its type. Data elements are usually either alphanumeric (words such as "Campbell's Pea Soup") or numeric (numbers such as "$1.22"), although various software packages may use different terms for this distinction. It is useful to make the distinction because letters can be stored in relatively little space. Numbers, on the other hand, take up more space because they must usually be stored in a manner that permits calculation. Defining a data element as a word rather than a number can often save file space. For an alphanumeric item (words), the record space required would be determined by the length of the longest word or label to be stored. If a label is too long, only the letters that fit in the space available are stored, and the end of the label is cut off. The space required by a number would depend upon the possible size of the number and the degree of precision needed. Whole numbers, being less precise than decimals, require less space.

In some systems, the size of each data element must be specified, so that the length of a record can be determined. As explained above, records consist of fields, which are positions for letters or numbers. The field for a data element consisting of a name might need to be 30 characters long to accommodate long names. Storing a number for calculation might require a field as large as a series of many characters, depending upon the magnitude and degree of precision.

Next, a record format must be defined, consisting of the sequence of the data elements in the record. For example, "name" might go first, "age" second, and so on. Since the sizes of the data elements would already have been described, information on the sequence of the data elements permits the computer to construct a hypothetical "map" of the complete file.

When a data base consists of more than one file, individual records may be linked by pointers. These are items in a record describing the locations of other records in other files containing additional information on the person, case, or object. For example, a file of names and addresses would contain in each record for each person the record numbers corresponding to that person in other files.

The last step is to give each file a name or label, in case more than one file is to be maintained on the computer. If the number of records are known, such as the number of employees whose characteristics are to be maintained on file, the size of the file can also be calculated.

Data Input

The next function entails entering specific information into the records. For example, a personnel information system might include such data as the employee's name, date of employment, and job title or category. Most information systems offer certain features to improve the ease and accuracy of data entry.

Most systems provide a prompting label to cue the operator as to what information to enter. Usually the prompt is an expression, such as "Enter name here."

Many systems also allow the operator to obtain additional information about how to enter the item. For example, if a code were to be used rather than an item name, and if the operator could not remember a particular code, entering a "?" rather than a number would cause the computer to proceed to a routine that lists possible codes.

Some systems allow for a familiar form to appear on the screen of the terminal, such as the one used as the source for the data.

This makes it easier to be sure that the right information is entered.

Some systems also permit automatic error checking, requiring reentry of information that falls outside of preset parameters. For example, the system would reject a letter in place of a number, or a number that falls outside a preset high and low limit.

Most often information is entered by operators using screens and keyboards. However, there are other methods to consider. Sometimes, a new data base is constructed from information that already exists in other computer files. A special program is written that reads the necessary information from the other files and writes it in a proper format directly into a new file. Sometimes forms are used that can be filled out directly by line staff, clients, or other persons. Usually the person completing the form must darken points with a pencil that correspond with numbers and letters. A device called an *optical scanner* detects the dark and light points on the form and interprets them.

It is even possible to enter typewritten information directly into a computer. Text that has been typed using certain type styles can be read by a machine that looks like a copier but that recognizes characters directly. This approach is more useful when written material must be entered into a computer for word processing or typesetting. However, in some cases, it can be useful in record systems as well. Devices also have been developed to recognize spoken commands and expressions. Such voice recognition systems are able to recognize only a limited range of expressions, usually comparing them to original versions of the expressions recorded by each operator. As processors become more powerful and memory devices more efficient, voice recognition systems may become the dominant method of data entry in record systems.

Sorting

Sorting is the process of arranging the data base in a predetermined order. The objective is to speed the process of locating any particular record or item of information, and to speed the processing of some or all of the records to produce summary reports.

Records within a file may be maintained alphabetically, or in an order of magnitude of some numeric variable, or in the order in which they were entered. Most organizations need information sorted in several orders. For example, in an inventory system, one employee might need to know about inventory by manufacturer, another by type of product, and another by storage location. The various file arrangements are necessary because people search for records using different starting information, reflecting differing tasks, interests, and sources of information. A personnel file that has been organized alphabetically would not permit an efficient search for a record based upon the age or identification number associated with the employee record needed.

There are many strategies used in data base management to enable different users to access one record or item of information even though they start with different information. One obvious solution is to maintain more than one file system, each organized in a different order but containing the same overall information. In any file, the records can be in only one order at any time. Duplicate files, however, are cumbersome because they take up twice as much space and because many storage and retrieval processes must be executed more than once.

Another solution is to approach the problem in the same manner as would a clerk responsible for a paper record system. The actual files are arranged in one order, and separate index files are maintained to locate a file using different starting information. The file itself is maintained within the computer system in the most frequently used order. Specialized auxiliary files contain lists of record numbers in the alternative orders. For example, the file itself may be kept in the order in which records were entered, while an alternative list would show files in alphabetic order. A report of names in alphabetic order could be produced by printing out the names within each record in the order contained in the auxiliary file. Such alternative files, called *sort files,* can be created by executing a "sort" under the procedures of the data base management program: specifying the item to be used for the sort and the basis for determining the order (e.g. ascending or descending order of magnitude, alphabetic order).

Another method is to organize records in hierarchies, where one record "owns" another, and that record "owns" yet another, and so forth. The ownership relationship is defined by the record number of the "owned" file stored as an item in the "owner" file. A sort avoids the necessity of reading all records because the pointers navigate the computer through the data base. For example, an alphabetical listing or search would begin at a record designated as the first in alphabetic order. This record would contain the number of the next record, and so forth. Several sorts can be maintained in one system by having more than one pointer item in each record. This type of file structure is very useful when several types of reports are required routinely.

There are several other systems as well, and in the computer programming profession, there is a history of efforts to define common standards for the more common strategies. This would ease the analysis of a file created under one computer program by someone who used a different program.

The method of file organization is usually not critical unless a file is to contain many records and unless the records must be processed in several different orders to produce routine reports. If the scale and complexity of a record system is great, then it would be worthwhile to obtain the services of an expert to help in the selection and development of a good program and to help in decisions about file organization for efficient sorting.

Manipulation of Records

Manipulation describes the processes for modifying the contents and/or formats of records. It may be necessary, after a record system has been created, to make room for some new data elements in each record, or to make room for and automatically compute a new item based upon data already in every record. There are a number of levels of manipulations: those that act upon the items in a particular record, those that act upon the items in all the records in a file, and those that change the format of all the records.

The simplest and most common manipulation is to change an item within a record because of a change in circumstance (such as a change in an employee's address) or an error in a previous entry. The operator would have to tell the computer which record must be changed, which item must be changed, and what it should be changed to.

A more complex manipulation involves changing an item in all the records in a file. This might be necessary if, for example, a policy of the organization was changed so that a new method to calculate the value of an item was adopted. This might occur in the case of a price change in an inventory system or a procedural change in calculating overtime hours for workers under a personnel record system. The operator would have to tell the computer how to calculate the new item value, which items in each record to use in the calculation, and where to store the result.

Even more complicated would be a change in format of all records in a file. This might be necessary should a procedural change call for new information to be maintained in each record. The operator would have to redefine the internal arrangement of records, and then the computer would have to create a new file providing for the additional space required. Then the new information would be created or entered in one of the ways described above.

Retrieval

Retrieval is the process of obtaining information stored within a record after the information has been stored in the computer system. Simple retrieval occurs when the user knows the exact record and item desired, and when the user needs only the item value itself, not an analysis of it. When these conditions exist, the computer can obtain and display the information very quickly.

Retrieval becomes more complex if the exact identity of the record is not known. Under this condition, a search is required. The computer must examine records to see if one or more meet a specified condition. For example, the computer might be instructed to identify all records in which the last name is "Smith" and the first name is "Bill." If the record is organized alphabetically, either literally or by means of sort files or pointers, then the search would be easy. If no alphabetical organization has been developed, then the computer would have to read each file to look for the specified condition.

Under most systems, searches can be performed for number items on the basis of the following types of relationships: equality (i.e., where age is 40), greater than, less than, as well as combinations of these, such as "all records where age is less than 40 and income is greater than $20,000." Searches for word items can be conducted matching identical words or combinations of letters in words.

Some searches will identify more than one record meeting the specified condition. For example, a sales manager might want the names of all salespersons whose sales are above average for the current year. This is commonly done in one of several ways. The computer may evaluate each record for the specified condition and indicate the numbers of any files meeting the condition. Alternatively, one might create a special sort file on the item in question, perhaps in order of magnitude of sales. Then salespersons with above-average sales can be easily identified and listed. The same basic strategy would apply under other methods of file organization.

Report Generation

Report generation entails the development of summaries of the information in the data base. Reports either appear on the screen or are produced on paper by a printer, or both. Generally, reports describe selected contents of a given record, summarize the contents of all the records, or describe the identity and contents of a subset of reports meeting a set of search criteria. To make a report, the operator must specify a screen or printer format—that is, the arrangement of the information in the report to be produced. Then the operator must indicate what items, or calculations of items, are to appear in the report, and where in the format each item is to appear. Sometimes the operator must specify retrievals, searches, and computational routines as well. Usually, once the instructions for development of a particular report have been written, they can be saved and recalled later if the report is ever needed again.

In some systems, reports can be created both interactively and routinely. The interactive approach allows a user to perform searches and construct screen and report formats to produce a new and unique report. For example, an executive can explore a data base to answer questions about organizational and employee performance. The routine approach sets up a standard process for producing a given report, which can be implemented simply by calling for that report. Production of a monthly sales summary might be an example of routine reporting.

GENERAL-PURPOSE DATA BASE MANAGEMENT SOFTWARE

The records management systems described above are for general application, allowing the user to identify the elements of the items to be stored and to create unique reports. Other systems are specially designed for specific functions, such as accounting, inventory, sales, and accounts receivable programs. The decision to use a general-purpose program instead of a specialized program depends upon several factors. Is the system likely to change a great deal in future years, requiring changes in record and report formats? This would call for a general-purpose system that can easily be changed. Is the function highly specialized, and is a software package available that accomplishes the function? If such a system is available at a feasible price, then it may be efficient to purchase it, since it would probably be more expensive to develop a specialized system out of a general-purpose package.

The major advantage of a general-purpose data base management system is that the user can organize and tailor the program to apply very specifically to the type of work involved. In an inventory system, for example, unusual characteristics of products can be included in each record, special reports can be created, and the program can be adapted very closely to the exact style and method of operation of the enterprise. A packaged inventory program might not permit inclusion of each of the product features desired and may only produce common types of inventory reports, but not all the reports one might need in an unusual business.

The problem, of course, is that the general-purpose system must be customized to the particular application. This requires the definition of file, record, and item characteristics, as well as the development of sorting and organizing systems and report generation routines. The customization process can take more than several weeks to perform and can require that the user learn a complex language of procedures, commands, definitions, and techniques. A specialized program package should be operational and ready for data entry soon after it is purchased.

Should one decide to use a general-purpose system, there are some important features to look for and issues to consider in selecting a package.

First and foremost, unless you already have a computer, or have an overriding reason to select a particular model, select your software first, and then select a computer that economically and efficiently supports the software you choose.

Read the manual that is provided with the software, to determine that the programming of the system does not exceed your abilities, interest, or time availability. You might also ask for any programs that automatically create the necessary code to produce reports and screen formats, based upon a few descriptive instructions. Such programs can simplify some parts of the customization process.

Check the type of sorting and file organization capabilities built into the program, and satisfy yourself that these will support your needs. You will have to balance the programming ease of simpler systems against the power (and programming complexity) of some other systems.

Be sure that the program can do a full range of file manipulations. Most certainly, after a period of development and operation of your information system, you will discover additional items needed in each record, as well as other deficiencies requiring file manipulation.

While the foregoing discussion applies primarily to small-scale record systems, the same general considerations apply to the selection and development of larger record systems as well. A very large system might require a general-purpose data base management system, because many large applications have unique features and report requirements. The trade-offs between ease of initial implementation versus user control and customization still apply even though programmers might actually customize and operate the system.

EXAMPLES OF SPECIALIZED INFORMATION MANAGEMENT SYSTEMS

Specialized data base management systems are generally known by the types of records stored and reports produced. The following application profiles review several important types of specialized software: accounting systems, resource management systems, and small scale filing systems.

SOFTWARE PROFILE 8:   ACCOUNTING SYSTEMS

Some of the earliest applications of computers were in financial management. This probably resulted from the extensive clerical work involved in the processing of such documents, the need for accuracy, and the need for very up-to-date information. Some common types of accounting systems include the following.

Accounts receivable systems organize and summarize the current assets of an organization, such as claims derived from the sale of goods and services.

Current assets in the more general form summarizes all that is owned by a business or organization, such as cash, legal claims, inventory, and prepaid expenses. Often systems will define current assets as those that can be expected to be converted into cash within a specified period of time such as 1 year.

Accounts payable systems summarize the claims against a business or organization by vendors, suppliers, and employees.

Current liabilities are broader forms of payable claims, including notes payable, legal claims, as well as specific payable accounts.

Employee payroll systems retain records of information necessary to pay employees and to produce other documents necessary to the management of the personnel function.

Many accounting software packages not only provide standard summary reports, but also provide information about the financial health of a business based upon the following types of ratios.:

Merchandise turnover.
Current assets to liabilities.
Acid-test ratio, which is the readily available assets divided by the current liabilities.
Plant and equipment to capital.
Long-term debt to capital.
Earnings to sales.
Sales produced per dollar of investment.

In computer-based accounting systems, an organization usually will maintain several files, one for each type of source document. Thus, there may be a file in which each record is a bill from a vendor or supplier, and another file where each record describes the payroll status of a specific employee, and a file where each record represents a receivable account owed to the business.

Because accounting systems are used to manage large amounts of money, special attention should be paid to the security of the software and the hardware. The following are some factors to consider in developing and operating an accounting system.

As a general rule, any precaution that you would normally take in a manual accounting system should also be taken with one supported by a computer. For example, the forms used to create checks should be stored securely. This type of precaution may seem obvious, but errors are commonly made. One reason is that the persons operating or supervising the system may not have a background in account management and therefore may be unfamiliar with routine security procedures. Careful attention should be paid to the maintenance of appropriate source documentation for transactions entered into the information system. Procedures should be established to independently check and audit the accounting system, to assure that program and data entry errors are discovered and corrected.

Accounting systems are probably among the most common uses of computers in support of management. There is great potential for improvements in employee productivity, as well as for increases in the timeliness and accuracy of reports. However, such systems require special attention in their development and ongoing operation.

SOFTWARE PROFILE 9:   RESOURCE MANAGEMENT SYSTEMS

There are many other data base management systems commonly used in management. Most deal with the human and material resources used by the organization. Common examples include those that manage personnel records, and those that track inventories.

Personnel record systems maintain information on employee performance, qualifications, training, and career background, so as to assist managers in such areas as career development, promotions, salary and bonus determinations, and related issues. Security and privacy of information are special concerns in personnel record systems. In an insecure desktop computer system, an unauthorized person could obtain information if he or she understood how to turn on and operate the computer. Most "user-friendly" software packages would guide the unauthorized user to the desired information, prompting the user whenever necessary. In a larger multi-user system, access to information by unauthorized persons could be achieved through terminals deployed for other purposes.

Inventory systems enable organizations to keep track of material assets, including finished goods, materials used in the production of finished goods, general equipment, and furnishings. Some specialized software and hardware packages permit automatic maintenance of inventory records, through connections to electronic cash registers, production machinery, and other equipment. This eliminates much of the record keeping needed in the past, although periodic audits are still necessary. Inventory software may also produce reports when supplies run low and reorders are needed.

Some inventory systems have a built-in capability to apply inventory modeling as described in Chapter 3. With such software, a manager can optimize purchasing decisions considering the product cost effect of interest rates, transportation, volume purchase discounts, and storage costs.

As a general rule, the larger and more complex the record system to be managed, the greater the benefit derived from the use of a general-purpose data base management system to customize a system for the application involved. As the application grows in size, chances increase that unique item and record features will be required, as well as special sorting and reporting features. The initial cost and inconvenience of a customized system will be balanced by the long-term flexibility and adaptability afforded.

SOFTWARE PROFILE 10:   SMALL-SCALE FILING SYSTEMS

As the technology of microcomputers and enhanced terminals has evolved in recent years, data base management systems have been economically and practically applied to individual and small-scale applications. Managers and people who work with managers have small record systems that pertain to important aspects of their work. These records would not have been supported in a large computer system because the number of records is too small, the information is not sufficiently standardized, or the productivity improvement value of the application is too limited. The software packages that currently support such applications are very powerful and flexible file storage and retrieval systems, allowing variable record formats. Many systems can process records created on standard word processors.

Most small-scale applications involve records that are usually maintained by one or two persons. They may be maintained in an unstandardized fashion, with variations in record contents not only between two different employees but even between two records maintained by one employee. A personal telephone list may include notes and comments unique to particular entries, such as birthdays (only for close friends and relatives), and business as well as home addresses (for business associates). A standard data base management system could not handle the unusual variation in material.

The following are some examples of common small-scale records management applications:

Mailing lists can be maintained, including descriptors that allow the user to target a mailing to a subset of the list. A very flexible system would allow the addition of comments and notes as well.

Records of telephone numbers and addresses can be maintained so that a user can find a number or address on the basis of a name, a location, or some other piece of information.

Records of correspondence, memoranda, contracts, specifications, and other documents can be maintained.

Some software packages work much like more fully developed data base management systems. In such systems, the individual record is usually the document or specific piece of information needed. Other packages are more flexible, accepting as input material lists typed on a standard word processor. They may require designation of key words so that a sort file can be developed for searches against each key word. In effect, each entry is treated much like a three by five card. The cards can be arranged by the computer in any order, and any card can be promptly retrieved.

COMPUTERS IN PROCESS CONTROL

Process control is a very different use of computers in the support of management operations. In process control, a computer directly controls a machine or work process. This type of application is sometimes difficult to distinguish from engineering. In fact, process control by computers often replaces managers when the coordination of logistics and schedules becomes sufficiently predictable that a computer can take over. The following are some examples of process control applications:

Collecting production and inventory information in a factory production line.
Controlling material handling in a production process.
Monitoring the quality of material produced.
Controlling production machinery including robots.

High-level management process control systems include scheduling programs used to coordinate the activities of many workers for large and complex projects. (Such programs are used for decision making support in planning and organizing, but they become process control devices when they are used to coordinate ongoing work.) Lower level programs do not control people, but rather they control production equipment, machines, computers, and other devices.

In general, there are several basic elements to a computer-aided process control system. First and last, there is the computer and the process. In between, there must be a program that instructs the computer as to what to measure when, and what to do about the measurements. In addition, there must be a connection or interface between the computer and the work process.

There are several common types of interfaces that enable computers to control processes. A very common, flexible, and high-level connection is the terminal screen itself, or other similar peripherals, which can instruct a user with words, numbers, or sounds.

The next level is sometimes called the universal interface. It is a multipurpose electrical interconnector that can include a range of outlets and connections, including conventional electrical outlets as well as terminals specific to selected electronic devices and appliances. It can be connected to a computer through an RS-232-C port in much the same way as a printer is. However, when characters are sent from the computer to the universal interface, it does not print them. Instead, the character signals the device to perform some function, such as turning off the power at an outlet or sending a "high" electronic signal out of an outlet. These events can be used to control such devices as lights, heating and air conditioning systems, security systems, and manufacturing machinery.

The next level is the interface that is specific to a function or device. Such a connection may be built into the device itself to permit a computer, or a specific brand and model of computer, to control the device. Finally, the last level is the use of a microprocessor as a part of a device itself. This is common in automobiles, paper copiers, and other sophisticated devices.

Programs that coordinate by means of a computer are usually quite simple. One type of program merely emits signals repetitively in a cycle of seconds or minutes. This is common in systems that control traffic signals for a city. A master cycle of 5–10 minutes includes changes in lights every 20–60 seconds, with certain events occurring less frequently. Programs that constantly monitor systems have very short cycles, such as 1000 times per second or faster. These types of programs could enable the computer to monitor the temperature of a device or environment, and take action if the temperature falls outside the required range.

When a program is very specialized and when the device is relatively small, the program is usually stored in ROM, or

read-only memory, or it is built into the electronics of a microprocessor developed especially for the function. This is faster and
less prone to breakdown, which is especially important when the
device is to function in a relatively inhospitable environment. A
computer that controls traffic signals, however, might have a program stored on a disk, permitting flexibility in changes of signal
patterns.

Process control is a highly specialized use of computers. It is
unusual for managers to participate directly in the planning and
design of such systems. Instead they are purchased as part of a
larger device designed to carry out a specified function. The only
general exceptions are systems that control a management process, such as a project coordination system that might be developed for a specific organization.

CONCLUDING OBSERVATIONS

There is one factor that distinguishes a computer used for operations support (whether records management or process control)
from a computer used in decision support. In operations support,
the computer will be used over a long period of time, and many
employees and clients will be affected by the efficiency and effectiveness of the system. Employee morale and productivity as well
as customer satisfaction is at stake. On the other hand, decision
support applications are used relatively briefly. Although the results of a wrong decision can be substantial, the long-term damage from an operations support system can be greater.

As a result, a manager should be very careful in the planning
and development of a computer system used for operations support. Additional time and resources expended in pilot projects,
employee involvement and feedback, and careful analysis of affected operations will pay back many times over as the system
performs successfully over the years.

CHAPTER 5
THE OFFICE
OF THE FUTURE

The new terminal at my desk was exciting, intimidating, and a bit humiliating. I had felt that I had been putting off learning to use a computer too long, so this was an opportunity to catch up with some of my colleagues, and even my children. However, I felt uncomfortable with the idea that I would entrust important documents and projects to a machine that stored them in a form which I could not directly see or touch. I also worried that once I became proficient on the machine, I would lose some of the secretarial support which I have always relied upon. I think now that I intentionally never learned to type because it assured that link to a secretary which has been so useful and convenient. Losing typing services also seemed a bit humiliating, since that had always been a sign of status. Depending upon how I looked at it, the terminal made me feel both promoted and downgraded.

Computers are directly affecting executives and other office professionals. In the 1980s, the office—the working environment for the clerical and management employee—will be the target for a major wave of innovation.

Innovation in office systems follows upon several earlier developments. In the 1960s and 1970s, computers provided automated management record systems, while at the same time, other types of office equipment—copiers, typewriters, dictating machines, and filing systems—became more powerful, less expensive, and capable of a more diverse range of tasks. As the cost and size of computer systems have decreased, computers and general office equipment are increasingly combined. Integrated systems providing internal and external telecommunications, computer systems, word processing, and a variety of other services have emerged.

This management revolution is sometimes called "office automation," leading eventually to "the office of the future." Many think that this consists primarily of substituting new equipment for old, and "smart typewriters" for "clackers," and installing telephones with more and more buttons. Actually, the change is much more profound, and it will lead to basic revision of office operations and management procedures in the years to come. Managers and business operators not familiar with these new office systems are in for some disturbing surprises:

Changes in such jobs as secretary may occur, and the unprepared manager may not be able to work effectively in the new ways.

Jobs may be eliminated altogether, and some people may lose their jobs to those with more appropriate skills for an automated office.

Businesses and organizations that do not invest in the new technology, in terms of equipment, environmental change, procedural development, and employee retraining, may find themselves at a competitive disadvantage.

In the automation of the headquarters of a medium-size business or government agency, it is not unreasonable to expect that

10–30% of the secretarial positions might be eliminated, so that many of the remaining secretaries support more than one executive. It is also likely that some of the executives who formerly supervised clerical employees might be replaced by computer professionals operating the automated office equipment. The organization can experience reduced costs and higher levels of production. ⌐

Employees and organizations can benefit from office automation, or they can be competitively eliminated by it. To capitalize on the opportunity both personally and organizationally, managers must understand (1) what office automation consists of, (2) where it is going, and (3) how it might best be implemented.

THE CONCEPT OF OFFICE AUTOMATION

Office automation consists essentially of the application of computer and telecommunications technology to office work. It involves the substitution of new equipment for old, but it also involves totally new types of equipment, new ways of doing work, new roles for workers and related changes in the mix of employees, as well as changes in the physical and organizational environment of the office. To understand office automation, we must begin by understanding the office itself. What happens in an office?

> People communicate, to inform, decide, or to coordinate activity. They communicate one to one, or in groups in meetings, or on paper through reports, letters, and memoranda.
>
> People gather information from one another or from documents, reports, and record systems.
>
> People analyze information in quick and simple ways, such as scanning a document and discarding it, or in more complex ways, such as research, planning, and evaluation projects.
>
> People transform information from one form to another, such as developing a summary report from filed records or translating a plan into specific procedures.

People store information in various types of electronic, facsimile, and paper record systems.

Most offices, whether parts of large organizations or small independent businesses, have already automated some of these functions. Electronic typewriters and dictation systems, office telephone systems, and computer-based record systems are now commonplace. An advanced automated office, an "office of the future," will automate each of these functions in an integrated and coordinated manner, so that each system can support every other system. As a result, the time and expense of transforming information or work processes from one technology to another will be reduced. Offices will progress gradually with automation, in three typical stages:

A *Stage 1* office has automated some of the above functions, such as word processing or records management, but other functions are still done in much the same way they were done during the 1960s.

A *Stage 2* office has automated each of the basic office tasks to a substantial extent, but the systems are not necessarily compatible. For example, word processors do not communicate with copiers, or with the automated record system, or with the office telephone system.

A *Stage 3* office, a truly automated office, has automated the basic functions in an integrated manner, so that letters typed on word processors can be transmitted through electronic mail or stored in the computer-based record system, and reports from the management record system can be sent through the organization's internal electronic mail system to the managers requiring the information.

The experience of a small law firm illustrates a common process of office automation through distinct stages. In the late 1960s, the firm progressed to Stage 1 when it leased a primitive electronic typewriter and a copying machine. Copies of letters, contracts, and routine documents, such as wills, were stored on magnetic cards. This reduced the time required to prepare such documents. However, the typewriter was operated by one secretary and was used only for the production of routine documents. Everyone found that it was easier and faster to prepare one-time letters and documents the old way.

In the mid-1970s, the firm acquired microcomputer-based word processors for each of the secretaries and added several more lawyers to the staff without an increase in clerical staff. This economy paid for the word processors, and the secretaries found their work to be more interesting as well. Even the most simple letters and documents were produced on the word processors. The secretaries began to take on some of the paralegal tasks involved in creating routine wills and contracts. An electronic backup filing system was established that involved the use of a diskette for each client or case. This permitted many documents in a case to be stored on one or two diskettes. However, the lawyers usually kept physical copies of documents in files as well, since the inconvenience of printing out documents stored on disks was too great.

In the early 1980s, the firm acquired a multi-user networking microcomputer with a large disk capacity. This enabled the word processors to be linked to a shared disk and also permitted each lawyer to have a terminal as well. Software was installed to perform billing, time accounting and analysis, as well as document storage and word processing. While the lawyers still used paper copies of documents for some purposes, reliance on electronic filing also increased. The system was also linked over telephone lines to a computer-based legal research system which often improved the production speed and quality of legal briefs.

This case illustrates several of the reasons why automation of office activities is desirable. First, it can often lead to greater production in less time. Letters can be written and typed more rapidly, and reports generated and distributed more efficiently.

Second, automation can lead to higher quality work. Computational and writing errors can be reduced or eliminated, reports can arrive when they are really needed, and work can be planned and coordinated more accurately.

Third, an automated office can be a more pleasant and satisfying place to work. Less time will be spent in the routine mechanical functions of gathering, storing, and transforming information, and more time can be spent in actual communication and analysis, leading to real problem solving.

A Stage 3 office has implemented the five basic physical elements of office automation: (1) a communications system to the external telephone system; (2) a multipurpose computer called a central processor, which coordinates the entire system and does many computing chores; (3) a local telephone and telecommunications network; (4) a system of employee work stations providing most employees with direct and continuing access to the system; and (5) a system of specialized peripheral equipment not needed by each employee (See Figure 5.1). In the Stage 3 office, each of these five system parts are interconnected to function in coordination and support of each other.

To best appreciate what such a system can accomplish, let us examine each of the five elements in some detail, to see how each contributes to the overall result.

External Communications

External Communications is the connection between the office and the external telephone system. Just like an office telephone system, it allows calls to be placed to or received from outside of the office. In addition, it allows electronic mail to be transmitted to and from other organizations, and it permits connection of the office system with computer networks outside of the office itself. These capabilities generally exist today, and therefore no major changes in national and regional telephone systems are necessary, although some improvements in the speed and quality of communication should be forthcoming. The big changes must come from within the office to make full use of the opportunities available. Potentials exist in the areas of improved speed and reliability of communication, electronic mail, and expansion of external computer networks.

Communication by computers over telephone lines commonly occurs today. High-speed communication requires a very "clean" telephone connection (a *data line*), which is often leased from

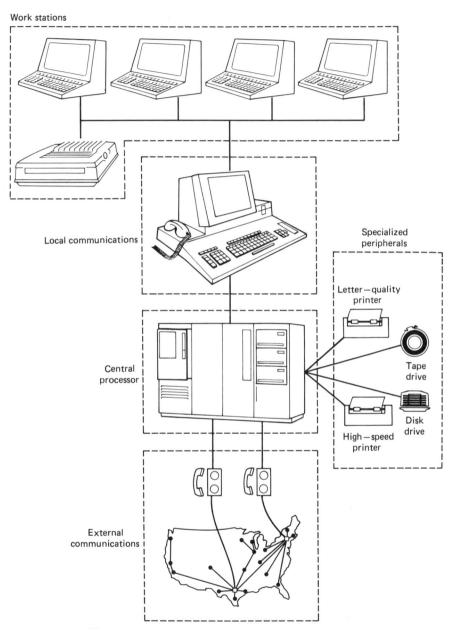

Figure 5.1. A General Model of the Automated Office.

116

telephone companies, especially for a large computer system with many faraway terminals. Computer communication over telephone lines used by the public for conversations usually takes place at a slower rate. Faster communication works if the line is of high quality or if the equipment is sophisticated. Efficient electronic mail systems will require such faster communication, at rates of perhaps 20–30 lines per second or faster. Unless such speeds are achieved, it might take an hour to send 10 or 15 business letters, or one 30-page report. This is practical for emergency correspondence or for transmission of short communications and small tables, but it is impractical as a general way of doing business. There are several approaches to achieving the more rapid communication.

Modems that enable computers to "talk" over the telephone can be made more powerful and sophisticated, so that they catch errors in communication, recover when something unexpected occurs in the telephone line, and detect information even when line quality is poor. Organizations with a frequent need to communicate may develop their own external links between offices as extensions of their internal communications system. Such systems might use technology that is more efficient for data communication than that used by the average telephone company for voice conversations.

One such technology is the use of fiber-optic connections in place of electric wires. Since these lines are made of flexible, clear glasslike materials that carry beams of concentrated light rather than electricity impulses, they are faster and less subject to distortion than are electric wires. Another technology involves a change in the method of communicating information over the line. At present, most computer communication over a telephone line requires that the modem transform the information into a series of sounds. Changes in the pitch of these sounds correspond to the numbers or letters being communicated. This is called acoustical or analog communication. An alternative system is called digital communication. Under this approach, more precise signals directly corresponding to numbers are sent over the line. These are more efficient because more information can be sent in a given period. Such signals are also easier to check for accuracy by the modems on each end of the line. It is unlikely that the nation's telephone system will soon be changed to a digital system, because this would require major expense for new equipment, including new telephones for everybody. However, the use of such a system within an office or for specialized lines is feasible.

Electronic mail exists today, although few systems in use are fully electronic from user to user. Probably the most common example of electronic mail is the telegram, which is electronic from the sending to the receiving office, although not from the originating person to the receiving person. Some organizations and many people who own microcomputers send messages and documents over telephone lines. Some computer telecommunications networks enable people and organizations with computers to send messages to a central data base to be stored until a receiving computer system requests the message. These networks will also print out the message on selected types of paper, in various offices across the nation, for delivery in the local mail. The number of such services and the types of services provided will expand greatly in coming years.

Specialized services will be developed, tailored to specific types of users. Examples include purchasing supplies, access to decision support models, up-to-date news services relevant to certain businesses, and electronic access to travel reservation systems. Large organizations or governments may develop their own networks to permit, for example, electronic mail between government agencies or corporate offices.

The Central Processor

The central processor is a specialized computer that coordinates all of the elements of the automated office system. In a minimal system, the central processor is hardly more than a switchboard to connect terminals that have their own processors. In a more sophisticated system, the central processor maintains a large shared disk as well as numerous specialized devices. When a minicomputer is used as the central processor, sometimes the work stations share the central processor rather than operate independently.

Selecting a central processor often determines the brands and types of equipment that can be used for the remainder of the office system. Therefore, selection criteria should include factors such as the eventual size of the office, the functions needed, and features of compatible work stations.

Local Communications Network

A local communications network is an expanded and enhanced version of the system of telephone extensions most offices have today. However, the Stage 3 office will have a network integrating the internal telephone and intercom system and the computer terminal network. It will allow people to initiate or receive electronic mail at their desks and to incorporate material from a computer-based record system directly into reports and letters. It will also permit reports typed at a work station to be transmitted electronically to the duplication machine without first having to be printed out on a typewriter or printer.

There are a variety of local network systems available on the market, and they vary in several ways:

The physical design of the network sometimes provides for connection of each terminal to the central processor, and sometimes provides for chaining of terminals, so that one terminal is connected to another, which is connected to another, and so forth. Such chains sometimes loop back to the central processor.

In some systems only one terminal can use the network at a time, so that messages do not collide. Other systems detect collisions so that messages that do not reach their destination can be sent again after a random delay.

Some systems allow only one message on the network at a time. Other systems allow several messages at once by segmenting the signal into frequency levels, in the same way as citizen's band radio channels.

Some systems use telephone lines, and other systems use more traditional data communication cables. The advantage of the phone lines is that they are already installed, but the data communication lines often can carry more information more quickly.

Some systems allow only messages consisting of words and numbers, while others support voice, graphic, and video transmissions as well.

Eventually a few approaches to local networks will become standard, and each will be compatible with the other. Until a common approach evolves, selection of a network system should be based upon the immediate needs of the organization. Systems should be preferred which offer compatibility with other networks.

Work Stations

The most exciting aspect of office automation for employees will probably be the work station itself. This is the terminal to the automated office system, which permits each employee to put the system to work. There are basically three kinds of stations for three different kinds of office functions: executive work, clerical or support work, and specialized work.

The executive work station in a Stage Three office helps an executive to do the following tasks:

Write, review, and edit letters, messages, and reports, with or without support from clerical employees.

Initiate telephone calls automatically, dialed by the terminal, which may ultimately include a telephone as an integral part. Store frequently used phone numbers in the terminal for automatic dialing. The terminal may also retain the return phone numbers for any telephone messages to be answered, so that the return call can be placed with the press of a button.

Receive messages from other terminals. If the executive is at his or her desk, messages can be answered directly; if the executive does not answer or is not present, the work station will take a written message and a call-back number.

Provide access to computer-based management information

systems, either on external networks or operated by the executive's organization.

Maintain and operate specialized computer programs used by the executive in routine work. For example, the executive might maintain several decision support computer programs or a specialized data base related to his or her job. Perhaps the executive might even keep a few games available for after-hour diversion.

Provide access to office-wide scheduling and time-accounting systems to facilitate scheduling of meetings or to bill clients accurately for services provided.

To support these tasks, the work station should be able to maintain a clock and calendar, run programs such as word processing, communicate with other computers, store documents and records, perform calculations like a calculator, and create graphic displays. Perhaps most important, it should be able to help the user by answering questions about how it works.

The clerical or support work station is one used by a secretary or administrative aide. Such systems can decrease the time required to do conventional secretarial work. Such tasks as typing reports and letters, filing and retrieving information, and scheduling appointments can be done more quickly and with greater quality and reliability. As a result, the role of the secretary will gradually change as such systems are installed.

Two types of changes in clerical employment may occur, depending upon the needs of the organization. One approach is to increase the number of management and professional employees served by a typical secretary. In addition to reduced costs, this approach can increase the coordination of a work team, because one person (supported by one clerical work station) can be aware of what each worker is doing, easing coordination problems. Another approach involves upgrading the role of each secretary to encompass a greater number of management functions. This might include answering routine mail, using standard letter drafts maintained in the work station memory as a starting point. In addition, the secretary could update and run some of the specialized computer programs maintained and operated for a particular executive.

Generally, the clerical/support work station will include all the features and capabilities of the executive work station, as well as several more:

It may include special equipment for transcribing dictation, including the eventual use of direct speech recognition systems.

There may be specialized programs for checking written material for spelling and typographical errors, as well as for clarity of drafting.

The station may provide the ability to answer incoming communications at the clerical station, even though the destination of the communication is a particular executive station.

In some cases, several executive work stations will share a fast and a slower letter-quality printer located at the clerical/support station.

The third type of work station is the specialized station. These are terminals that include capabilities for performing a particular type of work. The following are some examples:

A station may be set up solely to enter one type of information on a high-volume basis, such as orders in a mail-order center, or some accounting and inventory documents.

A station might be used by a designer, engineer, or draftsperson and require computer-aided design capabilities. Such a station might also have a local printer capable of producing paper copies, such as blueprints.

A station might be used only as a switchboard and provide only basic information, such as employee telephone numbers and locations, to the switchboard operator, and to help the operator in transferring calls.

A station might be used to support the operation of specialized peripheral equipment, which will be described below.

Finally, a very limited station may be used, which works as a smart telephone with limited word processing abilities, but little else. Such a station would enable workers who do not need sophisticated systems to communicate with the office network.

Unspecialized work stations are computer terminals or microcomputers with an ability to communicate and share equipment with other microcomputers. As work stations become more specialized and adapted to the needs of office environments, many new capabilities will become available.

Software that tells the microcomputer work stations what to do is already being produced in great volume by many organizations. As computer-based office systems become more prevalent, greater numbers of programs will be developed with greater specialization. Thus, software for law offices, architectural firms, corporate offices, insurance offices, schools, government agencies, and many other types of organizations will be developed to integrate not only the computer-based record processing systems that have been available for many years, but also the capabilities of an automated office tailored to each type of organization.

Work stations will become more portable, so that full-function stations can be carried in a car or taken onto an airplane as carry-on luggage, used with battery-pack energy when electric outlets are not available, and capable of full communication with the home office when a telephone line is available.

As microcomputers become more powerful, the capabilities of office work stations will increase accordingly. Larger memories, faster processing speeds, greater disk capacity, and improved systems for communications will make the stations support a major increase in office productivity. Such capabilities as speech recognition of as many as 50,000 unique words will eventually become feasible as the memory size, processing speed, and program sophistication of work stations increase. This will permit the transcription in draft of dictation at much greater speeds, as well as the editing and correction of dictated material by nontypists.

The integration of work stations, telephones, and telephone systems will eventually occur, so that the work station will have a built-in telephone capable of both voice and data transmission.

The functions of typewriters will be built into work station systems, but the technology of the typewriter will change radically, as the difference between a typewriter and a computer printer fades, and finally as the difference between a printer and a copier fades. Work stations will send written texts electronically directly to the copier for reproduction, without the need for a mechanically produced paper original.

Specialized Peripheral Equipment

The fifth component of an advanced office automation system consists of specialized peripheral equipment. These include very fast printers, printers designed to produce such specialized products as blueprints or large drawings, and large disks for shared record storage for an entire office. The specific equipment used will depend upon the nature of the work done by the office. The following are some examples of existing or soon to be available equipment.

Letter-quality printers exist already or are under development that, because of various new technologies, can work very quickly to produce a wide range of characters or impressions. One approach allows a word processor to send text material directly to a copier. A "smart" copier can be equipped to generate a wide variety of type styles and characters. Another approach to achieving high speed, high quality, and great flexibility is the use of a mechanism that squirts a small stream of ink, the direction of which is controlled by electromagnets so as to form the desired characters.

Optical character readers already can recognize material typed on paper to enter it into the memory of a computer. However, as the equipment evolves it will be able to recognize a wider range of character types even when copy quality is poor. Such a system may become very important to the full automation of an office, because it may allow automated communication with organizations that still function largely on paper. An additional feature involves the ability to check spelling as documents are entered and to recognize and implement proofreading remarks and symbols. This is important for systems used in printing and publishing.

Printers and copiers will require more advanced paper-handling systems. A printer used to produce letters and reports must have the capability of feeding single sheets of paper of a variety of styles of paper, from plain white to the company letterhead. Many devices can handle small numbers of paper options, but they cannot accommodate the large numbers of options appropriate for serving a large organization. One solution is to use several printers at once and only one or two types of paper for each printer. This approach works well for letters, but it has limitations when a report uses several types of paper as well as several cover stocks.

A printer or copier used to produce bound copies of documents and reports will have to be able to collate and bind the copies. Often collation is done mechanically, but as copiers produce documents directly from electronic signals from work stations, collation may become electronic rather than mechanical. The work station, or a memory within the copier, will determine the exact sequence in which copies are made, enabling the direct production of copies with the correct page order.

As disks become smaller in mass and larger in their information storage capability, it will be possible to maintain very large record systems on very compact storage devices.

SOFTWARE FOR OFFICE AUTOMATION

Two types of computer programs are basic to an automated office: word processing and executive support programs. Such programs are commonly used at work stations. Many examples of bot types are available today, but they will be constantly improved and upgraded as automated office systems and terminals improve in computing power and capacity.

SOFTWARE PROFILE 11: WORD PROCESSING SYSTEMS

Word processing basically is typing using advanced computer equipment that makes the work easier and the result more accurate and better looking. Word processors store typed information in memory, so that it is possible to edit it and save it on a disk prior to printing it. The following are some common features of word processing systems:

Cursor movement refers to the location and relocation of a pointer indicating where text will be entered next or where some other action will be taken. If one wishes to add text to the middle of a paragraph, then the cursor must be relocated to the point at which the text is to be entered. Generally, word processing programs permit movement up and down, or over one or more words, sentences, or paragraphs.

Insertion refers to the process of adding text to a document. Most often this is done by merely typing in the material to be added. It is usually also possible to add the contents of another file or document. This allows a new document to be created by merging several older ones.

Deletion refers to the process of removing text from a document. The most common approach uses a "delete" or "rub-out" key, which moves backward removing each character it passes over, much like a correction key on a typewriter. This is very convenient for a typist who makes many errors, because correction is simplified. It is usually also possible to delete whole words, sentences, paragraphs, and documents as well.

Search and replace refers to the process of finding and possibly deleting, changing, or replacing a word or expression in a document. Generally, the operator designates the expression to be located and indicates whether the computer is, for example, to search forward or backward in the document, or to recognize the expression only if the upper-case and lower-case letters match exactly. The operator may also indicate that, if the expression is found, it is to be replaced by another expression. This is useful if a word is misspelled throughout a document or if a name should be changed throughout a contract.

Text formatting refers to the arrangement of the test on the printed page. Most programs start with a standard arrangement, unless the operator instructs otherwise. Options include varying the length of the page and the width and justification of margins.

There are numerous other features of word processing systems, and the software is evolving so rapidly that the best source of current comparative information about alternative software packages is recent issues of computer and office equipment magazines. Some desirable features include the ability to check spelling, insert footnotes at the bottom of appropriate pages, and present two separate sections of a report on the computer screen simultaneously. Compatibility with other software, such as spreadsheet programs, is another desirable feature.

From the standpoint of physical equipment, there are generally three types of word processing systems on the market. The *electronic typewriter* has a built-in memory that permits the typist to correct errors, store short documents, and perform some other functions as well. The *dedicated word processor* generally has a keyboard and screen, as well as a type-writer-printer. These machines are microcomputers designed specifically for word processing, so the are keys correspond to various functions and the operations are relatively direct and unambiguous. *Microcomputer word processors* are microcomputers running word processing programs. Initially, these were not as easy to use as the dedicated word processors because the machines and their keyboards were not developed and targeted for the word processing task. However, currently available software allows keys to be dedicated to specific jobs (such as moving the cursor up or down), and specialized screens and other peripheral equipment are available so that there is practically no difference between the dedicated and general-purpose machines. Another big difference in the past has been the ability of the microcomputer based system to perform other data processing functions. The dedicated machines usually have this capability now as well.

Word processing is probably the most immediately useful component of an automated office system. As a result, it is often the initial step taken in a longer term process of office automation. There are probably few people who would return to manual document preparation after learning to use a word processing system. The changeover to word processing is usually so satisfactory that favorable attitudes and expectations are created toward subsequent steps in office automation.

SOFTWARE PROFILE 12:   EXECUTIVE SUPPORT SYSTEMS

Work stations for executives must be able to support a wide range of activities. Here is a list of some of the purposes to which executives may put their work stations:

Drafting of sections of documents.
Analysis of information.
Maintenance of schedules.
Sending and receiving of documents and messages.
Storage and retrieval of phone numbers and addresses.
Storage of small but important records.
Storage and analysis of personal financial data.
Project planning and cost estimation.
Maintenance of evaluative information.

A system to help an executive perform these functions must meet several criteria. The system must be capable of many different activities. While a clerical work station may require a powerful word processor and several other programs, an executive work station may require a reasonably good word processor, a scheduling program, a spreadsheet calculation program, a communications program, and several other specialized programs as well. The programs must be relatively nontechnical, since the executive must personally use many of them. Executives are not likely to use programs that require a great deal of time and effort to use effectively.

There are several ways by which these goals can be met. One approach employs a program that interprets and translates the operating system to an inexperienced and nontechnical user. The result is that the executive can turn on the computer and immediately see a menu on the screen. The options on the menu correspond to the programs available on the system. Once an option is selected, the computer loads the necessary program, and the executive can proceed. Some programs employ graphic symbols rather than words and numbers to represent program options.

The major advantage of this approach to providing software for the work station is that programs can be added, changed, or deleted as the needs of the executive change. It also does not restrict the executive in choosing a particular word processor, spreadsheet program, or other aid. Any program operational on the computer can be added to the menu of options.

An alternative approach involves use of programs specially written for executive support. The advantage of these programs is that they are uniform across functions with respect to simplicity and basic operating technique. Thus, for example, pressing the "escape" key would achieve the same result in the word processing program as in the spreadsheet program. The major disadvantage is the lack of flexibility, since only a limited set of software packages can be available in any one system. If several of the packages are unsatisfactory, or if a needed capability is not available, the executive is out of luck.

As executive work stations become more common, the quality and flexibility of the available software will inevitably improve.

DEVELOPING AN AUTOMATED OFFICE

The Stage 3 office will use each of the five basic elements of an automated office in a coordinated manner. The evolution from an office with no automation at all to the sophistication and coordination of the Stage 3 office, will present many challenges, problems, and opportunities to management and employees alike.

Organizational Environment

The evolution of an office to Stage 3 requires more than the acquisition of equipment. Office automation implies major changes in the physical and organizational environment as well, which are critical to the successful operation and use of the equipment. An "organizational environment" is determined by the roles of employees in an office and the ways that employees work together in these roles.

A major area of concern is the impact of office automation on the freedom, initiative, and individuality of employees. No one knows what the ultimate outcome will be, but there are several perspectives one might have on this important problem.

One perspective is pessimistic. Since practically every employee will be working with and through the office equipment system, and since that system will function according to specific rules and procedures, an automated office will be in some ways a more structured and controlled working environment. There will be "one best way" of doing many aspects of the work process, and variation or innovation by individuals simply will not work. Some people view this as a dehumanizing trend, as individual identities, initiatives, and working styles are superceded by the requirements of a machine.

Early experience with certain word processing and office automation systems illustrates this perspective. Some offices were reorganized so that clerical employees were pooled, and their relation to specific functions and employees were severed. In many instances, the clerical employees perceived that they were no longer dealing with identifiable projects or persons. Instead, they dealt with a constant in-box of work, to be processed in an assembly-line fashion. Some workers transcribed dictation, others did revisions, and others produced final copy. The deterioration in morale and productivity associated with such office reorganizations led to the development of alternative organization strategies for office automation. The perspective of the more recent alternative approaches is more optimistic. It begins with a realistic assessment of what many offices, and what many jobs in offices, are like today. They can be very routine and very standardized, because of the need for the overall organization to integrate and coordinate work processes. In addition, the "one best way" that much paperwork is done is inherently dehumanizing as people carry out endless iterations of work that is almost mechanical in nature. If the automated office can relieve office workers of much of the drudgery of paperwork, then the remaining aspects of their jobs, even if they remain somewhat externally controlled, can be more fulfilling. A further consideration involves the degree to which each worker can have control over his or her own work station. Even though there may be organization-wide procedures for communications and record storage, an employee can develop or acquire a wide range of programs and systems at the work station for individual use. A program might provide for the management of a data base of use to only a few managers, or it might even provide for the collection, recomputation, and presentation of information within the organization's record system, but not maintained or generally reported in that fashion. Thus, the automated office may provide for even greater individual initiative than a Stage 1 or unautomated office would permit.

Probably the key issue in the planning and development of an automated office system that will maintain employee freedom and initiative is the degree to which the system (1) can be controlled at the terminal to perform unique functions, and (2) can perform organization-wide functions in an easy and flexible manner. This means that the process of communicating or storing records, for example, must be reasonably simple for an authorized employee with little training and must not require memorization and exact execution of complex instructions.

There are other foreseeable effects of the automated office upon the organizational environment. It is likely that in the Stage 3 office a high percentage of jobs will require training and special qualification, and involve the exercise of judgment and discretion with regard to important functions. The relationships among employees will have to change when fewer jobs are defined almost entirely by procedure or supervisory instruction. Chapter 10, dealing with employees and computers, will consider these relationships in much greater depth.

Physical Environment

The physical environment of the office will also have to change. The introduction of computer equipment into a work place that previously has not been automated can create numerous problems unless the physical design of the work place supports the equipment and the new needs of those who must work with the equipment for extended periods. There are several aspects of the physical environment of the office that should be considered, both in planning a new office or in redesigning and renovating an older one: mechanical and electrical systems, work area layout, and furnishings.

Mechanical and electrical systems include heating and air conditioning, lighting and electrical systems, and communications systems. In some instances, the adequacy of these systems can be determined by any manager or office employee; in many instances, however, adequacy must be determined by a qualified professional.

Heating and air conditioning should be capable of handling the changes in heat generated by the equipment. This may require more air conditioning in the summer and less heat in the winter. In the past, there have been very strict requirements for the temperature range for the operation of a computer, so that internal parts are not damaged. Some more recent equipment has a wider range of temperature tolerance, so that employees may become uncomfortable before their equipment is at risk and such discomfort may reduce work accomplished. Another result of the combination of heat-producing equipment and heat-extracting air conditioning is that the air can become very dry. This can be uncomfortable for employees and may also cause static electricity that can interfere with the operation of electronic equipment. Therefore, it may be desirable to check the adequacy of humidifying equipment.

A big mistake in considering the adequacy of heating and air conditioning would be merely to render the office adequate for the equipment. Since the equipment can tolerate an increasingly wider range of conditions, it is of primary importance to develop the office so that the needs of the employees are met. If the employees are comfortable, probably the equipment is comfortable too.

An adequate source of electric power is clearly necessary to operate an automated office. This may require that more power be brought into the building, or it may simply require that additional outlets be installed at appropriate locations throughout the office. Since utility power can sometimes go out, and since in many locations the electric power is "dirty," meaning that it has slight but significant surges and losses of power from time to time that can affect equipment performance, it may be useful to consider special devices to connect to the power source to provide power to all computer and computer-related office equipment. Such devices can carry out some or all of the following functions:

Compensate for slight surges and losses of power, so that the power delivered to the computer and the office equipment is of evenly high quality.

Provide an ongoing alternate source of power when the utility breaks down, so that the computer system can function during a power brownout or outage.

Provide alternate power for a short time, so that the system can be turned off without losing the information.

Communications wiring is the physical wiring of the local communications network. This is comparable to the wiring of telephone extensions in a conventional office. Wiring needed will vary with the type of office system to be installed, but several types of local networks are available. Some make use of existing telephone lines, on the assumption that most offices already have such wiring so that this is therefore a convenient system to build upon. Problems with telephone wiring for automated office systems involve the ease, speed, and reliability of transmission of data as opposed to voice communications. Often computer equipment communicates most efficiently using 5, 10 or even more lines of communication at once so that many aspects of coordinating several complex machines can be simultaneously performed. This would call for more complex wiring schemes. Other systems, such as the use of fiberoptics as explained earlier in the chapter, have distinct advantages but would require rewiring.

The layout of the work area is the second consideration in the physical environment of an automated office. A satisfactory office layout must respond to a variety of considerations, including the need for particular employees to be near other employees or office areas, the provision of sufficient space for employees to work effectively, and the overall need for efficient patterns of movement in the office. Two additional factors especially important in an office of the future are lighting and acoustics.

Adequate levels of light are necessary in any office. A major problem in an office using computer terminals is glare. Direct glare occurs when a light source shines too brightly into the eyes of a worker when he or she is looking into the screen of a computer terminal. Ceiling lights behind the terminal might create direct glare depending upon the position of the terminal and the brightness and location of the light. On a sunny day a window located behind a terminal can have this effect as well. Indirect glare is bright light that bounces off walls, furniture, or even the screen of the terminal itself. Providing the right levels of light, and providing it evenly without glare, can be achieved through the proper selection and location of light fixtures and through the use of venetian blinds on the windows.

Acoustical problems can also be complex. An automated office often has too much or too little sound. Some printers can make a great deal of noise, disrupting communications nearby. This can be minimized through proper location of the printer or through sound insulation either as a part of the printer itself or by means of a covered enclosure. The clicking of terminal keyboards, on the other hand, can provide insufficient levels of background noise for the office, resulting in employees distracting one another. This problem can be resolved by adding some background sound.

The third dimension of the physical environment of an automated office is the furnishing of the office. Of course, it is pleasant to have office furnishings that coordinate and reinforce the pleasing designs of much office equipment. However, there are some very immediate problems with the use of conventional office furniture for computer equipment, problems that go beyond appearance and image.

If a manager of a small office were to have work stations installed while keeping the conventional office furniture, several problems would be likely to arise. First, most computer terminals (or work stations) do not fit in the space where a typewriter fits. The terminals are too deep, so that the keyboard projects out far beyond the edge of the table. Also, the communications cables do not fit at the back of the table, unless the terminal is placed so far forward that it is precariously close to falling off. There are two obvious but unsatisfactory solutions to this difficulty. One might be to put the work station on top of the desk. This works, but it leaves the worker with no clear desk space. An alternative is to buy a small "computer terminal desk," which would hold the terminal but may not provide the employee with a nearby surface for the material being worked on. Probably the best solution is to get a new desk that can accommodate the work station, the printer, and other peripherals, and provide some clear work space as well.

There are other problems with the use of furnishings not designed for computer equipment. Placing a computer on a conventional desk, for instance, may place the keyboard at a level too high for comfortable typing over long periods.

The following are some questions to ask when considering furnishings to be used with a work station.

Is the middle row of the keyboard of the terminal at the same height as your elbow? If not, your arms may be held in an uncomfortable position. This is why typewriter desks are usually lower than table tops or desktops for writing by hand.

Do your legs fit under the desk when you sit close enough for your hands to touch the keyboard and your elbows to rest directly below your shoulders. You should not have to reach for the keyboard.

Do your feet rest on the floor or on a footrest? It is usually not an effective solution for you to raise the chair to adjust for a desk that is too high. It will be uncomfortable for your feet without a footrest. It will make the use of foot-operated equipment, such as a dictation transcriber, difficult or impossible, and it will make movement inconvenient.

Is the display screen 20–28 inches from your eyes? This is the optimal range from which to view the screen without eye strain.

Is there adequate work space adjacent to the terminal so that you can see and manipulate two or more source documents while you are operating the terminal?

In evaluating a table or other piece of furnishing for a printer, there are several other questions to consider.

How does the table accommodate the paper that the printer uses? When a printer uses continuous paper, the paper either passes up from underneath, comes in from the back, or follows a path similar to that of paper in a typewriter. The table should have a place for paper to rest before it is printed upon and a place for it after printing.

Should the table provide an acoustical enclosure? This will depend a great deal upon the nature of the printer and its location in the office.

Just as in the case of a manager who acquires a computer system and is subsequently surprised by the additional expense of software, the acquisition of advanced office equipment without consideration of the environmental requirements of that equipment can be equally surprising and dismaying.

PROBLEMS AND CHALLENGES

There are several problems and challenges that often arise in the process of implementing an automated office system. These are specific to office systems, rather than generic to management computing systems, and therefore are not covered elsewhere in the book. They result from unrealistic expectations.

The first problem results from the expectation that the office of the future is a paperless office. This is a pleasant idea but very difficult to achieve. The goal of eliminating paper is unrealistic for several reasons. This would require that the rest of the people and organizations the office deals with give up on paper as well. In addition, it would assume that the organization had no need for original copies of transactions or that it could microfilm all of these. Finally, it would assume that people could work together on problems without paper. Conferences and meetings, for example, would be held at tables equipped with terminals for the participants. Thus, a paperless work process is possible for some highly defined functions, but not for the average office. People may even disagree as to whether the automated office will reduce the amounts of paper used. It is possible that the equipment will enable some work to be done without paper, reducing the level of paper use. On the other hand, the automated office system can be viewed as one that increases the ability of an office to produce paper documents. Ideally, however, the additional paper documents should be of current value, while the generation of paper documents for storage should be reduced.

The second problem that arises as a result of unrealistic expectations is a tendency for employees to do sloppy work when word processing equipment is initially introduced. The equipment redefines the expectations between the executive and the secretary. The executive may be led to believe (often as a result of advertising) that rewrites of documents are "as easy as the press of a button" and therefore may redraft reports and letters more frequently than when such revisions were done manually by the secretary. Compounding the problem, the secretary may not check drafts as carefully and may not make minor revisions of language, because under the new system the executive is assumed to be responsible for editing draft material. Rather than causing the same number of drafts to be done more quickly and accurately, the new system may lead to more drafts than before. This problem can be dealt with through training.

Office automation will be a major target of innovation as computer equipment develops in the 1980s. Managers and organizations prepared to take advantage of this new opportunity will be rewarded with greater productivity and more satisfied employees.

CHAPTER 6
COMPUTERS FOR SMALL BUSINESSES AND AGENCIES

I left a sales position in a large computer equipment company 5 years ago, and opened up my own computer store. I soon discovered a big difference between my previous clients, generally big corporations, and my new clients, small local businesses, such as retail stores, professional practices, and restaurants. Small businesses cannot invest a lot of time and money in planning and developing a computer system. They cannot afford the expense and the risk. These businesses need computers and programs that quickly fit into their operations and produce immediate bottom-line results. Unusual and innovative applications can be explored later, once the computer is in place and earning its keep. As a result, in my store I focus most often on about 10 basic computer applications that really contribute to a small business.

During the 1980s, the greatest expansion in numbers of management computer systems will occur in small businesses and the smaller government agencies. Special characteristics of these organizations will place new demands upon computers and the people who use them. Realistic decisions about computers for small organizations must reflect these factors.

An important difference between the organizations buying and operating a computer today, as contrasted with their counterparts of 20 years ago, is the size of the budget available to pay for the computer project. In a large organization, a relatively expensive computer system is often only a small percentage of overall expenditures. In a small organization, the cost of a computer system, as well as the cost of implementation and ongoing operation, can require a major portion of available funds. Computer projects therefore represent a greater risk to such an organization. As a result, projects for small businesses and agencies generally must meet several criteria:

The overall cost of the project, including equipment, software, and implementation, must be relatively low.

The savings to result from the computer project must be relatively high, offering a payback in not more than 3 years.

The savings must begin very quickly, as small organizations often cannot support duplicative expenses (the computer and the process it is to replace) for long.

Another difference is that the volume of a single work task in a large organization might make full or nearly full use of a large computer system. In a small organization, the necessary level of volume might not exist, requiring the computer to be used for several functions in order for it to pay its way. This calls for a computer adaptable to a broad range of functions. The flexibility and range of the system can become more important than the power of the computer to carry out one function quickly. Externally induced changes, arising from new laws or because of new market conditions, may require that the computer be put to use for purposes not originally intended. This is another reason why flexibility is important.

Finally, the performance of the computer system must be close to what was originally planned. In a large organization, a project worthwhile in the long run can be allowed to underperform or run over budget for a while without great harm to the organization because the unexpected cost is small compared to overall ongoing expenditures of the organization. A relatively small series of losses can be tolerated if in a reasonable period of time the effort can be expected to pay off. In a small business or agency, tolerable limits are stricter. Since the project may represent a greater percentage of overall expenditures, serious adverse impacts of underperformance or overexpenditure can occur much sooner.

Accordingly, small organizations cannot (and need not) merely imitate in small scale the types of projects and implementation approaches employed in larger organizations. Differences between small and large organizations influence the types of computer projects that are useful or practical.

PRACTICAL COMPUTER APPLICATIONS FOR SMALL ORGANIZATIONS

It is valuable, therefore, to consider ways in which computers can make a practical contribution to the operation of a small business or agency. Managers of such organizations often favor computer projects with relatively simple and direct benefits and explicit costs, thereby reducing risk. The following is a summary of ways in which a computer can directly contribute to the productivity of a small organization. Some are applications such as word processing and inventory management. Others are approaches or styles in the use of a computer that can make an existing system more profitable. Each has been selected because it is potentially useful to a wide range of small enterprises; it can can pay for itself quickly; it does not cost a great deal to implement; the necessary equipment and software are broadly available; and it is not difficult to implement.

Clerical Productivity

One of the most common small computer applications is word processing, that is, using a computer in typing, editing, and producing letters, reports, and studies. Initially, word processing systems were largely electronic enhancements of typewriters. Today, most word processing systems on the market are microcomputer based, permitting data processing activities as well.

For a small organization or individual business, word processing can pay for itself in several ways. The most obvious savings is in reduced clerical expense or increased production. Some organizations have reduced the number of clerical employees, and some organizations have even eliminated clerical staff altogether for certain functions. Growing organizations may reduce unit costs, enabling growth in production without a comparable rise in costs.

There are several indicators that a manager might look for to determine whether word processing might be cost-effective. Are many documents and letters relatively standard, so that there are only minor revisions each time the document is used? Typical examples include form letters, contracts, standard proposals, and commonly used legal documents. A word processing system can produce these with only the changes in content entered for each document. Form letters used with mailing lists can be personalized. Are documents and reports a major work product of the organization? Reports are time consuming to type, and revisions or modifications can be even more complicated and expensive.

Word processing is discussed in greater detail in Chapter 5 which examines office automation. One alternative should also be considered for the enterprise that generally produces a limited set of standard documents, such as invoices, response letters, and other paperwork. Instead of a word processing system, some managers write simple programs in BASIC. The program initially presents a menu on the screen listing the types of document options available. The statements on the screen might look like this:

Which document is needed? Pick a number.

Invoice 1
Price list 2
Letter: Delay to fill order 3
Letter: Sent wrong amount 4
Letter: Payment overdue 5

For each document or situation, the computer calls for the necessary information, such as the products, dollar amounts involved, and name and address of the client. The computer then prints out the necessary paperwork or letter, inserting the appropriate information in the message.

This type of program can be developed to work independently, or it can be part of a larger system of programs, using names and addresses from an address file, product information from a product inventory file, and so forth. Such a program can be more efficient than a word processing program when only a few types of messages are sent.

Executive Word Processing

Computers can aid managers in ways that can be very cost-effective. Indirectly, improved clerical productivity can lead to improved executive productivity, as documents are prepared in final form in less time and with greater accuracy.

Executives can use computers directly as well. Sometimes, when the creation of a document requires only a few revisions of key areas, an executive can take over the editing process, entering the revisions directly into the text on a terminal. This permits the executive to control the production process directly and lets the executive see the revisions immediately within the context of the document.

Another use for computers is in the preparation of statistical and financial reports. Calculation programs based upon spreadsheet concepts allow executives to develop, and quickly update and revise, relatively complex tables and supporting reports. Projects that would otherwise have taken hours and days can be completed in minutes, with much greater accuracy and reliability.

In assessing the desirability of greater direct use of computers by executives, several questions are worth considering. Do the executives themselves draft reports and work products that require much calculation? A computer can greatly improve the speed and accuracy of such efforts. Is the relationship between clerical and executive employees as efficient as it should be? Sometimes clerical employees merely type material that has been handwritten by executives. But it may take executives no longer to draft their work directly on computer terminals, eliminating some duplicative work load for clerical staff. In addition, the executives get immediate turnaround of their work.

Clearly, significant savings are possible by reducing the staff required to accomplish a given level of work or by improving the speed and quality of production.

Cash Management

Most small businesses and agencies have less-than-optimal cash management. Receivables are not collected as soon as possible, and bills are paid sooner than might be necessary. It is time consuming and complicated for an employee to keep track of much of the details of day-to-day cash management.

A computer can efficiently and economically track funds owed and funds receivable. Timely reminders can be sent regarding past-due bills owed to the business. Bills due others can be paid on time, but not earlier than necessary. Not only can this result in lower interest costs or higher interest revenues, but it also can cut time and expense in managing paperwork aspects of the accounting process.

There are several indicators of cash management opportunities for a small agency:

If an organization has a relatively high cash flow in and out, such as in rental property management, the benefits of improved cash management increase proportionately.

If a business receives most of its income in cash, in payment for labor, there are fewer opportunities for gains through cash management, since income is immediate and expenses are limited.

If current cash management is sloppy, so that accounts receivable age unnecessarily or late charges are paid out on due bills, improved cash management can be economically significant.

Finally, if the management of accounts receivable and payable is already time consuming and complex, benefits may result from improved employee productivity.

Often cash management is only one aspect of a larger accounting system introduced to improve accounting staff productivity, and to provide more timely information about the financial status of the organization.

Inventory Management

The management of inventories can become increasingly expensive as interest rates and storage costs rise. The complex process of inventory management frequently can be accomplished more efficiently with the aid of a computer.

Inventories have several important functions in management. First, they "store" labor, since they permit the products of today's labor to be sold in the future. Second, they permit work to be done more quickly and efficiently, with materials on hand, than could be possible if necessary materials had to be ordered. Third, inventories permit lower costs through quantity purchases.

There are a variety of indicators of inadequate inventory management that suggest the need for a computer-aided process. One area to examine is the timeliness with which orders are filled. Problems to look for include delays in shipment due to the unavailability of goods, unnecessary order backlogs, high numbers of customer inquiries, special orders, and other irregularities in the fulfillment of orders. Another area to examine is the purchasing of raw materials. Are the orders as large as they might be, if sufficient discounts are available for larger orders? Are materials ordered specially, or are nonstandard parts used or built to meet priority orders? Two important groups to consider are sales staff and customers. Are they frustrated about delivery and availability dates of goods? Are sales lost because of such frustration?

A computer, of course, cannot solve all of the many problems involved in meeting orders on a timely and efficient basis. Often there are valid reasons for order backlogs and delays, when the cost of stocking inventory is expensive and the demand for the product unpredictable. However, computers can make important contributions to improved inventory management. They can monitor the number of units of each item in stock, to identify when reorders should occur, and perhaps automatically prepare the order paperwork. They also can calculate for each item the optimal point at which to reorder, based upon the recent frequency of sales, the cost of the item, prevailing interest rates and other carrying costs, the profit on each sale, and the supplier's quantity discount structure. Such computations are complex and would be impossible on an inventory-wide basis without a computer. However, they are cost-efficient only if they are calculated on each item individually, and only if they are recalculated from time to time to reflect changes in purchasing patterns and underlying costs. An additional useful capability is the identification of items that are overstocked relative to their demand and carrying cost.

The use of computers in inventory management has some additional benefits as well. The clerical paperwork involved in an inventory system can be complex and expensive. This is the type of work that a computer can do easily, accurately, and quickly. A computer-based inventory system can also be checked more frequently, enabling more timely identification of irregularities and unexpected conditions.

These advantages of computers for inventory management have been available to large organizations for many years and account for some of the cost advantages that larger organizations have had over many smaller competitors. The lower cost and higher levels of performance of new-generation small computers can bring these competitive advantages to the small business and organization as well.

Employee Motivation and Retention

Because small businesses have fewer employees than larger ones, the loss of any one employee can represent a proportionately greater loss of experience and production capability. As a result, employee motivation and retention can be very critical to the ongoing performance of a small organization.

In a small organization, key work loads may be the sole responsibility of one or two persons, and when increases in sales or demand occur, or when additional paperwork and related procedures are required, the work falls to these few persons. In the small organization, a critical problem is likely to surface much more quickly and demand rapid attention. In a large organization, such changes are spread across a larger number of workers. If a computer can be introduced in such a way as to reduce routine and repetitive work, employee dissatisfaction can be avoided while production can be increased.

Chapter 10 reviews in detail many of the ways in which computers can contribute to or impair employee satisfaction. Not only can the computer contribute through the work it can perform, but it can also improve the extent to which an employee is interested and creatively involved in his or her work.

Customer Satisfaction and Service Quality

In all organizations, it is critical that the clients or customers be satisfied. Often the computer is described as a source of customer frustration and alienation. One thinks of erroneous bills for outlandish amounts of money, charges for purchases not made, communications that refer to the customer as a number rather than as a person, and restrictions on the ability of employees to personalize service or make reasonable exceptions because of the requirements of a computer program.

Each of these types of problems have lead to more than a few businesses going under or experiencing significant losses. Computers can be used to contribute to customer satisfaction as well. They can enable an organization to personalize mass communications that otherwise might have to remain impersonal. They can also permit service enhancements at low cost to the providing organization, thereby improving customer relations and sales. For example, computers have enabled pharmacies to provide customers with annual summaries of medicine purchases for tax purposes. For a pharmacy that is operating a computer already, this is not expensive or complicated. Yet customers appreciate it, and the attraction and convenience of the comprehensive report may lead them to concentrate their business in one pharmacy. Computers can enable employees to provide quick and complete services to customers, as in the past when there were fewer customers to serve.

In implementing computer systems, much attention is given to internal logistics, but sometimes the opportunity to improve and to personalize customer services is not fully developed, even though the additional cost may be small.

Documentation and Records Organization

As a small business or organization grows, inevitably the number of records to be maintained increases, along with the complexity of those records. Some records relate to the performance of ongoing operations, such as assignments of work and schedules. Some records relate to income and expenditures, such as contractual documents or records of expenses. Some records relate to taxes. If a record cannot be located when it is needed, or if the process of locating records and converting them into useful summary reports and action documents requires too much time and effort, the performance of the organization will deteriorate. Deadlines will be missed, assignments will be confused, income will not be fully realized, and tax records may not be as complete as necessary.

Good records management can cost less than inefficient records management on an ongoing basis, even if one considers only the actual clerical process itself. Inefficiency can compound itself, consuming many hours of totally unproductive time. The major benefits, however, come in more indirect ways:

Projects can be performed efficiently, with full coordination and awareness of deadlines and responsibilities.

Bills can fully reflect all allowable costs, in a manner that can be easily documented if necessary.

Disputes that can be resolved through reference to original source documents can be readily handled, reducing conflict and expediting work performance and payment.

Tax returns can take advantage of all legitimate deductions and credits. A properly planned system can provide full backup documentation, including summaries, as well as information needed to locate original documents and receipts should they be needed to support claims.

Good records management, if the volume of records is considerable, usually requires the use of a data base management program, as described in Chapter 4. Such a program can be used to locate records, maintain desired information from the records in a form that can be processed for summary reporting, and to produce ongoing management reports.

Analysis and Evaluation of Problems

Most of the benefits of a computer to a small business are relatively direct, providing for less expensive methods to get work done. An important indirect advantage of a computer is the ability to investigate and assess problems quickly and thoroughly.

A small business may experience a variety of problems from time to time, involving slack sales of a particular product line, higher than expected costs, or irregular and unusual occurrences such as inventory losses. Appropriate action by the key manager can sometimes be critical. The first step in solving such problems is to describe the problem so that it is fully understood.

If sales are declining, which product lines are most affected? Is it a general decline, or it is limited to higher or lower priced items?

If costs are running higher than expected, which items or work tasks are responsible? Is this true across the board, or only on particular projects?

In cost reduction programs, what can be eliminated with the

least impact upon the bottom line? Which product lines are contributing most to profit?

These types of questions can be answered in several ways. First, using a data base management system, it is possible to produce reports that break down costs and expenses in as much detail as the specificity of the input documents permit. It is also possible to supplement this information by doing special analyses using a spreadsheet calculation program in ways described in Chapter 3.

Managerial Control

One characteristic of good management is close control over performance and costs. As a business or organization grows, it becomes increasingly difficult to maintain a close and direct sense of day-to-day performance. It becomes necessary to depend upon the reports of others or upon secondary impressions based upon limited information.

A data base management system, with access to daily records about such key organizational functions as inventory, sales, and production, can provide a manager with current information based upon hard data rather than secondhand impressions. This can contribute to improved organizational performance in several ways. For instance, problems can be prevented or resolved early, before they can harm overall performance. Also, employees can be advised of priorities, based upon which activities are currently most needed or profitable.

Such close managerial control can be especially important in a small business or organization, since many have been developed through the efforts of one or two people, and one of the major competitive strengths is close control and accountability. A computer can provide an alternative means to the achievement of such control as the organization grows.

Cost Analysis and Estimation

In many businesses and government agencies, a major management responsibility is the accurate estimation of costs and the subsequent operation within the constraints of estimated costs. A computer can provide a small organization with comparable or greater levels of knowledge about costs, allowing effective competition with larger organizations having sophisticated information systems.

When a computer processes basic information about a business, such as sales, inventory, employee time and effort, and related measures, it is possible for reports to be constructed that summarize the cost of products and services on an ongoing basis. This allows a manager to act in a timely manner to adjust prices or to control unnecessary costs. Even when a computer is not used to process routine detailed information from which cost profiles can be constructed, some organizations develop programs to generate routine project cost estimates that are used as the basis for proposals. The program can be adjusted on an ongoing basis to correct errors, oversights, oversimplifications, and changing market conditions, so that future cost estimates can reflect past experience.

Accurate cost estimation can increase profit in several ways. Unnecessary losses can be avoided. Bids for projects can be made as competitive as possible. Marketing and project development costs can be reduced when paperwork processes are streamlined.

FINAL OBSERVATIONS: OVERALL MARKET STRATEGY

Growth is often a necessary condition for the survival of a small business or organization. In the initial stages of operation, growth is critical, since the enterprise must grow to the point that operating costs and revenues break even. As the organization matures, it is competing in a marketplace where those with the greater market shares have the opportunity to achieve economies of large-scale operation sooner than their competitors. This results often in the failure of the weaker and less efficient operations.

For a small business, achieving growth in local market share depends upon the ability of the business to do several things. It must be able to attract new customers while retaining the old ones. This is, of course, the basic objective. As the volume of sales grows, it must also be able to reduce the cost of the product or service in comparison to the competition as this is the key to continued growth.

A computer can help a small business accomplish these two objectives in four general ways:

> The computer can help the business to lower costs, enabling more competitive pricing and higher profits.
>
> The computer can help to position the business to service a greater number of customers without direct and proportionate increase in costs. A given level of fixed operational cost can support an increase in work load.
>
> The computer can help the business to offer customers a better service, while the cost of the improved service is limited. The computer can help the manager to plan and manage the business more precisely, recognizing and solving problems early.

To use a computer effectively, the manager must learn to recognize the opportunities to apply computers to significant problems. It is especially important to recognize the opportunities that offer quick paybacks, so that the extra cost of computerization is limited and the business gets a low-cost head start toward the added competitive advantages of further computerization.

Table 6.1 is a summary of indicators that a small business or organization might introduce a computer at a low cost with an early payback or break even-point. If a manager can identify such opportunities and capitalize upon them, then the business has a greater chance to achieve growth, which is a key to survival and prosperity.

Table 6.1. Summary of Indicators for Computer Use

Indicator	Type of application		
	Office Automation	Data Base Management	Executive Computing
Inefficient typing	Yes		
Much executive report development	Yes		Yes
Many routine reports	Yes		Yes
Many accounts receivable		Yes	
Poor inventory management		yes	
High employee turnover	yes		yes
Customer frustration	yes	yes	
Disorganized records	yes	yes	
Misunderstood problems		yes	yes
Loss of managerial control	yes	yes	yes
Inaccurate cost analysis		yes	yes

—— CHAPTER 7 ——
IMPROVING PRODUCTIVITY
WITH COMPUTERS

Our real estate appraisal service had been the leader in the city. Our leadership was due mostly to quality, which means personal attention, and thorough property research. Our business began to decline, however, when several real estate agencies began to offer lower quality appraisals at lower prices. In a cost-conscious market, our quality advantage was not enough, and so it was necessary to meet the competition's price. Today, we are back in first place. We reduced our costs while improving quality, using a microcomputer to store records on property characteristics and past sale prices, to compute appraised values based upon these stored records, and even to develop, edit, and print drafts and final copies of our reports. With the computer system, we have been able to lower prices while focusing more of our effort on what makes an appraisal excellent— thorough research and personal attention.

To improve productivity is to obtain greater output of goods or services for a given amount of labor and materials. This is an important goal for all businesses, large or small, because it is the key to profitability in a competitive economy. It is also a critical priority for government services. This chapter will explain what productivity is, illustrate how it can be measured, and describe some ways that computers can be used to improve productivity. There are some basic principles that should guide a manager in attempting to improve productivity using computers.

Some productivity improvement occurs through the substitution of computers for labor-intensive work processes. These improvements include, for example, the use of office automation systems such as word processing or computer-based record systems.

Additional improvement occurs as a computer system helps a manager make better, more accurate decisions. Work processes may be carried out as before, but sales projections are more accurate, and inventories are neither too high nor too low.

Further improvement occurs as employees become more satisfied and challenged by their work. They may be relieved of boring paperwork, or they may be able to find needed information with less effort and confusion. They may be encouraged by recognition for their contribution to increased productivity and by the rewards they receive for it. Or they may be challenged by the opportunity to use the computer in their own work to make more accurate decisions.

Finally, once the most obvious productivity improvements have been achieved, measurement becomes critical to sustained success. Measures of productivity permit monitoring of new methods over time, thus allowing a manager to use rewards and incentives accurately. Measurements allow the manager to make informed decisions about further improvements and changes.

Productivity improvement is a major rationale for the introduction of computers to businesses and agencies. However, increases in productivity are not automatic with computer systems. Productivity improvement projects must be well planned and executed. The remainder of this chapter is intended to help improve such projects. The concept of productivity is defined, and approaches to its measurement are presented. Then methods are presented to make the process of computer use more efficient, and contributions of computing to productivity improvement are reviewed.

MEASURING PRODUCTIVITY WITH COMPUTERS

Productivity has been defined in many ways. Webster's dictionary defines it as "the quality or state of yielding or furnishing results." In business, the term is often used synonymously with profitability, which would be determined by the market value of produced goods and their cost of production. From a national perspective, our productivity is measured by comparing the total output of goods and services in the private economy, to the work-hours of all persons engaged in the production of those goods and services. Historically, national productivity per employee has usually increased each year. More recently, the rate of increase has slowed, and in some years it has declined.

Generally, productivity refers to the relation between inputs (such resources as material, labor, and capital), and outputs (services, tasks completed, or physical products). Productivity improvement is measured by dividing outputs by inputs, resulting in an index that can be compared over time or across production units. Productivity is measured in many ways, but the general formula for any productivity measure is:

$$O/I$$

where O is a measure of the outputs of the process under analysis and I is a measure of the inputs. For example, O might be 200 reports, and I might be 20 employee hours, resulting in a productivity index of 10 reports per employee hour. In this case, a computer could contribute to a productivity increase by increasing O, or decreasing I, or both. To reflect the relative cost to introduce the computer, however, another index might be created, which would be the number of reports per $1000 expended, including both the cost of employees and computer as a combined

I. Presumably, the production per $1000 would be greater with the computer than without it. The following are some typical indices of productivity for small businesses and professions. In each case, the output measure is followed by (*O*), and the input measure is followed by (*I*).

Number of clients serviced (*O*) per professional hour (*I*).
Number of sales (*O*) per thousand pamphlets mailed (*I*).
Number of meals served (*O*) per server (*I*).
Number of products produced (*O*) per 100 worker hours (*I*).
Number of forms typed accurately (*O*) per hour (*I*).

Managers have sometimes observed that profit is the most critical measure of the success of a business and that other measures seem less important. Profit or loss, however, can be due to many factors, and it is therefore difficult to bring about sustained favorable results without more precise information. Productivity measures can permit a manager to focus on specific components of a work process, in order to identify opportunities for improvement and to monitor progress achieved.

Instituting a measurement system to monitor productivity improvements is a key to sustained progress. Without such a system, improvements tend to occur only temporarily, where and when the attention of the manager is focused. Furthermore, planning and decision making about additional improvements is less accurate. Thus, one important use of a computer system in a productivity improvement project is to provide accurate information about progress achieved. The computer may play no part in the substance of the improvement and yet still contribute significantly to an effective process.

In large organizations, productivity measures can often be constructed from records already available on the computer. Sometimes information about inputs (such as personnel time and earnings, material cost and utilization) and production outputs (such as products or services delivered) are maintained separately. The development of productivity improvement measures involves the combination of such measures on a single set of reports.

For a small business or professional practice, or for a team of employees in a large organization using an enhanced terminal, the necessary data are not always available within the computer system. A solution is to use the computer to manage a record system, in order to monitor the production process. To do this, a data base management system, or DBMS software package would be needed. This type of software is discussed in Chapter 4.

An alternative solution, which is simpler but sometimes less accurate, is to devise a program to produce productivity measurement reports on a periodic basis, such as monthly. The information, provided by various employees, would be entered into the computer at the end of each month. The computer would perform the necessary computations and produce a report providing the productivity measures for the month in question, comparing them with previous months. For this type of project, a spreadsheet computation program, such as VisiCalc or T-Maker, would be needed. These types of programs are discussed in Chapter 3.

Once a basic approach has been selected, the next step is to determine what measures should be used. Usilaner and Soniat (in Washnis, 1980, p. 95) have identified some important characteristics of I and O when used in the development of a productivity index:

Mutually exclusive: Can the input required to produce the output item be separated from other inputs? A sales representative might have difficulty, for example, in precisely identifying time expended in closing a sale as distinguished from time expended in training the client to use the product.

Process definable: Are the same steps required to complete the operation each time? It might be unfair, for example, to compare the time required to inspect a certain number of stores in urban versus suburban districts, if there are different steps required to get the job done.

Countable: Can the number produced be counted? Sometimes the essence of satisfactory production is difficult to quantify, such as "customer satisfaction," as contrasted with the "number of clients served."

Uniform over time: Will the nature of the product remain relatively stable over a reasonable period of time? It would be inaccurate to compare over time the production of architectural draftspersons if some months they work on relatively simple projects and other months they work on complex ones.

Mission oriented: Does the item represent all or a significant part of the mission of the activity being measured? Misplaced precision can result in needless effort, such as a requirement for salespeople to document client contact detail when the organization compensates them only on sales actually made.

Quality definable: Item quality becomes a problem only when it changes, but definition is needed to determine if change has occurred. If changes have occurred, these can usually be factored in to adjust the productivity equation.

Data readily available: To what extent are data available from existing sources? Not only is this more efficient, but also the data that are collected for other purposes are less subject to manipulation, since the process of collection is already established and often carefully controlled.

Directly measurable: Are the measures direct? Or, if indirect measures are necessary, is there a rational relationship between the output and the measure? Very gross and indirect measures, such as the number of workers per 1000 units of production completed per year, can be explained by many factors other than production efficiency.

In monitoring a productivity improvement program, the role of the computer in the computation of measures can be independent of the use of computers in the actual improvement effort itself. It is often useful to build such measures into computer systems that are installed primarily to improve the speed and accuracy of a work process.

INTERNAL PRODUCTIVITY: OPERATING COMPUTERS EFFICIENTLY

The productivity of a computer system can be classified as internal or external. Internal productivity pertains to the efficiency and effectiveness of the computing process itself, from data input to data output, including all the resources involved in the data processing system. External productivity refers to the contribution of the data processing system to larger application processes. Computer systems can be either internally or externally productive, or both. Internal productivity contributes to external productivity. First, we will review internal productivity, and then external productivity.

Internal productivity involves the efficient performance of the computing process itself. For a small business operator or professional, a high level of internal productivity means that information is put into the computer and reports come out of the computer with a minimum of effort and delay, and a minimum of time and resources expended on maintaining and operating the computer. Internal productivity can be measured by dividing outputs (such as reports generated, information stored, computations made, or programs written) by inputs (such as programmer time or equipment costs). The following are some traditional examples of indices of internal productivity of computer systems:

OUTPUT $(O) \div$	INPUT (I)	INDEX
Programs written	Programmer hours	Programming efficiency
Hours system is	Hours system is available	Uptime index operational
Hours system is	Maintenance cost	Maintenance cost operational index

Enhanced terminals and desktop computers also can be more or less internally productive. However, because the systems are smaller and more advanced in design, measures of internal productivity focus more upon the hardware and operational characteristics of the system than upon the performance of those responsible for its operation. Thus, the importance of internal productivity in a desktop computer will depend greatly upon the way the system is to be used. The following are some characteristics of a computer and its software that may contribute to improved internal productivity:

Ease of installation and movement.

Speed in storing and retrieving information stored in memory.

Speed in searching for and sorting files.

Ease of maintenance.

Ease of training for new users.

Ease of programming for persons unfamiliar with computers.

Computers are sometimes "benchmarked" to determine their internal efficiency. The process is much like a race between the various models of computers. For example, one might determine how long it takes for each system to perform 100,000 addition operations, or to store and retrieve a piece of data 1000 times. For certain large, frequent, or highly precise purposes, such benchmarks can be important factors in the equipment selection. For most management purposes, however, the types of available software, purchase cost, quality of maintenance, and other practical factors become more critical.

Internal productivity refers to the operations of the data processing function itself, rather than to the value of that function to the larger organization. Sometimes a task prior to computerization can be so costly that a relatively inefficient computer system can still provide a valuable productivity improvement for the organization served. Typically, however, internal productivity is a basic factor in external productivity, especially because of the leverage involved. Improved productivity of the computer system reduces the input side of the productivity equation for all the functions of the organization, thus contributing to the overall productivity of each of the many functions served by the computer.

Reduced Cost of Equipment and Software

One way to increase the internal productivity of computer systems is to reduce the cost of equipment needed to achieve a given result. The declining costs of computer equipment have been remarkable, especially for small business operators and professionals. Lower prices reduce initial purchase costs, as well as ongoing interest and lease costs, maintenance and replacement costs, and operating costs. Two factors have contributed to the reductions in equipment costs achieved over the last 20 years. First, costs of computer components, such as integrated circuits, and various types of data storage devices, such as disks, have declined as a result of technical innovation and greater manufacturing experience over time. Second, overall increases in demand for computers and peripheral devices have enabled economies due to greater production and distribution volume, even for components that have not become less costly as a result of experience and technical innovation.

A second contributor to improved internal productivity can be lower software costs. This may be achieved through the purchase or use of software packages already available on the market, instead of the development of software from scratch for each application. Initially, such packages were available only for the most prevalent applications and the most widely used equipment. More recently, however, greater specialization of software by function and equipment applicability has permitted the cost advantage of packaged software for a larger number of users. This trend will be especially important for microcomputer users, as certain popular operating systems now allow many different types of machines to operate the same application program. Use of packaged software saves money, not only because of lower direct acquisition costs compared to internal development, but also because the user can examine the final product—the software— prior to purchase, to ascertain that the package will do what is needed. Internal development, either through a consultant or by the business operator, might result in a package that does not perform as planned because of organizational communication problems or program and development error. Also, the time between the decision to computerize and implementation can be reduced when software is purchased. Since the decision is probably motivated by expected lower costs from the computerized function, the sooner these savings begin, the greater they will be.

Efficiency in the Management of Computing

Certain design characteristics of an overall computing process can contribute to lower costs of computing. Large systems place responsibility on final users for entering information into the computer, for the accuracy of such data, and for the production and delivery of reports and other products. When final users directly enter data and receive outputs, not only is internal productivity increased, but efficiency for users is greater because they do not have to deal with computer staff as go-betweens. For desktop systems, comparable efficiency and convenience is achieved when software is flexible and "user friendly." This permits changes and innovations in computer use without the need to deal frequently with outside parties, such as vendors and computer programmers.

Computer systems that are structured so that the employees who directly operate the computer do not function as go-betweens in data input, verification, and output can grow without being constrained by the size of the staff to operate it. To increase the number of files maintained in the system and the number of output reports requested does not require a corresponding increase in operating staff to support the computer. One must usually plan in advance for flexible system expansion. In some larger data processing departments, a major source of programmer and operator work load is generated by nonroutine requests for reports that have to be specially programmed and run. To minimize this problem, programs have been developed that permit end-users to make inquiries of the system data base without the direct assistance of the operational staff. This further supports growth in the work load capacity of the computer system without a corresponding growth in the input resources.

For smaller systems, or desktop computers and enhanced terminals, the critical objective is to use "friendly" software, written so that most employees can use it without extensive training. This reduces the number of times that one employee must rely on another to use the computer. When the need for assistance is reduced, employees spend more time actually working rather than learning to compute, and error due to miscommunication between employees is reduced.

Another way to use a computer more efficiently is to increase the amount of work that a system performs, thereby lowering the cost per unit of work completed. A common issue in developing an adequate level of production for a computer system involves the achievement of "critical mass." Because several functions may interrelate (or share source information), even in a relatively small and simple computer system, producing a certain report (about productivity for instance) may often require an adequate level of use of some other function (production, material use, or sales) that provides some of the source information. For this reason, new computer systems can be unproductive until a "critical mass" of use is achieved. In the implementation of a new system, it is sometimes necessary to give priority to functions that interrelate so that one function can stimulate use of and support another function.

Some systems have taken on additional work for outside organizations on a time-sharing or batch basis. This permits additional output and can increase productivity if the operating staff does not have to provide substantial support for such activities. Such a practice was especially prevalent when computer systems were larger, requiring much greater operational support levels, and less dedicated to a single organization. With the advent of minicomputers and microcomputers, time-sharing is less prevalent.

EXTERNAL PRODUCTIVITY: USING COMPUTERS EFFECTIVELY

External productivity improvements refer to increases in production and decreases in input resources that occur to the organization, business, or professional practice as it performs functions with the aid of the computer system. There are many ways in which external productivity improvements can be achieved, but there are two broad categories: those that involve modifications of production processes and goals, and those that involve improvements in employee skill and motivation. These approaches apply to large organizations as well as to small businesses and professional practices.

A great deal of the productivity improvement under way in the nation today does not involve computers directly. Unnecessary or inefficient work practices are suspended, workers are motivated more effectively, or production volumes are increased enabling economies of scale of operation. Nevertheless, each method might involve computers in some aspect of the logistical support of the process to be improved or in some part of the planning, decision making, and monitoring of the effort.

Some approaches involve heavy use of computers. Automation of production methods usually involves the installation of machinery controlled by computers. Product redesign often involves computer-aided procedures for design, documentation, and evaluation. Resource management often requires more rapid and accurate information about inventories and demand trends, usually provided through data base management systems run on computers.

The following is a review of some basic approaches to productivity improvement, including a review of the contribution and potential of computers in each area. Several application profiles are presented as well.

Modifying Production Goals and Processes

Improvements in productivity are often achieved through the elimination of unnecessary tasks or functions in a work process. Similar economies can be achieved by combining like functions into new production units that can produce more efficiently. Not all such improvements require worker layoffs and terminations, as productivity improvement can be achieved by increasing production using the same number of employees.

The key to a successful redesign of an organization or program is the identification of tasks or functions to be combined or eliminated, and the implementation of such reductions in a manner that reduces organizational conflict and turmoil, and keeps economic harm to employees at a minimum. Computers can play a role in the planning and analysis of such efforts in several ways:

Data base management systems, or automated record systems, may provide descriptive statistics on production processes to allow identification of activity levels and costs of various steps in a process. These types of programs are discussed in Chapter 4.

Programs that aid decision making, such as financial modeling programs, can help a manager to make a more accurate decision or to take more factors into consideration. These types of programs are discussed in Chapter 3.

Programs can be used to perform studies of alternative work processes in order to identify better methods, as described below.

Computer systems can be used to monitor production processes while they occur.

Productivity improvement can be achieved by directly substituting machines for workers or by substituting more efficient machines for those that are obsolete. Computers are an integral part of many robots or production machines. The use of such machines has been cited as a major factor in Japan's productivity edge over the United States in certain industries.

Another approach involves evaluating methods of work so that employees can produce more goods and services in the same time period, without added effort. Time-and-motion studies have identified "best ways" to perform many tasks that are elements of production processes. Similar studies of production lines and larger scale processes can identify ways to reduce unnecessary effort and time. Increasingly, computers are used in performing the complex computations required for a reliable and valid study, and computers are sometimes set up to provide ongoing measures of task performance efficiency.

Improvements in production processes are also achieved through improved inventory management. Toan (1968, p.68) describes several functions of inventories. Because items on hand can be used, inventories make it possible for a company to manufacture and deliver goods more quickly than if the company had to wait for needed items to be made, or bought, or delivered. Inventories also reduce costs. They make it possible for items to be bought, made, or delivered in larger quantities than are immediately necessary, and thereby permit goods to be made, bought, sold, and delivered at lower costs.

Inventories achieve these objectives when the cost of maintaining the inventory is less than the savings achieved. As carrying costs increase, especially because of higher costs of money, the most effective achievement of these objectives depends upon accurate information and effective management response. The goal, of course, is to reduce the inventory to the minimum amount consistent with the achievement of shorter deliveries and reduced purchasing costs.

The role of a computer here is apparent. It can provide more timely and accurate information about the status of inventories and orders. It can also enable the rapid analysis of alternative courses of action to optimize the relationship between the costs and benefits of inventory.

Organizational Development and Employee Motivation

Another way to improve productivity involves the motivation of employees to produce more and the development of an overall organizational environment that promotes goal-directed effort rather than bureaucratic infighting. There are many ways that this can be accomplished.

Incentives and rewards can be structured so as to encourage improved productivity. Traditional salary compensation alone is often insufficient to motivate higher levels of production because it is not keyed to such production and because it is an inherently expensive reward. Other nonmonetary incentives, including greater supervisory autonomy, opportunities to adjust one's work schedule, and status incentives, have proven effective. Computers can be used to measure production and allocate incentives in a manner that is less costly (than manual approaches), more explicitly targeted to each employee's production, and more immediately responsive to changes in performance than would otherwise be feasible.

Computers themselves can serve as rewards for excellent performance while they also serve as devices that increase production levels. In the past, highly structured and expensive systems could not readily be used in this manner. With more individualization of computers and greater flexibility of application, this approach becomes more and more practical.

Changes in work patterns, both with respect to the time and location of work, can be facilitated with computers. Complex "flextime" schedules can be managed with computer assistance, allowing employees some opportunity to determine, according to their individual preferences, when they come to work. Some employees are already electing to work at home on computer terminals linked to a computer system at the work site. This reduces the costs of commuting to and from work and permits some flexibility in child care. Finally, work at home in individual professional practices can be supported by the technology of the modern office at a cost that is practical for the individual worker.

Chapter 10 further examines the implications of computers for employee development, supervision, and motivation.

COMMON COMPUTER APPLICATIONS FOR PRODUCTIVITY IMPROVEMENT

The following are some examples of programs and applications that permit computers to contribute to productivity improvement.

SOFTWARE PROFILE 13:   MANAGEMENT ANALYSIS WITH COMPUTERS

How can a manager use a computer to identify better ways to organize a work force and to structure worker's jobs? Here are some approaches that can be carried out on a desktop computer, although more sophisticated specialized software is increasingly available as well.

One approach is often called "task analysis." There are many precise and complete versions of how to conduct such a study, but the basic concept is quite simple:

Identify the tasks that make up a job.
Determine how long it usually takes to complete each task, in hours or parts of hours.

Then determine how many times each task is performed each week. Multiply the frequency of each task by the number of hours it usually takes to complete it.

Then add an allowance (in hours per week) for breaks, training, staff meetings, and other activities not directly associated with the main work.

Total the task hours and allowance hours per week to find the total hours the job requires.

Divide this number by 35 or 40 hours (depending upon the number of hours an employee works per week) to find the real number of employees required for the task.

The number of employees recommended through the analysis can then be compared to actual or proposed numbers of employees, and adjustments can be made. A simple system for task analysis can be developed on a desktop terminal or computer using a spreadsheet calculation program. More complicated applications may require specialized software.

Computers can also be used in the analysis of organizational structures and organizational staffing plans. Numbers of line employees can be proposed or evaluated using task analysis procedures. Then numbers of supervisory positions can be determined, for large organizations, using span of control ratios. While a computer can be used to develop a recommended number of employees at each level of an organization, perhaps a greater contribution can be in the ongoing calculation of total numbers and associated costs of a staffing pattern. Thus, a manager may use a great deal of judgment and experience, informed in some instances through task analysis, in the development of a staffing pattern and table of organization. The contribution of the computer can be in the ongoing determination of the cost of the recommendations generated. The bottom line implications of alternative decisions can be immediately considered as well.

SOFTWARE PROFILE 14:   COMPUTER-AIDED DOCUMENT RESEARCH

Document research is involved in the development of research projects, legal materials, and reports used in management planning and analysis. Such research is expensive because it is often highly technical and always very time consuming. Several additional factors affect the quality of any search. As the number of documents searched increases, the detail and precision of the resulting report should inprove, provided that the search is intelligently planned and directed. Access to an up-to-date source of documents can affect the timeliness and relevance of the resulting report. The skill and diligence of the researcher can also be a critical factor.

Computers are used in document searches in a large number of fields, including business, public management, medicine, and law. Such systems can improve the efficiency and effectiveness of a document search in several ways. First, they reduce the time required to locate the key documents of interest. Then they can provide the text of the document or a contact for acquisition. Finally, they can assure a more systematic search of a large collection of documents than a person could complete in a comparable period of time.

A search system requires a data base, which must be maintained on a continuous basis. The most extensive data bases keep the actual texts of documents so that they can be searched and generated in the original form. More limited systems keep abstracts, which summarize the source document, classify it as to key topics discussed, and describe where the document can be acquired.

To search a document, a user must identify the topic of interest, or key words and phrases to be located. A very powerful system can search the text of thousands of documents for certain words and phrases. Simpler systems can provide listings of all documents that were classified by abstractors as relating to certain terms or that include those terms in the abstract itself. The actual process of document searching is in many respects an art rather than a science, and therefore the quality of a search can be greatly influenced by the skill and experience of the researcher.

If the researcher is familiar with the descriptor terms used in the particular system, careful selection of terms can provide a more complete and more relevant list of documents. Familiarity with the search logic of the particular system can also improve accuracy. Systems permit a researcher to find documents that include a particular word or phrase, but this can be qualified as to the date of the document (e.g., nothing published before 1960) or as to other terms (e.g., the document must include both the word *computer* and the word *accounting*). A wide variety of other conditions can also be specified, such as the type of document (books, journal articles, newspaper articles, etc.) or the origin (e.g., only documents published in the United States). Obviously, if the researcher is not familiar with the system used, many irrelevant documents can be generated and many important and useful documents missed.

SOFTWARE PROFILE 15:   NETWORKS

Time-sharing is a way to provide computer services without the need to own and operate the computer itself. It is discussed in Chapter 3 as one approach to the configuration of a computer system. Initially, time-sharing systems consisted only of large computers connected by phone to large numbers of terminals that served the users leasing time on the computer.

As microcomputer systems have become more available, an alternative time-sharing approach has evolved that fills the gaps between what a microcomputer can do and a user's need for large-scale computing power, access to data bases, and connection to a telecommunications network. Large networks, such as Compuserve and The Source, offer services that supplement microcomputer capabilities, and they charge for these services at rates that correspond largely to the actual time the network is used. Networks can provide the following types of services.

A user can send and receive electronic mail. Most messages must go between two users of the same network, although it is also possible to have a message printed and deposited in the local mail near to the intended recipient.

Data bases are maintained by the networks, so that a user can get recent stock market information as well as other types of statistics.

The networks often provide access to text search systems as described in the preceding application profile. An investor can search the records of several newspapers for recent reports about a particular company.

Networks can provide the ability to perform calculations and statistical analyses that might not be possible in a particular microcomputer system or local terminal, either because of the size of the local computer or terminal or because of a lack of necessary software.

Some networks operated by users' groups (particularly those supporting the CP/M operating system) provide free public domain software that can be transmitted to your computer over a telephone connection.

Use of networks can increase the performance of a small computer system at a relatively low cost, since the user pays only for the services actually used. Costs of maintaining a large computer system and costs of maintaining large and complex data bases are supported commonly by all who use them, rather than by a few users.

SOFTWARE PROFILE 16:   COMPUTER-AIDED TRAINING

Training has an obvious and important role in employee productivity. Yet, it can also be very expensive, especially when one considers both the cost of mounting the training effort itself as well as the cost of employee participation in the program. Computers can be used to provide, in a relatively inexpensive way, some elements of a comprehensive employee training program.

Microcomputer software is available that provides a relatively "friendly" introduction to the use of computers and common programs, particularly for word processing and data base management programs. Many recent software packages include self-instruction programs. Packages are also available that introduce other management concepts and techniques as well.

Larger and more complex time-sharing systems, such as the Control Data Corporation PLATO system, provide training in more technical areas. The PLATO system includes a library of existing courseware, as well as a program that trains and supports a teacher, trainer, or instructor in the development of a new course. The course includes learning activities, as well as evaluation and grading systems. Most of the courses are structured so that, if a student cannot answer questions correctly, more basic learning activities are immediately available to teach the student the correct approach.

Some computer systems build instructional sequences into operational programs. For example, if an operator using a corporate information system encounters an unfamiliar situation, there is a "help" command that provides relevant instruction and training.

With a computer, a trainer can approach training in ways that are often not possible without one:

Target the learning activity to the needs and ability level of the trainee.

Assess performance on a continuous basis.

Provide immediate information to the trainee about performance.

Individualize the learning activity itself, to assure that each trainee is participating.

Randomize aspects of the learning activity so that exercises are different each time a student encounters them.

Provide the reinforcement and graphic interest that computer game technology can introduce.

Introduce the complexity of a real situation through a well-designed simulation.

But not all computer-aided training takes advantage of these capabilities. Paper flashcards, with the question on one side and the correct answer on the other, can sometimes be as effective. Programmed learning texts can often provide the same level of individualized attention.

When designing a training program, the trainer should try to use the best approach possible. A computer may be the best approach when individualized attention, continuous feedback, and graphic interest and reinforcement, and situational complexity are important.

FINAL OBSERVATIONS

Computers will occupy a central position in efforts to improve productivity in the decades to come. Not only will computers be used for automation of tasks, thereby reducing labor costs, but they will contribute to the indirect enhancement of productivity through employees, helping them to make more accurate decisions and to carry out their jobs more effectively.

As small, flexible, and decentralized computer systems become more prevalent, the individual manager will become more responsible for planning and operation. As a result, if productivity improvements are to occur, the individual manager will have to be trained and developed as the major agent of effective change.

PART

III

IMPACTS ON THE
MANAGEMENT
ENVIRONMENT

CHAPTER 8
MANAGEMENT PROBLEMS WITH COMPUTERS

After several years of experience in selling computers, I learned to spot "problem" customers early. These were customers who would be dissatisfied with their computer soon after it was installed and operational. Some customers have such positive yet unrealistic ideas about these machines that they become easy prey for retailers who only care about the sale, but don't have to support the customer afterwards. For me, the best indicator of a problem customer was a rushed and unstudied approach to a big and complicated task. Sometimes the best approach to these customers was to get them to find a system doing what they had in mind. The typical result was a more scaled-down and practical project.

Computer systems offer the opportunity of improved productivity and profit for large and small businesses, professional practices, and individual activities. Computers also offer the opportunity for expensive mistakes, as managers cope with a complex and changing technology. During the 1960s and 1970s, many large businesses and government agencies installed computer systems. During the 1980s, many small businesses and individuals will apply computers to their operations, if they have not already done so. Even though much of the collective experience with successful and unsuccessful computer systems relates to large organizations with large systems, the lessons learned may help individuals and small business operators to avoid expensive problems as well. To further that end, we will examine some common management problems associated with the implementation of computer systems. The lessons are relevant, regardless of the size of the organization or the computer.

When managers interested in the development of a computer system for their businesses or agencies identify some possible future problems that might be encountered, the most common response involves largely technical bugs. One common concern is equipment failure due to power shortages or the failure of some critical component of a computer system. More sophisticated managers will express concern about software errors and malfunctions, causing the wrong people to be paid out of organizational funds, or causing some other major and traumatic error.

When such problems develop, the consequences can be devastating. However, there is another dimension of problem that can be far more destructive. This type of problem involves the failure of the application—the function and purpose—of the computer system. When a system has been planned and developed to assume a critical role in an organization, such as the storage of records or the processing of accounting functions, failure of the system to fulfill this role can delay, impede, or destroy the remainder of the organization. Often in such cases, the computer equipment (the hardware) and the programs (the software) perform as specified. The source of the problem may be an error in the original specification of the system, or a negative reaction of the organization and its employees to the system, or the inability of the organization to support the input requirements of the system in a timely and accurate manner, or the inability of the organization to make effective use of the output of the system.

Several authors have investigated reasons for failures of computer systems to perform to the satisfaction of the user organization. While the subjects of their studies were large organizations, their findings often relate to small computer environments as well. Garrity (1963), in an extensive study of successful and unsuccessful computer installations, identified the quality of management direction as the most important factor, ahead of the technical skill of the staff operating and programming the computer, and the technological sophistication or sheer computing power of the system used. Two other authors, DeMarco and Campbell, developed more refined observations based upon the expectations of managers and the characteristics of the hardware, software, and user organization involved.

DeMarco (in Gruenberger, 1972) attributes application failures to mistaken beliefs about computers on the part of managers responsible for them. He has identified six mistaken beliefs that lead to application failures:

1. *The Emperor's New Clothes Complex.* Managers who see other managers using computer systems in their businesses and professional practices may proceed with a system even though they can see no real value of such a system to their own organization, because they feel that otherwise they might look outdated.

2. *The God Equals Love Complex.* Managers who do not understand the problems of their own businesses may understand computers even less. Irrationally, they therefore assume that the latter is an appropriate solution to the former.

3. *The Never Throw Anything Away Complex.* Business operators and professionals may plan to use a computer system merely as a new way to hoard old and useless records. The computer probably is more efficient than filing cabinets for hoarding records, but such an investment is not likely to lead to greater profitability or production.

4. *The Money Complex.* Some managers perceive that more expensive solutions are generally better than less expensive ones.

5. *Paranoia.* Some managers mistrust other employees, especially subordinates. Their effort, therefore, is to use computers to replace or closely control such employees. DeMarco cites early efforts in computer programming for businesses where computers were used to replace management groups, such as accountants or planners. This, of course, has not worked, although computers have proven to be substantial aids to middle managers.

6. *The Any Oracle in a Storm Complex.* For managers operating businesses that are in chaos, computer-based reports, even if they are based upon unreliable data, can appear valid and provide a comforting appearance of order.

Campbell (in Gruenberger, 1972, p. 119) has identified 10 reasons for application failures. The author has classified Campbell's reasons into three groups: those attributable to hardware, those attributable to software, and those attributable to the users and management. The following are causes of application failures due to hardware failure, or equipment problems:

Costs of physical communications, interfaces, and terminals can quickly eliminate claimed economic advantages.

Overhead costs of hardware, control, systems programs, and storage required for efficient operation exceed compensating economies.

Human/machine interfaces, such as display and display-to-hard-copy terminals, frustrate employees and create unnecessary work.

The following are causes of application failures due to software operation, design, or development:

System design and implementation is exceedingly complex, and design subtleties are often lost in translation for implementation.

Effective query languages for management have not yet been developed.

The following are causes of application failure that are due primarily to the users or the managers of the user organization:

The systems designer has exceptional difficulty in determining what the application is about.

Much of the data most keyed to management decision making are unsuitable for machine processing.

The organization of data files, with respect to information labels and locations, is poorly understood and presents substantial organizational problems.

Mechanisms for getting accurate and timely information into the system are often inadequately planned and developed. They are as important and as difficult to implement as mechanisms for getting information out.

Claimed operating economies cannot be achieved unless the system reaches "critical mass," implying massive expenditures ahead of promised economies and substantial control problems afterward. If the system does not "go critical," it does not work.

It is the experience of the author that major failures of computer systems occur most frequently because of application failure, as opposed to software or hardware defects. Application failures occur for several basic reasons:

A computer system, including hardware and software, may be acquired without adequate consideration of function. Sometimes this is done in imitation of other organizations, or because of a very intensive sales promotion, or because of a practical problem for which computerization is perceived as a solution.

A computer system might work in one business but might fail in another because of incompatibility with the nature of the work, organization, or management style of the business or agency.

A system might be acquired without sufficient involvement of employees in the design of the system. As a result, output reports might be inappropriate, or unfeasible types and amounts of information might be required to be entered into the system.

Most of these problems apply to large computer systems in large organizations. However, an individual computer purchaser or small business is perhaps more vulnerable than in large organizations, because they have fewer overall managerial controls to limit impulse decisions. For this reason, awareness of the management problems experienced by other computer users can be especially important for those interested in small systems.

COMMON APPLICATION FAILURES

The rest of this chapter reviews 11 common application failures of computers. In each of these types of problems, the hardware and the software of the computer system can be operating perfectly. The basic source of the problem is in the function and role of the computer within the business or professional practice, and in the management of the process of planning, design, acquisition, implementation, and ongoing operation of the computer system.

Wrong Equipment

A small hardware store chain purchased a minicomputer system for inventory management. The system printed price labels, prepared various reports on levels of inventories and number of sales for each store for each type of product line, and generated a weekly list of products for reorder. The system was located in the main office, and stubs from the price labels were shipped to that office to be entered into the system. This was a bit cumbersome, but it worked satisfactorily. In an effort to reduce the time involved in entering data, the chain purchased electronic cash registers that enabled clerks to enter the necessary data at the point of sale and allowed the accumulated data to be transmitted to the central system over telephone lines every night. This worked well until two things changed. Two additional stores were opened, and the software was changed to enable more information to be entered for each transaction and to develop more complex sales and cash flow reports for the stores. At this point, the system began to function more slowly because it had much more work to do. The time involved in doing the accounting reports left less time for completing other reports, and the performance of the system became unsatisfactory. The solution to the problem was to purchase a new central computer system with more memory and record capacity and a faster processing speed.

A particular computer, including all its elements, may not be able to do what is needed. The deficiency may be very obvious, such as an inability to support the number of users in the organization or to store the available files, or the deficiency may be more complex, such as an inability to transmit reports to remote sites with satisfactory speed. There can be several reasons for such a situation to arise. There may have been inadequate planning of the function of the computer or inadequate specification of the hardware needed. Perhaps the equipment was purchased in advance and the functional planning followed, or perhaps the expectations of the computer system mushroomed after the acquisition was made. Sometimes such a problem can result from greater than expected success and acceptance of a computer system, so that it is used more often than planned. Or the situation may be intentional, to stretch out the useful life of old equipment as long as possible, or to delay equipment purchases in anticipation of a new generation of more powerful and less costly equipment, or to allow an organization to determine more precisely its exact needs.

The obvious solutions are to acquire the equipment needed or to limit operation of the computer system to the high-priority functions of the organization.

Unexpected Costs

A small mail-order business purchased an over-the-counter microcomputer system to maintain inventory records, mailing lists, and accounting records, and to manage orders and deliveries. When the computer was purchased, a related software package was also purchased, which was designed to accomplish these functions. However, in working with the computer and the software, the owners were dissatisfied with the information maintained on the records and the nature of the reports generated. The basic problem was that over the years they had developed a set of codes that classified their product lines by supplier, type of product, and regional market. These codes were used in all of their previous records and in many of their previous management reports. The software worked, but it could not accommodate all of the codes and develop the reports based upon those codes. Thus, there were important differences between the owners' old record system and way of doing business, and the software package. The owners were faced with three expensive choices: to revise their old records and way of doing business, or to pay to revise the software package that they had already purchased, or to purchase a new software package and run the risk of making the same mistake twice. Their decision was to have the existing software modified by the company that developed it.

Early assumptions as to the cost of a fully effective computer system can often be inaccurate. A very common unexpected cost relates to the acquisition of software. Other, less obvious examples include the cost of in-house software development, which frequently takes twice as long to develop as planned. Problems can develop as a result of inadequate specification of the computer system at the time of acquisition or as a result of overoptimistic assumptions about in-house staff programming abilities.

Such problems are not easy to solve once they have occurred. Either one must live with less-than-optimal performance or pay the cost of additional equipment and service. The time to avoid the problem is when the system is planned. With respect to software, a small computer operator can be at a definite advantage over a large system operator if the small computer can use a variety of existing software produced for microcomputers. Most microcomputers are designed to use software from many sources, which reduces the initial cost of the software, thereby reducing the cost of any selection errors.

Eternal Adolescence

A mental health center bought a computer system along with a software package for a client services tracking system and accounting system. A programmer was employed as a consultant to modify the software to fit the agency's plans and to help the system to grow with the agency. It was anticipated that during the early stages, the system would be relatively simple, growing more comprehensive as time went on. After about 6 months of effort, largely devoted to input of client records, the first stage of implementation was achieved. At this stage, the system maintained a record on each client, including identifying data, address, type of problems, and assigned staff member. It could then produce simple but not very useful reports on case loads.

At the second stage of development, a controversy ensued within the agency. Originally, the system was merely to keep a record of services provided, and provide monthly invoices to clients for payment. However, the staff also wanted to track the progress of clients to compare the effectiveness of alternative treatment methods. This required that service records be maintained over a longer period of time and that data on the progress of clients be created and maintained as well. This was a tall order for the consultant, as it required much additional programming and even some additional record storage capacity.

To compound matters further, when the new tracking system was about 2 months from completion, the state changed some regulations in its processes for payment for services to certain clients. The system was now required to maintain specific diagnostic data and some client background data. If the information was not made available, reimbursement for services would be reduced. This required some additional extensive revisions to the program under development and to the program then in operation. The programmer became very discouraged. Upon hearing that the initial operation of the new system might be another 3-6 months away, the staff also became frustrated with the long wait and lack of tangible benefit from the computer system. Because they were not getting much out of the system, they became less dedicated about the quality of the information they put into it.

Inadequate computer systems often present the manager with a continuing series of trade-off decisions between current performance and future potential. For example, limited programmer time might be directed at immediate operational problems, or at future system development that would increase the overall benefit of the computer to the organization. Sacrificing either immediate performance or future capacity leaves the system in a state of constant inadequacy. It neither develops the confidence of current users, nor grows with the organization it serves.

The worst error for a manager is to fail to recognize the trade-offs associated with choices between alternative development priorities. If those to be affected by the decision can participate in it, they may fashion a less harmful approach, and discouragement about the decision may be reduced. Otherwise, the manager may blindly attend to one problem without recognizing a related one.

Computer Competition

A small department store chain was owned and managed by an executive who recognized the possible benefits of a computer system. However, he deferred such a project for almost a decade while waiting for more sophisticated equipment at a lower cost. He also hoped to learn from the efforts of others, especially his competitors. While the owner delayed, middle management employees in the main office and at the stores could see immediate benefits from computerization for their areas of operation. One by one, they either contracted for time-sharing services, developed small microcomputer systems, or arranged with banks and other vendors for services done more economically by computer. These actions were allowed because each could be justified on the basis of immediate cost savings. However, it finally became apparent to the owner that a coordinated program of computerization was necessary. The various separate computer systems created difficulties in communication and coordination between stores and departments. Information had to be put into each system separately. Perhaps most important, profits were beginning to grow at a slower rate than competitors because of higher over-head costs. An executive committee was formed to select a system, to acquire software, and to integrate existing systems to the fullest extent possible. During this process, a great deal of conflict arose, because each participant was attempting to assure that the new system would integrate with the existing subsystems already developed. Since this was impossible, it became necessary for the owner to decide. This upset more than half of the employees on the committee because their systems were to become obsolete. Conflict continued as the system was implemented, as employees resisted the new system and attempted to justify continued use of their older methods.

Continuing deferral of computerization, or a continuing pattern of underperformance in computerization efforts, may lead subdivisions of an organization to develop their own separate computer systems. This is not entirely undesirable, and it is certainly better than no computerization at all. However, there are several reasons why a coordinated program is preferable:

Uncoordinated development usually results in duplication of efforts and a resulting system that favors one area of an organization to the detriment of other areas.

Separate computer systems may not be capable of communication between terminals and sharing of records and other information. This results in employees having to enter data into the computers more than once.

Uncoordinated development also sets up the potential for resistance to a computer system by the "losing" subdivision, which must eventually implement the computer system against which it has been competing.

The problem reflects a perceived need for computerization within an organization that is not being met by management. If the system cannot be developed from the top of the organization down, elements of a system may be developed from the bottom up. This can give rise to expensive, inadequate, and badly coordinated systems that must be replaced by an entirely new one.

In Chapter 11, which describes approaches to implementing computer systems, a "bottom up" strategy for computer development is described. It has the advantage of flexibility and relatively low risk, but it is subject to the computer competition problem described here. The key to a successful "bottom up" strategy is careful "top down" preplanning in the selection of equipment and software so that as the new system evolves the parts are compatible with the whole.

Input Overload

The owner of a fast-growing real estate agency purchased a management information system. Because most management-level employees were brokers and paid by commission, few took the time to become involved in decisions about the computer and software purchase. After considerable review of real estate oriented programs, the system that the owner chose reflected his interest in detailed, accurate, and timely reports on the financial and operational progress of the agency, including reports of efforts and successes of the brokers, agents, and salespersons. During the first months of implementation, it became clear, however, that the data required to generate these reports placed great demands upon the sales staff, in terms of daily reports, sales documentation, and other paperwork. The clerical effort in feeding the raw data into the computer was also significant. After several months, the owner suspended use of the system because it was affecting employee morale and taking too much time away from sales work.

A computer program can require more information to be entered, and therefore more time and expense in "feeding," than can be justified by the reports and other information coming out. The development of relatively simple management reports can require extensive input of basic data, as well as updating of those data and creation of previously unavailable data. This problem can be a source of resistance to a new computer system, especially when remote users perceive that they are contributing more effort toward the computer than the system is saving them.

This situation can be the result of excessive efforts by managers to secure information, when greater attention is paid in the planning effort to management information and analysis than to the logistics of information management. A good rule of thumb in developing management report concepts is to use fully the information that is already in the computer (from existing programs and functions) before developing report concepts that would require additional information.

Computer Kingdom

A family-owned importing company was headed by a rather weak president who usually relied upon the company lawyer to make important decisions. This approach to organization and decision making arose, not intentionally, but because the president did not anticipate problems or make decisions, leaving the accumulated problems by default to the company's in-house lawyer. The decision to develop a computer-based accounting and inventory system caused a change in the balance of power within the business.

The vice president in charge of finance was responsible for the computer system because it dealt primarily with his area of operations. As the new system was introduced, the vice president seized the opportunity to change many procedures and production reports, ostensibly to improve the inventory system and to provide certain productivity measures. The production departments were not pleased, however, because the reports did not benefit them. In fact, they exposed the departments to possible criticism for legitimate short-term variations in production levels, the causes for which were not reflected in these reports.

Gradually, it became apparent to the lawyer that the computer system could provide the finance/accounting vice president with great new power and influence. The lawyer countered this influence by encouraging complaints by those concerned with the problems in the operation of the factories. Without the active leadership and involvement of the company president in these matters, a series of internal battles ensued that hurt the company and encouraged a lack of support for the computer system.

While much of the public mythology regarding computers and

their unusual powers is the stuff of science fiction, computer systems do provide managers with a high degree of influence over organizations. The increased influence occurs in several ways. The computer, through its programs and procedures, overtly or informally allocates access to critical resources in the organization, when priorities are assigned between divisions and functions. Authority over the computer also legitimatizes the ability of associated managers to determine operational rules and procedures in areas to be served by the computer. A manager should attempt to structure authority over the computer so that it best serves the interests of the organization. A satisfactory arrangement will usually reflect a balance of input and influence over computer operations by each of the key segments of the organization, and a clear delineation of where authority rests in decisions about the computer system.

Output Overload

A state government agency responsible for the distribution of certain federal grant funds to local governments planned a computer system to keep track of the grants. In working with the software developer, the team of employees responsible for planning the system developed a long list of reports that would be useful. In brainstorming the list, many reports were identified as breakdowns of a set of measures by grant number, or by county, or by type of recipient function. Some of these breakdowns were then compounded, so that, for instance, one could compare for each county the breakdown of funds distributed by function. Numerous reports were identified as useful. Once the system was developed, employees checked off on a distribution list those reports that they would like routinely to receive. The result was chaotic. Employees received foot-thick piles of reports monthly and even weekly. Over time, reports were consolidated so that essential information was concentrated on a few pages, and more detailed listings were placed in a central library for access by any employee needing them.

Computers are capable of producing large reports efficiently. Employees will request such reports by mistake, not realizing the magnitude of their order, or they will elect merely for status reasons to receive a report they do not need. Computer systems designed with inadequate participation by users can frequently be subject to this problem. Output reports and materials may be developed based upon the systems analyst's inaccurate concept of what the users needed, which is often not accurate. The result is output that is not of benefit to the users.

Duplication and Redundancy

A private medical clinic developed a computer-based record system for certain patient records. The system was expected to achieve a 50% reduction in paperwork. In the first year of implementation, both the computer system and the manual record system it was to replace were operated, to avoid a total loss of records if the system failed. It became very difficult during the second year to cease use of the manual record system because several key management, professional, and line employees continued to rely on the manual system. Even after an official deadline to cease using the manual system and to reassign employees working solely with that system to other duties, some employees made the extra effort of maintaining aspects of the manual records anyway.

When a manual process, such as a bookkeeping system, is being replaced by a computer-based system, sometimes the organization maintains both systems for a period of time to ensure that the computer system is fully operational and practical. This is often a very reasonable precaution. Such duplication also can occur, especially in a complex organization, because of lack of staff confidence in the computer system or because of staff investment and interest in the old manual system. When this occurs, some of the savings expected from the computer system are not achieved.

Useless Output

A cafeteria purchased a software package designed for restaurants. The software provided much of what was needed, including inventory and purchasing reports and plans, as well as records and projections of sales of menu items. However, the cafeteria served only a few items, and therefore did not need some elements of reports aimed at helping a restaurant predict demand for specific menu items.

Software packages designed for one organization or function and then applied to another do not always provide what is needed and often provide much that is not needed. The following are questions to consider when evaluating a program for adaptation from one function to another:

Can the program be adapted merely by changing names and labels (which is easy), or does it require changes in file contents, report formats, and formulas for processing information (which is much more complicated)?

Is the program written in a flexible and accessible language? A data base management program may be written in machine language. It may be easy to change labels and report formats using the features provided in the program itself. It may be very difficult, however, to efficiently and reliably change the processes used by the program for sorting data, as this would require rewriting the machine code. This is possible, but complicated and time consuming.

Generally, it is not economical or especially effective to attempt to modify a program written for one purpose to accomplish another purpose. Even the most highly organized and well written computer programs can become internally complicated after a series of adaptations and revisions are made. To add the burden of an entire revision of function is probably fatal. Especially for the small computer user, there are so many programs available so relatively inexpensively that the need should never arise. Even for the most unusual requirement, a general-purpose program probably exists that can be effectively used.

Implied Management Style Conflict

An office supply store, which markets products both at the store and through several sales representatives assigned to districts, acquired a used computer system to manage sales and ordering activity. The software had been developed for a local medical equipment supply store, which had previously owned the system. This company had very specific procedures and expectations for its sales employees. The employees were salaried and were encouraged to function more as consultants and advisors to clients. When the system was implemented for the office supply sales employees, they became very frustrated because of the need to document all sales activities, even though they were rewarded only for actual sales. Gradually, the computer system was changed to document levels of sales achieved, to plan sales objectives, and to coordinate such activities with other divisions of the company.

Organizations vary in approaches to management. In the above example, one organization emphasized rules and procedures, while the other focused upon outcomes. Computer systems also can have implied management styles, based on their focus for data gathered and reports produced. Sometimes computer management styles can conflict with organizational styles. For example, a marketing division might be assessed and supervised according to sales results, while the computer program might use a daily activity sheet that emphasizes frequency and type of client contacts. The computer system is focusing upon and rewarding behaviors and accomplishments different from those emphasized by the supervisor. It will also provide the supervisor with unnecessary information.

This problem arises from inadequate involvement by users in the planning of a computer system. There are several common ways this can occur. For instance, a software package may be transplanted from one situation or function to another. It may initially appear appropriate to the decision maker, but the details of the system do not fit with the method of operation of the new unit.

A manager may seek to change the management style of an organization through the computer system. For example, the goal may be to increase central control over operations or to increase the accountability of middle managers. This can be an effective strategy if the proper foundations are laid, but a weak manager can not take control of an organization using a computer if he or she could not do so without it. If a change in management style is deliberately planned and is broadly supported within an organization, a computer system can be used to reinforce such a change. An existing system can also be adapted to support change. Problems arise in the use of a computer system alone as a tool for change in management style and in the use of a computer program that is incompatible with the management style of the organization.

Computer Crime

An auto parts supply store purchased a computer to set up an inventory system. The computer maintained a current count for each item stocked by the store and provided weekly reports on items to be reordered and items not selling as frequently as expected. The computer program for the inventory system was very flexible, allowing the store owner to designate new items, as well as information to be maintained on each product. The system worked so well that the owner of the store put off his quarterly inventory for several months. At the time of the inventory, the owner discovered that the record system for automobile stereo equipment had been modified, so that several models had more than one record in the system. The added records valued the stereos at next to nothing, called for rather large reorders when inventory was low, and referred to the models by unusual names. As a result, the computer had suggested that more of these be ordered, and it was satisfied when they were sold at the indicated price. A rather intelligent store clerk had modified the system, bought the equipment, and left town.

An important and expensive problem can arise because of the opportunity presented by a computer system for such crime as embezzlement and fraud. Preventing crime is a complex and continuing problem, so serious and complex that is is the subject of Chapter 12.

AVOIDING TROUBLE: A CHECKLIST

The following is a checklist of very basic questions to consider as important decisions are made about a computer project. The questions reflect the lessons learned from the types of failures discussed in the chapter.

Does the equipment support the software I plan to use?

Have I considered all of the potential costs of this system, including not only the equipment purchase but also installation, maintenance, and software?

Have I fully considered what I plan to do with the system, and can the system accommodate these plans?

Can the system be coordinated in future years with computers elsewhere in my organization or with computers that serve my organization from outside? How much compatibility is feasible? Can an organization-wide plan be developed?

Can I, or my employees, provide the computer with the information it will need? Can this be integrated as much as possible with normal duties and tasks?

Will the computer change the responsibilities and authority of employees within the business? Are these employees prepared for this?

Are the reports the computer will provide really needed? Are they designed efficiently? Can they be modified as the system is implemented? Can the employees using the system make the modifications, or at least influence this process?

If the computer is to replace a manual record system or some other labor-intensive process, is the computer system really capable of the replacement?

CHAPTER 9
ORGANIZATIONAL DESIGN FOR COMPUTERS

The Records Unit, which I supervised, was the last one to get the computer. When the system came on line, it worked great, but there were some other factors which I hadn't counted on. One big difference was that we had yet another department, the data processing people, looking into exactly how we did things. My job as a supervisor changed too, as I became responsible for fewer people, but greater work flow. The big surprise hit last week, though, when the Records Unit was dismantled, and each of my workers was assigned instead to a specific department. I got a promotion in the process! Apparently, since one worker could handle all aspects of a record problem at once, and could get any part of any record needed regardless of which department created it, there was no longer any need for a central records unit any longer.

Computers generally operate within organizations. Even though some computers are operated under the control of one person, and lately many computers are owned by individuals, most people (and their computers) work with the routine support and contact of one or more organizations. Even the free-lance consultant who works alone often deals with organizations as clients. Because computers are complex devices, most require a cooperative effort between the persons using them, the specialists who maintain and perhaps operate them, and officials at each level of the organization who may be affected by a computer.

A manager should therefore be informed about how an organization can be structured to support a computer, to provide for needed expertise, coordination, and maintenance. A manager should understand the differences in approach to organizational structure appropriate for smaller and larger computer systems and should be aware of the changes that the small systems are bringing about even in large and traditional data processing divisions. The effects of computers on organizations is an important topic as well, since they may shape the ways in which organizational control and leadership are maintained in the 1980s and thereafter.

COMPUTER EXPERTISE WITHIN THE ORGANIZATION

How can an organization be structured to provide for the ongoing support of a computer system? When is it appropriate to develop a special team of skilled employees to operate the computer, and when is it appropriate to leave this to persons outside of the organization?

Until very recently, it was not possible for a manager simply to buy a computer and, with little more than a read-through of a manual and a few practice sessions, begin to perform useful work with the device. Even now, computer applications of any complexity often require some professional support. As a result, organizations using computers must have some source of expertise to guide planning decisions and to assist implementation. Organizations vary as to how they acquire and maintain such expertise, but there are several commonly used strategies.

Central Data Processing Model

The large scale and complexity of early computer systems required that they be operated by teams of specially trained personnel. As a result, most organizations using large computer systems developed departments or divisions responsible for the management and operation of computer services (see Figure 9.1). Organizations using complex megacomputer systems still must maintain these teams of skilled professionals. Generally, central data processing departments structured along this model have the following functions:

They provide overall management and planning for computer services, working with other managers to define long range priorities and goals and developing funding requests to support them.

They operate the computer itself, as well as such peripheral equipment as printers, disks, and telecommunications devices.

They develop application programs, so that the computer can perform the work of the organization.

They often provide user services, such as entering data, running programs, and interpreting output.

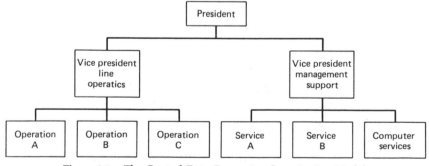

Figure 9.1. The Central Data Processing Organization Model.

Data processing departments have evolved along with computer technology so that there are several differences between the early units and their counterparts today. One basic difference is that the present-day center avoids, whenever possible, many of the traditional user-service functions, such as entering data and interpreting output. It is much more efficient and reliable to make the end-user assume responsibility for these, especially because of the great increase in volume of work processed by the computer itself.

Another stimulus to change has been the development of minicomputer and microcomputer technologies, reducing the central data processing staff's control over computing. Traditionally, the central data processing unit has controlled all computer services within an organization. This was desirable because it fostered coordination of data base management, integration of information systems, and economies of operation arising from volume. Within an organization having a central data processing unit, one result has been that divisions could not acquire computer equipment and services without working through the central unit.

The development of minicomputer and microcomputer technology has modified some of the basic premises that underlie the central data processing concept. In many cases, large-scale operations are no longer less costly than individual computer implementations. Diversity of applications, in response to the diversity of job roles and responsibilities of employees, can be more effective and efficient than rigidly imposed standardization. Sometimes greater sharing of information occurs with many dispersed one-to-one contacts than with a centrally controlled and coordinated process. Finally, individual employees and operating units have gained the ability to acquire microcomputers without the approval of the central data processing division. The previous rigid control has broken down because these computing devices, available from so many sources, can be purchased for such functions as typing, which are not traditionally under the hegemony of the central data processing division, and they can even be purchased individually by employees.

As a result of these trends, operating concepts of most central data processing units are under gradual revision. Since traditional autocratic control is no longer possible, more open and positive strategies are under development.

> Data processing departments are setting up the equivalent of in-house computer stores to encourage the use of small computers, while guiding the selection and application of the technology. Some offer a standard product at a discount. Such an approach can take advantage of the interest of individual employees in acquiring their own computer systems.
>
> Some departments have identified a microcomputer that can function both as a terminal to the corporate computer system as well as an off-line microcomputer and word processor. Many such devices are on the market, and they offer a technological bridge between the old and the new technology.
>
> Some departments have set up training programs and software-sharing users' groups to encourage coordinated development of microcomputer systems within an organization.
>
> Some departments have explicitly identified functions currently on the large corporate computer system that can be "shed" down to microcomputers and minicomputers, allowing the small and large systems to focus on what each can do best.

While central control of the organization-wide computer system is a practical necessity for some types of computer systems and applications, the development of competing technologies is requiring that traditional data processing divisions become more open and user oriented.

Time-Sharing Model

Time-sharing occurs when an organization pays for the use of a computer system operated by another organization (see Figure 9.2). Under such an arrangement, many of the functions of a central data processing department are fulfilled by the organization operating the computer. The development of special programs for a particular user may also be done by the computer operator, although an equally common approach is for the user organization to employ a small staff of computer specialists to develop such applications.

The basic advantages of time-sharing are that the user avoids the responsibility for acquiring and operating the computer, takes advantage of some of the economies of large-scale operation possible with a very large computer system, and pays only for the capacity used and not for capacity acquired to meet future needs.

The basic disadvantages are that the user is subject to the limitations and priorities of another organization. Should the operating organization need capacity elsewhere, it might reduce the capacity available to the user organization or it might raise prices in an effort to shed excess work load. These disadvantages are mitigated somewhat when computer time is acquired from a time-sharing company, because the company would presumably plan and develop capacity to meet its customers' expanding needs. Ultimately, the feasibility of time-sharing has to be considered on a case-by-case basis, and will be determined by the nature of the application and the capabilities and pricing structures of the leasing company.

The evolution of minicomputers, microcomputers, and enhanced terminals has had much the same impact upon time-sharing as it has had on the traditional centralized data processing concept. Some functions that in the past either would not have been computerized or would have been done through time-sharing can now be carried out with small in-house comput-

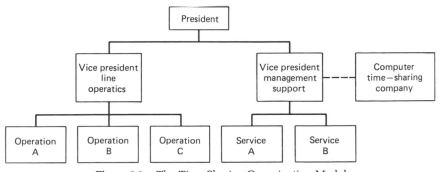

Figure 9.2.   The Time-Sharing Organization Model.

ers. As a result, a mixed strategy is evolving in which some functions are done internally and some externally.

Mini-Central Model

The mini-central model is similar to the traditional central data processing model (see Figure 9.3). It has evolved as minicomputer technology has developed, enabling an organization to implement independently a computer system dedicated to fewer functions than the large traditional systems. Although an operating and specialist staff is needed, a proportionately smaller team is required since only a limited list of applications is operational.

Because this approach has evolved from the development of the smaller computer technology, the introduction of microcomputers does not represent as significant a change in approach. In fact, some organizations are using a microcomputer network technology that involves the sharing of a large disk, but not a central processor. Under such a strategy, many of the capabilities of a large system are achieved, without sacrificing the flexibility and user orientation of the microcomputer technology.

Single-Vendor Organizational Model

Under the single-vendor organizational model, the vendor of the computer hardware provides ongoing maintenance and software, so that an in-house staff of computer specialists is theoretically not needed (see Figure 9.4). The great advantage of this approach is that, while the organization has the benefits of owning its own computer system, the entire cost of operation and maintenance can be defined in advance, and the risk and responsibility can

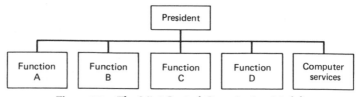

Figure 9.3. The Mini-Central Organization Model.

be borne outside of the organization. However, there are several problems that should be anticipated.

This approach leaves open the responsibility for organization-wide coordination and planning. It usually falls to the managers negotiating the contract with the vendor or to a consultant brought in to assist in long-range planning. In addition, the reliance upon one vendor for the full range of services can set up a conflict of responsibility. The client organization may rely too greatly upon the vendor to advise as to the quality and utility of its own services, and this may place the organization in a difficult negotiating position should the services prove to be inadequate.

When considering a contract for a full range of support services, it would be prudent to develop a contingency plan for switching vendors for some or all services. Ideally, such a plan would never be needed. It is also prudent to identify a source of expertise independent of the vendor to evaluate the quality and utility of services rendered or proposed.

Multi-Vendor Organizational Model

Under the multi-vendor approach, a computer may be purchased from one vendor, software from another, and maintenance from yet another (see Figure 9.5). The expertise may be purchased on an as-needed basis, rather than developed internally or contracted for in advance.

The major advantages are that the organization can innovate flexibly and that it does not have to rely on one vendor or one internal staff for its computer operations. If consistent and reliable working relationships can be set up, including good maintenance and follow-up service, such an approach may be satisfac-

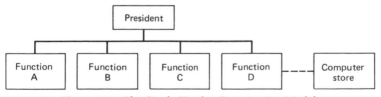

Figure 9.4.   The Single-Vendor Organization Model.

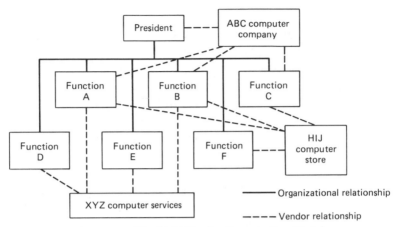

Figure 9.5. The Multi-Vendor Organization Model.

tory. The leading microcomputer models are usually supported by a variety of vendors in any market, and the many mail-order sources for equipment and programs supplement local vendor capabilities.

This approach is typical of organizations in which no basic plan for computer development has been articulated. As a result, employees and operating units all go in their own directions, and, through a process of trial and error, evolve systems that meet their needs. This can be a successful approach to computer development, provided that necessary organizational ground rules are established. An example of such a process of implementation is fully described in Chapter 11.

The basic disadvantages are of the multi-vendor approach are easy to visualize. Systems may be incompatible with each other so that one division cannot easily use the information and programs developed by another. One division may not learn from the mistakes of another or may duplicate some of the software and systems development expenses and efforts. Finally, the various vendors can become unreliable or antagonistic if purchasing and service practices between the various operating units become inconsistent, unpredictable, and arbitrary.

As the computer system becomes larger and more integrated, the feasibility of this approach diminishes, as fewer vendors remain capable of dealing with the exact system implemented. The same problem exists when one purchases a highly specialized device. Technical features of particular computer systems, such as networking technologies, are often unique and proprietary, so that only one or perhaps a few vendors can support them. Even in small microcomputer applications, decisions about software and peripheral devices can ultimately limit the number of vendors capable of providing support.

Thus, the long range practicality of such a strategy may be limited for most serious users. Gradually, as the computer system enlarges and becomes more integrated, reliance upon fewer and fewer vendor sources, and development of internal expertise, will become a necessity.

Developing an Organizational Structure

Table 9.1 summarizes some factors to be considered in developing an organizational strategy for providing leadership and expertise in computers. These observations apply to typical situations, but they may vary in their applicability to specific circumstances. They represent important considerations in the deci-

Table 9.1.   Summary of Organizational Models

	Central DP Unit	Time-Sharing	Mini-Central	Single Vendor	Multi-Vendor
Model Characteristic					
Expertise	Internal	External	Internal	External	External
Hardware Type	Mega	Mega	Mini	Mini	Micro
Hardware location	On-site	External	On-site	On-site	On-site
Operational responsibility	Internal	External	Internal	External	Internal
Operational Result					
Coordination	High	High	High	High	Low
Economy due to scale	High	Medium	Medium	Medium	Low
Cost of entry	High	Low	Medium	Medium	Low
Flexibility	Low	High	Medium	Medium	High
Diversity	Low	High	Low	Low	High
Ease of expansion	Low	High	Low	Low	High

sion to adopt a particular organizational strategy in the development of expertise and leadership in a computerizaton effort.

EFFECTS OF THE COMPUTER UPON THE ORGANIZATION

Thus far, we have discussed how to structure the organization to support the computer. Now we will examine the reverse process: how the computer changes the structure of the organization. These effects can be very surprising to an executive trained in traditional management concepts and techniques. They often occur unintentionally and unobtrusively, and are not noticed until a variety of critical operational problems emerge.

The computer is sometimes considered to be a neutral tool, enabling people to do faster and more accurate work, without changing the work or the people in the process. For example, a word processor may improve the quality of letters and reports, and it may help the typist to work more quickly, but it does not change the basic job of typing or the basic content of the letters and reports. Most technology, however, has had unanticipated effects upon its users and upon society in general. For example, the automobile has changed not only the dominant methods of transportation but also the patterns of urban and suburban development.

A computer-competent executive should be familiar with the results of the major studies of the impact of computers upon the organizations using them. Anticipation of the side effects of computer use can help a manager to assure the achievement of the basic goals of computerization, as well as the basic objectives of the organization. Some of the unexpected problems could do serious damage to an organization. The computer may change the patterns of authority in control and decision making, and the conflict that may arise as the new patterns of authority develop can inhibit productivity. Changes in flexibility of work processes, once a computer-based system is in place, can inhibit the ability of an organization to react to market conditions.

We will examine the findings of several of the major studies and consider their implications for computers and organizations in the 1980s. While the studies of the effects of introducing computers into organizations are very comprehensive and carefully done, the findings are limited by several factors. Most of the studies were done during the 1960s and 1970s, when large computer systems prevailed in businesses and other organizations. It is difficult to separate findings that are associated with computer use itself from findings that may be due to the large-scale computer enterprise. Major systems require extensive advanced planning and impose standard processes and procedures upon those who are to work with the systems. Individual flexibility is therefore often reduced, and the centers of control and authority in the organization may change. The cause of this impact, however, may be the size of the overall project, not the use of a computer. Therefore, many of the findings of these early studies may not apply to smaller organizations using the more flexible, adaptable, and user-controlled desktop computers and enhanced terminals.

Another limiting factor in the early research is that many of the findings were not inevitable impacts, but instead they were tendencies that appeared to varying extents from case to case. Because of this, the manager cannot apply these findings rigidly to a new situation, but rather must use them as guides or checklists of factors to consider.

Finally, there are some inconsistencies in the studies as to differences between intended and unintended effects. For example, in some studies increased standardization of procedures is considered to be a side effect, whereas in other studies it is considered to be a management goal, a basic objective of the computerization effort in the first place. As a result, there was variation between studies as to the likelihood of various effects, because of the differing conditions of manager motivation and intent.

The findings and recommendations of these studies cannot therefore be literally applied to computers and organizations in the 1980s. However, they do provide us with a framework for evaluating organizational side effects of computing, and they establish a preliminary list of impact areas for managers to consider. We will therefore examine the experiences of large organizations with their computer systems as reflected in the major studies, and consider the extent to which these findings apply to computing during the 1980s, in light of the major changes in the computer itself.

Each study has a separate way of classifying effects. Thus, definition of a common framework of analysis is necessary. In addition, some revision is necessary so that the classifications are readily applicable to computing as it currently occurs. Generally, anticipated effects can be classified into five broad categories:

1. *Planning effects* occur as a result of the process of decision making and specification in selecting a computer system. These effects include increased specificity of organization goals and increased awareness of the contributions of work processes to those goals.
2. *Changes in patterns of control* occur when a computer system increases one employee or division's ability to influence events at the expense of another's.
3. *Changes in supervisory patterns* occur when the standardization of work processes reduces supervisory discretion, or when the computer enables changes in the number of people or amount of work flow for which a supervisor is responsible.
4. *Changes in process specialization and flexibility* occur as the computer performs parts of the work process in a routine and standard way.
5. *Changes in task characteristics* occur when the computer modifies the nature of line and supervisory work itself.

These categories summarize possible organizational changes due to use of a computer that go beyond the specific changes intended when the computer was acquired and implemented.

Planning Effects

Planning effects occur as a by-product of the process of specifying and acquiring a computer system. In a large organization, this process can require a great deal of communication, priority setting, and decision making that would not otherwise occur. Stewart (1971, p. 13ff.) identified a series of effects resulting from the process of changing from a noncomputer to a computer method of work, including effects of the development and implementation process. Effects were identified in three distinct stages: the selection of projects, the identification of objectives, and the system design. In general, the effects include direct time demands upon managers, opportunities for managers and lower level staff to learn about existing work methods and problems, difficulties due to lack of understanding of the managers by the computer specialists and vice versa, and lack of acceptance of potential changes by staff.

It is likely that these effects would also exist as a result of a small-scale or even individual computerization effort. A manager might prepare for them in the following ways.

Anticipate that planning and organizing computerization will make substantial demands upon management time and attention at each level of the organization. Attempt to schedule the effort in such a way as to avoid competing demands.

Expect that the planning process will become an arena in which many conflicts and problems throughout the organization will be expressed, and perhaps resolved. The computer may become a tool in power struggles, ambitious career plans, and settlement of old grudges. Attempt to resolve conflict outside of computer planning, and to align key policy directions in computerization with overall organization plans and policies.

There is also a positive benefit to a manager in planning use of a computer. A set of concrete decisions must be made about the exact operational functions that the computer is to perform. In making these decisions, it is likely that the manager will come to understand better the work activities to be accomplished.

Changes in Patterns of Control

Changes in patterns of control occur as the computer enhances the ability of some employees and organizational divisions to influence events and inhibits other employees and units. Whistler (1970, p. 11ff.) identifies several effects: increased centralization of control, increased control by machine, greater control over individual behavior, and a blurring of traditional lines of authority and control. Klahr and Leavitt (in Myers, 1967, p. 129ff.) propose that computers have a centralizing effect on organizations performing routine functions and that they tend to decentralize control when tasks are open ended and not strictly defined. For example, computerization of the preparation of a payroll would limit the discretion and autonomy of the people who prepare it. An improved and expanded information system for district managers of a chain of stores could enable more decisions to be successfully made by those managers, rather than at higher levels of the organization. Delehanty (in Myers, 1967, p. 78ff.) suggests that organizational structure may tend to change toward a form that is consistent with an efficient computer system.

These changes would seem to be equally likely in the small organization or individual computer implementation as in the large organizations where the effects were initially identified. A manager might prepare for them in several ways:

Recognize that the computer must change the degree of influence that persons and organizational divisions have over tasks and functions. Those with access to the computer and responsibility for its operation may see increased participation and influence in any function that the computer performs. Others will see declines in their flexibility to make exceptions, innovate, or use nonstandard procedures.

Avoid conflict by clearly delineating where the authority and responsibility of affected organizational divisions and employees begins and ends. Assure that computer programs implement the same patterns of authority and responsibility.

Prevent those whose responsibility is limited to operating and programming the computer from assuming authority beyond their area of responsibility.

Of course, in a very small organization, the concept of centralization of control becomes less and less meaningful. However, an increase in control by machine is very likely, such as in a small law practice where time accounting and billing are completely automated. It is also reasonable that a computer might serve to extend a manager's control over a wider range of routine functions in a small organization.

Changes in Supervisory Patterns

Changes in supervisory patterns have been identified in several studies of the impact of computers upon organizations. Whistler (1970, p. 45ff.) suggests that the number of workers per supervisor should decline as a direct result of the increase in centralization of control. Another reason why the number of workers per supervisor might decline is that each worker would presumably be doing more work; thus, the number of workers would decline while the actual amount of production occurring under the supervisor's control would increase. Whistler also suggests that the number of clerical employees would decline in relation to the number of management employees and that the number of levels within a given organizational structure might decline.

These changes can also be anticipated in the small-scale computerization effort, and a manager can prepare for them in several ways:

Take early advantage of the opportunity to trim numbers of support employees when the computer makes this possible. Otherwise, work can expand to fill the time available, procedures can become structured and routine, and the inefficiency becomes harder to identify and more and more difficult to remedy.

Consider the potential for overall changes in organizational structure made possible and desirable because of changes in the mix of tasks performed by employees.

In a small business or organizational operating unit, the direction of reorganization might involve the elimination of specialized support divisions or units, provided that the remaining operating units can take over the functions with some of the redistributed staff and the computer. For example, some specialized support units, such as certain central records units, exist primarily to assure general access to all aspects of a case record by all units of an organization. Prior to the computer, each unit would otherwise have immediate access only to the records that it created itself, and would have to search out related records from other units. With the computer, each authorized unit can have access to all records.

Because the computer changes the tasks that workers perform, and because the nature of those tasks represent an important determinant of organizational structure, it stands to reason that a major computerization effort would lead to the opportunity for major reorganization as well.

Changes in Process Specialization and Flexibility

Changes in process specialization and flexibility occur as a result of the machine characteristics of the computer system. It may be able to do a few tasks with great accuracy and speed, leaving to the rest of the organization the remaining tasks (leading to specialization) and reducing the ability of the organization to change work processes in the face of problems and inadequacies. Whistler (1970, pp. 12ff.) suggests that computers lead to greater rigidity and inflexibility in decision making and more routine and narrow work content. A manager might anticipate these effects in several ways:

Recognize when a computer system may create an inability to respond flexibly to new problems, needs, and opportunities. If necessary, develop contingency plans not involving use of the computer at all to respond to important foreseeable changes in work loads and working procedures.

Develop a capacity to update a computer system on an ongoing basis, so that it is a stimulus to organizational growth and competitiveness, rather than a limiting factor.

Encourage experimentation, by both individual employees and organizational units, with new uses for the computer. This creates an agenda for future improvement in operations, after projects currently under way are complete.

For both the small and large computer application, a critical management problem is the tendency for such systems to lead to an inflexible working process. A key management role in the use of computers is the encouragement of continued improvement and the identification of critical problems to be solved.

Changes in Task Characteristics

Changes in task characteristics occur as a result of the use of computers to perform work previously done by managers. Whistler (1970, pp. 12ff.) identified a tendency for lower level jobs to become more routine and narrow, while upper level management jobs become more responsible. Klahr and Leavitt (in Myers, 1967, pp. 107ff.) suggest that "closed routine" management functions, which are those that involve following predetermined instructions (such as scheduling) will tend to be taken over by computer systems, while "open routine" management functions, which are those that do not have defined procedures (such as planning or coping with exceptional situations) will tend to increase as a proportion of the manager's work. A manager can prepare for these changes in several ways:

Critically examine your own work as a manager. Ask yourself to what extent your work is "closed routine," suitable for computerization.

Develop an ability to apply computer technology creatively to problem solving and decision making, improving your ability to manage in an "open routine" environment.

Plan and design line jobs to minimize the tendency for lower level jobs to become routine and narrow when performed with a computer.

The next chapter considers the effects of computers on individual employees and further extends some of the issues raised here.

FINAL OBSERVATIONS

A major consideration in the management of computer use in businesses and agencies is the development of necessary organizational supports for the computer and the anticipation of inhibiting and destructive conflicts over its introduction. A great source of failure in computer implementation results from a lack of insight and sensitivity to this problem.

It is important to identify an approach to providing leadership, coordination, and operational support for computerization. For a small organization, initially a single employee might be designated for this job, to work with outside consultants and vendors. As a system develops and becomes larger and more central to the operations of the enterprise, more structured support and coordination of the computer will become necessary.

It is also important to anticipate sources of concern and resistance to a computer application. Some of these arise because of lack of information, and others arise because of actual changes in job function and authority resulting from the introduction of the system. Many problems can be resolved through advanced planning and training, and those that cannot should at least be anticipated and managed in a conscious and deliberate manner.

Ultimately, the responsibility for effective use of a computer rests with those in charge of an organization. However, many of the recommendations and suggestions in this chapter have been directed at the individual manager, who may have significant responsibilities but may not be at the top of the table of organization. It is important to keep in mind that there are two dimensions to the effective use of a computer in management. There are the top-level functions of planning, coordinating, funding, and motivating. Then there is another, perhaps more important dimension, which is the ability of the individual managers (whether there are 2 of them or 2000) within the organization to implement the computer system and to capitalize upon the opportunities that it creates. During the decades to come, computers will be critical to business and government efforts to revitalize our efficiency and productive capacities. The most successful managers will be those who can respond to the challenge and the opportunity.

CHAPTER 10
EMPLOYEES AND
COMPUTERS

I've been the director of data processing for about a year now, and the job has been most frustrating. I have been trying to introduce new computer applications and office automation, but I always seem to be fighting the past. My predecessor introduced the first computer system to the business, and he did it in all the wrong ways. For example, as the system was introduced, employees were laid off, jobs were downgraded, and job tasks were made narrow and repetitive. Obviously, this raised the anxiety level and reduced the morale of many workers. The system itself was very inflexible and tended to frustrate those who operated it. Middle managers and supervisors became upset with the constant interference by the data processing department, since the computer programmers seemed to be dictating procedure, over the heads of the supervisors. Now when I mention a new application, supervisors get on edge and employees become anxious. Even the union begins to ask questions. People recall only the frustration and hassle of past disasters; only a few sense the opportunity, challenge, and fun of computers. Our company has probably been set back by several years, only because of the attitudes we created in our work force.

Ultimately, the work of small and large organizations is done by people. Some of this work is done directly, and some is done with the aid of machines. As a result, the attitudes and abilities of people who work with computers are critical factors in their successful introduction. A successful computer system must be a successful human enterprise. This requires that human factors be considered in the planning and operation of computing systems.

This chapter examines the effects of computers on employees, and the effects of employee performance upon computer performance. The introduction of computers affects the content of jobs at each level of an organization. This is the major way in which computers affect people. The abilities and attitudes of people can enhance or inhibit the performance of a computer system, either directly by inhibiting the efficiency of a computer or indirectly by limiting the effectiveness of the computer's role in the organization's work.

IMPACTS OF COMPUTERS ON EMPLOYEES

There are many studies that examine the effects of computers on the content of jobs. As in the case of studies on the impact of computers upon organizations, most of these studies were conducted in the 1960s and 1970s, and therefore most of the findings apply generally to large-scale computers in big organizations. In our review and analysis, it becomes clear that not all findings apply to small or individual organizations using desktop computers and enhanced terminals. When findings clearly do not apply for small systems in the 1980s, alternative patterns of impact are suggested.

Generally the findings relate to three distinct levels of workers: the line or support worker, the middle manager, and the top executive. The research suggests that the introduction of computers affects these groups of employees in different ways. The findings can be summarized in seven general categories, applying first to the line-level employees and working up the chain of authority.

Routinization of Line Work

The introduction of computers during the 1960s and 1970s, tended to make clerical, support, and line work more routine. Whistler (1970, p.126ff.) reported that early applications of computers, which focused heavily upon the work of clerks, have tended to increase central control and discipline with respect to procedures and time deadlines. Klahr and Leavitt (in Myers, 1967, pp. 116ff.) distinguished between object processing employees and information processing employees, suggesting that the computer tends to control the object processing function, whereas the employee controls the information processing tasks. Stewart (1971 pp. 16ff.) indicates that line staff resistance may occur as work becomes more monotonous and minutely demanding. However, each of these tendencies may not be due to the computer itself, but rather to the way in which it is implemented.

An alternative pattern of impact may occur during the 1980s. Computers are becoming more decentralized and less subject to central organizational control. Programs are written to be more flexible, responsive, and tolerant of errors and variations of approaches to operation. Rather than imposing inflexible task routines on terminal operators, new computers may make work less dull and repetitive. The most boring aspects of line jobs are increasingly automated, so that what remains are those tasks that are challenging and variable. For example, an automated office system may reduce the amount of draft typing and retyping done by secretaries, leaving them more time to become involved in administrative and management tasks.

Changes in Line Skills

The introduction of computers during the 1960s and 1970s tended to be followed by a decline in the average skill levels of line staff. The reason for this observation is not that worker skills declined, but that the level of skills required declined, since the computer determined much of what was to be done. Whistler (1970, 129ff.) found that actual skill classifications of employees for a given function were lower following computerization than before.

However, he recognized that an opposite effect could be supported by other studies: Computers could call upon the line employees to possess higher levels of skills. Karloff and Lee (1981, p. 315ff.) stress the importance of training line employees in the use of the system and imply that their actual level of skill will depend upon the exact nature of the system and the nature of the training provided.

This pattern of impact is probably less likely during the 1980s. While recent computer systems and application programs are not extremely difficult to use, proficient use often requires some training and some experience. Use of a program that aids decision making and report development, such as spreadsheet calculation software, may encourage an employee to learn more about his or her job.

Decreased Interpersonal Communication

The introduction of computers has been associated with a decline in interpersonal communication. In studies of this effect, employees with computers spent more time working alone and less time interacting with other workers or with supervisors. Whistler (1970, pp. 133ff.), in a study of 15 companies implementing computer systems, noted that the greatest decline in interpersonal communications was among lower level workers.

This problem becomes more pervasive as computers become more commonplace at work. Anyone who has played a game on a computer or worked on a computer program knows of the almost hypnotic effect that can occur as the hours go by. The outside world almost disappears into the background, as one deals with the complications of the problem at hand. People with microcomputers at home have noted the antisocial aspects of computing. Most games or programs are for one person at a time. Few people would find it interesting to watch from behind while another person works at the keyboard and screen. A really bad case of "home computeritis" even has symptoms: The family member begins to function on a schedule that is independent of the rest of the family, missing such routine events as meals. Some divorces have even been attributed to home computing, although these must have been extreme cases.

A compounding factor in the work place is that the computer often makes it possible to complete a work task without much help from others. No longer must one go down the hall to fetch records maintained by another employee; the computer fetches them in seconds from a disk. No longer must one work with a team of several clerks to develop a report that includes some complicated calculations; the computer can make the calculations in seconds.

A supervisor should make a concerted effort to encourage opportunity for employees with computers to interact with others. There are several ways this can be done. The supervisor may schedule work breaks more frequently and promote opportunities for people to converse. Jobs may be designed so that employees do not spend all day at the computer terminal. Tasks can be rotated so that part of the day is spent on other activities not involving the computer. Tasks can be structured so that it is necessary for several workers to cooperate. Each may check the work of the other. Or tasks may be structured so that no job is completely done by one worker. A pair of workers completes them together. A special emphasis upon human relations in management is probably more important in a work environment that is heavily computerized than in one that is not.

Increased Middle Management Process Responsibility

Computer use has lead to an increase in middle management process or work load responsibility, and a decrease in responsibility for employees. As a function is computerized, more work is often possible with a given number of employees. As a result, the level of work flow that is the responsibility of a middle manager can increase, while the number of employees doing the work can decrease or remain constant. The manager's role therefore can involve more attention to the work itself and less time and attention directed to the employees.

This pattern will probably continue, as it is an equally likely result with smaller computer systems. However, the importance of the supervisor's role as an employee supervisor probably increases even though the numbers of employees supervised decreases. This is due to the greater work load responsibility of each remaining worker and also to the greater need for human relations for the reasons cited above.

Changes in Middle Management Skills

Middle management skills may decline, according to several studies, with the introduction of computer systems. As is the case with the lower level employees, this is not due to a decline in skills themselves, but rather it is due to a change in the skills required of people in the middle management role. Deardon (in Myers, 1967, pp. 188ff.) observes that middle managers spend less time following computerization on such logistical problems as scheduling and ordering. Such a skill would be obsolete when the function is performed by a computer. Whistler (1970 pp. 130ff.) suggests that higher skill levels may be needed during planning and implementation of a computer system, but that lower skill levels would be needed once the system is in operation.

This effect may be likely when a larger system is introduced that automates a work process, so that much of the complicated work is done by the computer, not by the employees. However, small computers introduced into smaller organizations may demand broader middle management skills. A computer is likely to be used in several operations, and much of the implementation (using off-the-shelf programs and equipment) is likely to be a direct responsibility of a supervisor, rather than the responsibility of a consultant or data processing specialist. Add to this the human relations challenges of the computerized work environment, and a picture emerges of a middle manager who must have the old skills of task management as well as improved skills in computer management and human relations.

Decreased Middle Management Discretion and Authority

Implementation of a computer system may lead to decreased middle-management discretion and authority, and increased procedural control at the upper levels of the organization. Deardon (in Myers, 1967, pp. 180ff.) argues that the centralization of logistical functions will decrease the authority of the middle manager. He questions, however, whether upper-level administrators can use the computer to take over the expert decision making and analytical functions of the middle manager.

Decreased middle-management authority is a likely impact of a large computer system, which permits exacting control over field operations by a central staff. However, the newer and smaller computers introduced during the 1980s are less frequently deployed in such a hierarchical fashion. Instead, they are deployed locally, under the control of a few local employees. The middle manager equipped with a computer may be capable of studies and operations that previously could be done only with central office resources. A middle manager in a computerized office may also experience great increases in the work load under his or her responsibility, and with such an increase in production often goes an increase in influence, authority, and discretion.

Top Management Opportunities and Skills

The demand for greater skill levels in top management may increase as a result of computerization. Whistler (1970, pp. 148ff.) suggests that managerial jobs will develop higher and higher proportions of research content. In addition, he expects a greater level of involvement by top managers in operational decisions formerly delegated to middle managers. This deeper involvement in operations, in addition to other top-management responsibilities, would require greater competence. Computers may also increase the degree to which top-management jobs include creative and unstructured effort. Klahr and Leavitt (in Myers, 1967, pp. 116ff.) suggest that executive jobs that involve processing, assessing, and acting upon information will be creatively extended and augmented by the computer.

The increased use of computers, both large and small, will continue to demand that top management be informed and actively involved with computers at all levels of an organization. The inevitable introduction into the work place of small computers and automated office systems will demand that top managers understand radically different concepts and approaches to computer use. Central control of computing, and the extensive network of terminals dependent upon a central mainframe computer, will continue. But small computer systems, controlled locally and often individually, can change many patterns of management.

A candid assessment of all these expected impacts of computers upon employees and users suggests that all levels of employees, from top management to the line employee, can be positively affected as computers are introduced. However, middle management and line jobs can also be eliminated or rendered more routine, monotonous, disciplined, and constrained by the computer. This is not a desirable outcome, and it may inhibit the overall value to management of a computer system. Most studies have suggested, however, that most of the adverse impact of computer implementation is not unavoidable. Furthermore, many adverse effects may arise only in the traditional large-scale implementation and may not occur at all with smaller, more flexible systems.

FOSTERING PRODUCTIVITY AND EMPLOYEE SATISFACTION

How can a manager limit any adverse impacts of a computer system upon employees? As a generalization, the solution is to attempt to focus as much upon people as upon tasks in planning and implementing the system. In the past, many systems have been structured with a great emphasis upon designing the most efficient way to accomplish a set of tasks, such as filing or producing reports and documents. The predominant emphasis upon the task probably is a reflection of two factors. First, the large cost of computer systems in the past required that even marginal cost efficiencies be fully developed in order to enable the system to pay its way. Second, the kinds of people planning systems—hardware and software experts—were most experienced with tasks and things, not with the management of people. As a result, early systems tended to break down processes into specialized steps, much like a traditional industrial production line, so that each worker could do a small part of the production process very quickly and efficiently.

More recent systems are somewhat different in character, both because computers have become less expensive and more flexible and because the types of functions being computerized—office systems and management support functions—are less amenable to routine assembly-line solutions. As a result, it is possible to plan and implement such systems with more consideration toward the employee and the factors that lead to greater motivation and job satisfaction. However, these types of solutions to management computer applications are not limited to the more recent applications. Traditional, large scale systems can be made more interesting and satisfactory to users by both software revision and hardware addition.

There are seven basic factors to consider in attempting to make a computer system more motivating, satisfying, and interesting to the people who use it. They grow out of direct experience, trial and error with computer systems, as well as from the application to computers of motivational principles and concepts learned in other fields.

Job Design for Motivation and Satisfaction

There have been many studies of the characteristics of jobs that tend to lead to satisfaction or dissatisfaction. One concept that attempts to integrate much of this research and to enable the specific application of the findings to jobs is the concept of job enrichment. In simple terms, the process involves redesigning jobs to make them more interesting to workers. While several conceptions of job enrichment exist, Hackman and others (1975) have developed a relatively specific one, which has been tested successfully in evaluation projects and studies. They identify five elements of job enrichment: skill variety, task identity, task significance, autonomy, and knowledge of results.

The *skill variety* of a job describes the extent to which a job offers the opportunity to employ more than a few abilities and competencies. Enhancing this characteristic reduces the monotony of a job and offers a challenge to the worker. A computer job that involves only one function, such as entering a certain record into the system repetitively, would have low skill variety. A more satisfying job might involve several functions, and several different ways of using the system, and perhaps even some tasks that did not involve the system at all.

The *task identity* of a job describes the extent to which a job involves a process or product that is completed by and can be recognized by the worker. Jobs using a computer with low task identity might involve partial steps in a data entry process or in the process of creating a document, which other workers complete. Jobs with high task identity would involve whole processes, such as developing a report.

The *task significance* of a job to a worker depends upon whether the employee is aware of the ultimate purpose or value of the work. When a job focuses upon a particular function or goal, it can be more interesting and satisfying because the worker contributes to the achievement of the goal. Often the introduction of a computer to a work process divides up tasks so that each job supports various functions and goals, and the users of the system no longer sense that they are relating to a specific function.

Autonomy describes the degree to which a job offers the worker an opportunity to make decisions about how a job is done, within the framework of basic practical limits. Not only can this reduce monotony, but it can also permit the worker to discover new ways to get work done that may be more efficient and effective. The introduction of computers to a work process often requires the employees using the terminals to follow precise and minutely demanding steps to accomplish a task. This, of course, reduces autonomy and can lead to dissatisfaction and lack of motivation.

Knowledge of results describes the extent to which a job provides a worker with information about performance. The information can be important to enable the employee to make judgments about which methods of work are most productive. It can also serve as a reward by itself. Computers can be especially effective in this regard, because immediate feedback informing the user of errors or omissions can often be built into software packages.

When a computer system is being planned, job enrichment factors should be considered in designing the specific jobs to be done. In even a small system, there are frequent opportunities to assign work to different employees or to design a work process so as to increase the prevalence of job enrichment elements.

A good case in point involves office automation. There are two common approaches to the introduction of word processing systems. One approach involves the development of a stenographic pool equipped with word processing equipment. The typists assigned to the pool perform various specialized steps in the document production process. In concept, such an approach allows a typist to become more proficient in advanced word processing technology, and it creates promotional opportunities to supervisory positions. An alternative approach maintains the more traditional organization of clerical services, where one typist is assigned to one or more professionals and is responsible for each aspect of the production of a letter or report. The typist is provided with advanced equipment enabling the assigned work to be done more quickly and accurately, with greater ease of revision and correction. Sometimes, the equipment enables improved productivity so that additional duties can be assigned.

The application of job enrichment concepts to these approaches to clerical work illustrates some ways in which computers can make work more interesting and satisfying, and also some ways in which computers can make the work tedious and frustrating. Skill variety is increased under both approaches merely by the addition of the computer, since the worker must learn to use the computer. However, variety is lessened by the pool approach if an assembly-line system is developed. On the other hand, if the pool enables employees to work on new and different types of projects, variety can be increased. Under the traditional approach, skill variety can be increased only by adding new functions and duties.

Task identity and task significance are decreased if a pool approach is implemented in an assembly mode. The typist deals only with pieces and steps of the work process. Task identity is not increased, however, by the traditional approach, although task significance can be maintained if there is a sense of participation in the efforts of a team of workers to achieve certain goals and objectives.

Autonomy is decreased under the pool approach if the worker is expected to work from an in-basket of assigned tasks. Under the more traditional approach, there are several complicating factors. Autonomy may be increased if the scope of the employee's tasks is increased and if there is flexibility as to how those duties are discharged. In actually working with a computer, autonomy may be decreased unless the programs used are flexible and user oriented.

Knowledge of results is decreased under the pool approach, because the worker is usually only aware of the immediate task at hand. The computer can be programmed to provide some feedback as to the performance of tasks, but the pool concept does not naturally support individual feedback to workers about the results of their work. On the other hand, the traditional approach does not increase feedback merely because of the introduction of computer technology.

A safe generalization is that the computer does not absolutely promote or inhibit job enrichment, except to the extent that it represents an additional skill for the worker to develop and use. The degree to which a job will be satisfactory depends significantly upon the attention to job enrichment given in the planning and design of each job.

Participation in Planning

Participation in planning is another way in which employee satisfaction can be promoted when implementing a computer system in the work place. Much of employee resistance to computer systems arises as a result of a lack of information about the system and a lack of opportunity to structure some aspects of the work. Since a large computer system tends to impose a standard procedure upon those who work with it, it can be very frustrating if that procedure is perceived to be inefficient or wasteful by those who must use it. There are several ways to involve employees in planning.

Formal or informal advisory groups can be formed, to permit

employees to help in the design of their jobs. Not only does this provide management with early information about possible malfunctions and problems, but it also permits the employee to become more informed about new methods of work, easing the training task later on. Participation in this manner may also increase the acceptance of new methods when they are introduced.

Some computer systems do not have to be implemented in a highly controlled manner. Certain functions in office automation systems must be operated according to preset instructions. But employees can experiment with other functions, such as spreadsheet calculation programs, inventing and introducing new uses at their own pace.

Involvement of lower level employees in planning can increase management work loads and introduce complications and problems to the design of a computer system. However, the payoffs in greater employee acceptance and in avoided problems are usually worthwhile.

Recognition of Changes in Employee Role and Status

Nonmonetary status recognition can promote positive attitudes and improved performance. Sometimes the use of a computer in a job can be associated with a downgrading of the job. This has been a typical pattern in the implementation of many large computer systems (Whistler, 1970, pp. 12ff.). While the employment of workers with lower qualifications and status can lead to short-term savings, in the long run, it may be more productive to increase the status of employees who work with computers. This may help in retention and may also improve attitudes elsewhere in the organization toward future computerization efforts.

There are a variety of possible approaches to consider when introducing a computer system, to improve employee attitudes and perceptions about themselves and the equipment they operate.

The computer will probably require new furnishings, because the equipment often cannot fit onto or into traditional office furniture and because people have difficulty using the equipment if any critical part is too high, too low, too near, or too far. Since new furnishings must be purchased anyway, the added expense would be small for furnishings appropriate to the work environment of an important professional.

The computer will require added space. Often the space is provided at a location that is not "owned" by any employee. Provided that the equipment is not so loud or obtrusive as to interfere with work, and assuming that the computer is a small system, the operator might be assigned a large space that will also house the computer equipment. The area should be arranged and decorated so that the entire space is professionally appropriate. This approach provides an employee with the status associated with a larger work area.

Some innovative shift patterns may be feasible. One approach is sometimes called "flextime," which entails permitting the worker to come to work and to leave earlier or later than usual, provided that the worker is present during certain "core" work periods. Much of the work with a computer can be done independent of other workers, and the computer can be programmed to keep track of working hours as well.

Since the employee operating a computer terminal is very important to the performance of that portion of the system, an investment in better worker attitudes and production can be an investment in equipment productivity as well.

Training

Training can be a key to successful long-term attitudes and performance. If an employee's first experiences with a new computer are frustrating and confusing, these attitudes may be retained and they may inhibit later performance. Early training can promote successful first experiences with the computer system and thereby promote positive attitudes later on. Several other types of training should also be considered.

Employees should understand how their work fits into the total operation of a particular computer system. This makes the work more relevant and helps the employee to understand why certain operations are performed as they are. Employees might be exposed to other computer systems and computer-related jobs and functions within a large organization. This can build a sense of professionalism and provide the employee with an informal source of support and assistance for solving problems.

Employees should be trained, and their terminals and desktop computers equipped, to develop small programs and applications on their own. This may provide a source of new ideas for productivity improvement. Training should not be limited to instruction in carrying out a limited set of functions with the computer. This will lead to task proficiency, but will not necessary stimulate positive and creative attitudes.

Incentives

Rewards for the successful use of a computer system can be important, especially when the computer is planned to help a worker increase productivity. An increasingly common characteristic of many productivity improvement programs that introduce new technology or automation to increase work production involves "gain sharing." Under this arrangement, some of the savings or profits due to increased productivity are distributed to the employees according to a formula. Some employee incentive systems include a desktop computer as a reward. Not only is this sometimes a prized incentive, but it also builds an opportunity for further training and career development. A carefully planned incentive system can provide employees a stake in the successful implementation of computer projects.

Growth Opportunities

When employees can develop new computer skills, either on their own or as part of a structured program, they often subsequently propose new and effective computer applications. There are a variety of strategies to promote this result.

In some organizations, the central data processing department has arranged for discounts (or even subsidies) for computer equipment and software purchased by employees for their own personal use and for work-related activities. This encourages employees to develop new skills and interests, and to explore new work-related applications for computer systems. It also tends to assure that all of the small computer systems owned by employees are compatible.

Formal and informal users' groups have been developed within organizations to promote and support employee competence and innovation with computer systems. These efforts promote interest in computer systems and provide for an informal coordination system.

In the past, computer systems have sometimes tended to reduce opportunities for employees, especially those in lower levels of an organization. With the introduction of microcomputers and enhanced terminals, greater opportunities for lower level employees may develop.

User-Friendly Software

The quality of software can be critical in promoting a successful experience by employees with the computer system. Programs that are difficult to understand, that tend to "crash" when errors are made, and that are inflexible can frustrate those who use them. In the selection and development of software, the following characteristics are important.

Instructions should be easy to use and remember. Terms should be meaningful and remind the user of what the instruction does.

Common errors should not cause the program to "crash" or require that work be redone. Recoverability is critical. It becomes particularly important if the error is routine and frequent. For example, in one word processing program pressing a "wrong" key causes work to be destroyed, but that key is adjacent to a routinely used key. A slip of the finger leads to disaster.

Programs should be as flexible as possible, to permit operators to choose their own sequence of procedures to accomplish a task and to allow innovation in methods as work characteristics change.

Programs should prompt users to the extent needed. When a user is just beginning, many prompts are needed. Later on, the user should be able to instruct the computer to reduce the level of help so that the program and the user can work more quickly.

The ability of computers to function in a "friendly" manner to their users is increasing from year to year. The increasing availability of advanced peripherals, such as graphics, color terminals, and voice recognition devices, as well as the increasing power of processors will lead to more and more intelligent programs, capable of flexible response to operators.

A CLOSING PERSPECTIVE

A business or government agency that is positioned to make effective use of computers will have a significant advantage over competitors. Creating such a climate involves planning, equipment development, and employee training and encouragement. Managers often underestimate the relative significance of employee attitudes and skills in the overall computerization effort. Fearful and suspicious attitudes, creating resistance to even the most worthwhile and well-planned projects, can be a critical limitation on the advancement of a computer project. Conversely, when employees view the computer as a source of interest and challenge, and when the organization is structured to take advantage of the ideas and suggestions that employees will develop as they work with computers, major advancements in productivity often are the result.

CHAPTER 11
IMPLEMENTING COMPUTER SYSTEMS

As the information systems manager for a large insurance company, I work with about 30 field offices each year, as they start to use our computer system. We have a very detailed implementation plan, describing the exact steps to be taken each month, both before and after the equipment is delivered and in operation. It is interesting to me that even though the offices are implementing the same computer system for the same basic tasks, some offices get the system up and working much more quickly than others, with fewer hassles. There appear to be several factors at work. The attitude of the top managers is probably most important. If they don't want the system, or if they distrust it, this gets down to the employees, and generally everyone's worst fears come true. A second factor is the organization and preparation of the employees. If they really follow through on the early steps in the implementation schedule, such as the general orientation, the visits by employees to other field offices using the system, and the training, then all goes well. The problems happen because the manager didn't fully prepare the employees for the system.

Computers can contribute to improved productivity in many ways. A manager must select projects that are economically and operationally practical. Certainly this is difficult, but once the decision is made to proceed, the implementation process is even more challenging. Many systems are theoretically practical, but not all of these can be translated, through management, into operationally practical and beneficial applications.

The failure of a system to live up to expectations is often the result of either inadequate initial planning (choosing to apply a computer to the wrong problem) or inadequate early project management (developing the system in the wrong way). This chapter will help a manager to avoid both problems.

Most books and articles on the implementation of computer systems describe an often lengthy series of steps that should be followed, much like a long and complex version of a recipe in a cookbook. As with recipes, however, the results of computer implementation processes do not always meet expectations. Sometimes this occurs because one or two of the steps in the process, critical to the overall result, might be inadequately described or emphasized, or difficult to complete correctly. Very precise instructions might not relate to the environment in which they are to be applied, as each business or organization has unique attributes and circumstances.

Much of management is not done by the book. There is an element of intuition, creativity, and hands-on experience, which is critical to genuine accomplishment and which must be combined with the application of objective and time-tested principles developed through the analysis of many prior experiences. A manager responsible for the implementation of a computer system must balance these two sources of decision making judgment. Managers generally approach this challenge according to one of the following styles.

The traditional style might be called the *comprehensive approach.* It assumes that successful implementation can be achieved through the correct application of a series of rules and procedures. One such approach (Long, 1982), written largely for large systems and organizations, defines 62 separate steps involving committees, draft reports, priority lists, feasibility analyses, and planning matrices. These all culminate in the development of a long-range plan for information services that, if followed, should lead to a successful result. Another approach (Perry, 1982) is oriented more to the smaller business and agency, and includes numerous steps and over 30 specific and helpful worksheets to aid the manager.

An alternative style might be called the *incremental approach.* This method is more subjective, relying to a greater extent upon employee motivation and initiative, as well as numerous trials, successes, and errors, while attempting to reduce initial outlay costs (and therefore immediate risks) as fully as possible.

The comprehensive approach invests great time and resources in being right the first time. The incremental approach employs trial and error, reducing the outlay of time and resources for planning. The strategy assumes that it may be ultimately less costly to be partially right four times and completely right the fifth. The comprehensive approach tends to be ordered and controlled by top management, whereas the incremental approach attempts to encourage line employee insight and initiative. A book by Graham Allison (1971) offers an interesting analysis of these approaches to planning and implementation, applied to foreign policy.

There are several factors that, if present, favor the application of a comprehensive approach:

When the size of the application is large, such that a mainframe or minicomputer configuration is probably necessary, then major long-term organizational commitments are required up front. There is much less opportunity to recover from a basic planning error, and therefore careful and thorough planning is a necessity.

When the complexity of the project is great, involving the integration of complicated procedures, then careful planning is also necessary.

If the implications of error are great, such as in accounting and inventory systems, the risks associated with a sloppy planning process may have an intolerably high cost.

If the ongoing cost of the tasks to be computerized is great, then the expense of unexpected dual operation of the existing as well as the computerized system for a long period of time would also be great. Careful planning is needed to prevent these costs.

There are circumstances, however, when a thorough and detailed planning process can entail an investment in misplaced and unnecessary precision. These usually involve applications where it is relatively easy to fall back to a manual operation should the intended system not operate successfully. For example, consider the free-lance consultant who purchases a microcomputer to use for small statistical analyses and for word processing. Extensive planning is not needed because the system costs relatively little and because it would be easy to return to a manual operation if the computer should not work out as well as planned.

As a general rule, a comprehensive approach is necessary in most mainframe and minicomputer applications, especially when the system is dedicated to a small number of functions. The comprehensive approach is less necessary when one or more microcomputers are to be used, because of the smaller scale of most microcomputer applications.

THE COMPREHENSIVE APPROACH

To plan and implement a computer system following a comprehensive approach entails the same general process that an architect would follow in designing a building. Ultimately, in building design all of the details have to be specified so that a construction contractor knows exactly what to do. A comprehensively planned computer system would be described in the same level of detail. Nothing would be left to trial and error or to employee initiative.

Such an approach to the implementation of a computer system entails seven basic steps: assessment, planning, acquisition, transition preparation, installation, transition, and operation. The complexity of each step depends upon the nature of the application involved.

Assessment

The objective of assessment, the earliest stage in the implementation process, is to decide whether use of a computer would improve the work process under consideration. It is always possible to pull back from the project at a later point. However, as a project proceeds, the amount of time and resources expended makes modifications expensive.

A project usually begins with the identification of a problem or an opportunity. Perhaps records storage and retrieval has become increasingly costly and unproductive. Or perhaps, even though records management is working moderately well, someone has seen or heard of a competitive organization using a computer system for records management, achieving good quality with lower cost. Assessment entails the following types of activities.

The precise problem or opportunity must be defined. Surface impressions might prove partially wrong, because the exact nature of the problem is different than initially assumed. Perhaps, for instance, the records problem can be solved through destroying old and unnecessary files, rather than by developing a faster and more efficient way to retain such files.

Descriptive information should be obtained on the cost and productivity of the process to be computerized. The information can be analyzed to determine roughly what the computer would have to do and how much it would cost (both initial acquisition and ongoing operation costs) for it to make an effective and productive contribution.

Related processes might be assessed to determine whether use of a computer could produce additional benefits or additional burdens for others. Sometimes a system, only marginally cost-effective for one central function, can be justified because of additional contributions to the productivity of related functions. The reverse can also be true, that the apparent cost reductions associated with the computer are really based upon a hidden transfer of work load to others.

Usually, before proceeding beyond the assessment stage, a potential project should be supported with credible estimates as to initial and ongoing costs and savings or benefits associated with its implementation.

Planning

The goal of the planning stage is to describe the computer system: How it will work; what it will cost in terms of staff, equipment, implementation, software, and operational expenses; and finally, how long it will take to make the system operational. Generally, the following types of activities occur.

The functions to be computerized are studied in detail to determine exactly what the computer must be designed and programmed to do. This information will guide the development of equipment and software specifications, as well as the development of operational manuals.

Draft procedures are developed for the tasks to be performed with the computer, so that users (employees in the organization) can review and react to them. Procedures are also developed for the management and ongoing operation of the computer itself. When such procedures are defined, staff time and expense of ongoing operation can be estimated.

It is desirable to define as precisely as possible the information to be stored within the computer system and how it is to be manipulated. This means that each piece of information should be listed and described as to type (alphanumeric or numeric), size (usually the largest possible range of letters and numbers), source (where you get this information), and disposition (what it will be used for). This information is combined to create an estimate of the amount of secondary memory (such as disks) the computer will need.

A master schedule is developed, showing the key steps in the implementation process. If the system is complex, management systems such as PERT or CPM (described in Chapter 3) can be applied to allow very important tasks and deadlines to be identified.

The end result of this stage should be a set of documents describing the computer system and its operation in detail.

Acquisition

Acquisition involves the purchasing or leasing of a computer, necessary software, and peripheral equipment, such as terminals and printers. There are several common approaches to acquisition, depending upon the nature of the computer system. The process begins with the development of a purchasing specification. It may serve as a competitive bidding document, or simply as a shopping guide.

In developing a computer specification, it is usually best to start by specifying the software. This, of course, must respond to the descriptions of tasks to be performed. There are several ways to acquire software:

A standard data base management system might be specified, assuming that employees within the organization will be able to tailor the package to perform the necessary tasks.

A specific type of software might be specified, such as an accounting system, developed solely for this purpose and operational immediately without further modifications and refinements.

The "software environment" might be specified if it is necessary or desirable to leave open the definition of a specific software package. The specification would then describe the nature of the operating system, types of peripheral equipment to be operated, and number of terminals.

Sometimes the acquisition process is subdivided, so that a software package or vendor is selected first, and the computer is selected later. Once the software is selected, the task of selecting hardware is simplified, since the software will probably be able to run on some but not all machines. In selecting the software first, one should consider portability, since software that can run on many computer brands and models can permit an open equipment selection process. If a software package can be identified, usually the manual (or the vendor organization and staff) can be of great assistance in the development of specifications for the computer equipment to support the software.

Open and direct equipment specifications permit the widest number of competent vendors to compete. Otherwise, many vendors do not participate, or they simply bid available equipment, with vague statements about how the it can be made to comply with the specifications. However, if the specification contains 5-10 key system performance characteristics, vendors can respond more specifically, or they will not bid if they cannot fulfill the specification.

Generally, a hardware specification contains the following types of information:

Processor and memory requirements.

Secondary storage requirements (disk and tape drives, etc.).

Quantity and characteristics of terminals.

Peripheral equipment needed (printers, modems, etc.).

Speed and output quality of peripherals.

Physical environment constraints (size of room, power, etc.).

Software compatibility requirements.

Maintenance and support requirements, including warranty.

In evaluating bids, one must remember that computers are much more complex than other equipment, such as cars. Usually, no one bid is best in all areas, as some vendors will be stronger in support, some systems will be more flexible and compatible with software requirements, and some systems will be less expensive for some elements and more expensive for others. Other more intangible considerations involve the background and stability of the vendor, or the "upward compatibility" (future expansion capacity) of the system in future years. A final consideration is the relation between performance and cost. An initially inexpensive system may cost less because it works more slowly or less reliably, which could translate into higher operational costs as the equipment is used in months and years ahead.

The final decisions in the acquisition process are not easy, rarely occurring without difficult selections between competing features of proposals, such as higher performance versus lower initial costs, or lower costs versus greater vendor experience and integrity.

Transition Preparation

The goal of transition preparation is to prepare the organization for the installation of the computer, so the change from the old to the new work methods can be as smooth as possible. Preparation usually occurs prior to the installation of the equipment. There are several activities common during this stage.

Employee training and orientation in three areas is critically important. There should be a general orientation and introduction to computers, to help employees become familiar with the devices and to allay unreasonable expectations and fears. There should be a program to assure that employees understand any shifts in organizational structure and task responsibility associated with the computer. Most important, employees should understand how the computer will affect their individual tasks.

Preparation of the environment for the computer is also important. This involves not only changes in the immediate location of the computer itself, but also any alterations in work stations that will house terminals, soundproofing of locations with noise-generating devices, such as printers; and any modifications of the mechanical system of the building to assure proper temperature levels for workers as well as for the machine.

Sometimes it is necessary to hire additional temporary staff to assist in the transition process, since existing staff may not be sufficient to carry out everyday tasks and also to complete the necessary training, initial data entry, and other tasks associated with the new system. Extra help may be employed during the transition period, so that permanent employees can be trained and can have the necessary time to get the computer system up to date and reliably operational. It is not wise to bring in the extra help only at the last minute. If temporary staff is to be hired, it may be desirable to begin early training and orientation for these workers before the "crunch."

The quality of preparation during this stage will influence greatly the ease and speed with which the overall system can be implemented.

Installation

The actual installation of a computer may take only minutes, or it may take weeks, depending upon the size and complexity of the system. This stage usually involves several types of activities.

The installation itself may be somewhat disruptive if it also entails the installation of communications wires throughout an office building or if it requires related mechanical and electrical work as well. Once the computer is installed and operational, it is desirable to test it to assure that it works properly. Proper testing procedures vary from machine to machine, but they usually involve preliminary exercises, such as a memory test, where information is stored and then subsequently read from every position in memory to assure that every point is operational. Additional tests involve the operation of the computer for a period of days (sometimes called "burning in'), to again assure that all is in proper working order and to stress any weak elements in the system. Thus, potential breakdowns would tend to occur during the warranty period. Some of the initial testing is done by the vendor, in accordance with any installation contract. But it is wise to do some additional testing internally.

Physical installation of "canned" software usually entails little more than mounting a tape or disk, reading the program into the computer, and making necessary backup copies. Thus "bringing up" the software can occur in minutes or hours. However, configuring the software to a specific computer system can take longer, as terminals must be specifically identified, peripherals defined, and minor incompatibilities resolved. The difficulty of software installation generally depends upon two factors: the degree to which the software has been used by others, and therefore debugged, and the type of equipment it is to run on. Installing a standard word processing package on a compatible microcomputer is, for example, very quick and simple. Installing a complex data base management system on a multiterminal minicomputer can be very time consuming because the software must be adjusted to work with the specific features of the system.

At the end of the installation stage, the organization should have an operational computer in place, with the software up and running.

Transition

During the transition stage, employees begin to use the computer, and eventually cease to perform designated tasks manually. There is a range of opinion about the best way to approach this activity. One approach is to make the transition as quickly as possible, once the computer system is operational. This is much like teaching people to swim by throwing them in the water. The argument for a clean break is that this is the only way to assure an end to previous methods. Otherwise, employees tend to cling to old procedures and processes—a costly crutch. Another approach entails a deliberate and gradual changeover from one method to the other, even if this means that the organization bears the cost of duplicate operations for a while. The advantages are that computer malfunctions do not cripple the organization and that employees can become accustomed to the computer system before they must rely on it totally.

Probably the best rule of thumb is to apply the clean-break approach when the chances of success are high, the cost of malfunction is low, and it is possible to revert to the previous method if the system or the employees do not perform as expected. Otherwise, the deliberate and gradual approach may be best. There are several concepts to consider in managing the transition. Often it is not possible to implement an entire system at once. Management must then choose to focus upon one part of the system first. The decision may be a difficult one, since choices about the relative priority of service for sections of an organization can be troublesome, especially when there are contradictory trade-offs that have no clear resolution. For example, often two or three functions will share the same file of records, such as a personnel record system that includes information on payroll, employee time and attendance, and records of the application of time to projects.

The complete execution of any one function requires information provided through the other functions. If all three cannot be brought up at once, it is difficult to bring up any one fully. The resolution of the dilemma involves either (1) solving the problems that limit bringing up all systems at once (e.g., by hiring more staff), (2) delaying implementation of all three until the computer operational staff is prepared to have all come up at once, or (3) selecting one or two subsystems to come up at once and developing creative approaches to overcoming the limitations of the data base.

Whether the transition is sudden or gradual, management should recognize that this period entails additional work loads for employees. If no additional staff is provided, the employees are expected to (1) continue their regular duties, (2) enter the existing records into the computer system that are necessary for ongoing operations, (3) learn to use the new system, and (4) perform their regular duties under the new system so that it does not fall behind. This can lead to a work load crisis and give employees a very negative introduction to the new computer system. Transition is complex and demanding enough without a doubling or tripling of work loads.

If the transition effort is well planned and organized, and if major problems are foreseen and resolved in advance, then the process can be relatively easy. It is, however, a period when computer systems can be most frustrating.

Operation

The ongoing operation of the computer system is subject to the same complex of changing conditions and influences as is any organizational activity. Work loads may increase or change in character, and new demands may be placed upon the organization. Thus, a computer system involves an organization in a continuous series of small-scale implementations of new subsystems and changes in existing subsystems.

Sometimes a system is initially implemented smoothly, with great attention to all of the critical aspects of the process. Subsequently, as additional subsystems are brought into operation, management perceives that the system is already largely implemented and therefore becomes inattentive to the critical details and required support of subsequent efforts.

It is also useful to provide for a comprehensive evaluation of the computer system from time to time, to identify those activities that are working as well or better than expected and those that should be changed or abandoned.

A comprehensive approach to implementation is critical when a system is large, highly complex, and dedicated to specific functions. Failure in implementation can result in substantial wasted equipment expenditures, costly delays, and unsatisfactory performance.

THE INCREMENTAL APPROACH

The arrival of microcomputers and enhanced terminals, and the rapid increases in their computing power and capacity, opens up opportunities for computers to be used in new ways and in new environments. However, much of the advice about the use of small systems has been developed by people whose background is in the mainframe tradition. When implementation of small systems is discussed, it is natural that a comprehensive approach is assumed. For a person used to operation of larger scale computer systems, the painful lessons of inadequate implementation processes are difficult to forget.

Many executives and small business and agency managers are approaching the problems of implementation in an entirely different manner. They do not apply lessons from large-scale systems that do not appear to be immediately applicable to their circumstances. Their approach generally follows the following steps outlined here:

Obtain a microcomputer or get access to an intelligent terminal, play with it, and become familiar with its capabilities and potentials.

Introduce co-workers and key managers to the devices, and encourage them to obtain them also, to play with them and to become accustomed to what they can do.

Encourage experimental efforts to make the systems perform useful work, providing modest support for software development and employee time to devote to such efforts.

Develop an informal coordinating group to identify useful and promising applications of the devices on the job and to stimulate wider adoption of such applications throughout the organization.

Build a larger and more complex system from the bottom up, gradually introducing a local communications network within the office, so that workers can communicate from machine to machine, share a large and fast disk with multi-user files, and share access to specialized peripheral equipment.

Such an approach can work only when the equipment is relatively inexpensive and flexible, when employees are creative and motivated, and when the tasks to be computerized are relatively simple. These criteria apply to many small businesses and agencies. The stages of the incremental approach are somewhat less defined than those of the stricter comprehensive approach, but they can be generally described.

Introduction

The general purpose of the first stage is to introduce small computers to a wide range of employees in the organization. In an organization of any size, the process has probably begun on its own already. By 1985, there will be at least one microcomputer for every 20 citizens in the United States. As a result, most businesses and agencies will have workers who own and operate systems whether they promote them or not. There are several advantages to an intentional effort to promote computer use.

A passive approach may result in the wrong people taking the lead in this area. For example, it is likely that the staff operating any traditional, large-scale computer system may be among the first to become interested in the small systems. Sometimes a traditional computer unit within an organization may feel threatened by the small systems, because they can lead to a lessened role of the traditional computer staff. As a result, the traditional staff may attempt to restrict the use of small systems. Another example of the "wrong people" problem occurs if key managers and opinion leaders do not become interested in the systems. This can lead to a pattern of ongoing discouragement of innovation and experiment, and to many lost opportunities.

An active approach can permit the organization to coordinate the acquisition of equipment so that compatibility is assured. This does not necessarily mean that each employee must have identical equipment, but it should mean that the potential for an interconnected system is preserved. An active approach can also coordinate official organizational purchases with personal purchases by employees. As mentioned earlier, some businesses are establishing the equivalent of a subsidized computer store within the organization to provide discounts and other incentives for purchasing personal computers that are compatible with those that the organization generally uses. Others have established discount and employee purchase subsidy arrangements with independent stores.

Depending upon the size and complexity of the organization, there are various strategies that may be employed to introduce computers. A common pattern is that one or more key employees, such as the owner of a small business, may purchase computers and operate them at home as recreation. In this way, they become familiar with the operations of the computer and become capable of many basic operations and functions. They then encourage other key employees, including secretaries and other lower level staff, also to develop some basic computer skills, perhaps by purchasing several computers for employees to borrow and take home. At home, there is less pressure for immediate performance, and less risk and embarrassment if progress is unsteady. In time, a key group of employees is competent, and presumably interested, in computers. It is then difficult to restrain the development and implementation of creative ideas.

The overall goal of the introduction stage is to develop a group of employees competent and motivated to enter into a creative process of applying the computer to the work place.

Experiment

The experiment stage involves the development of useful and cost-effective computer applications. Opportunities for such applications are identified largely by employees, who are at this point familiar with their work as well as with computer capabilities and potentials. Some ideas are rejected initially as unfeasible. Other ideas are attempted and, at some stage of the process, fail to live up to expectations and are discarded. Many ideas succeed initially and are subsequently implemented throughout the organization wherever applicable. There are several tactics that a manager may employ to coordinate and encourage effort.

An informal users' group may be created to provide interested employees with basic ideas to consider and to assist in problem solving. The users' group may also be employed to select from among a number of proposed projects those that deserve initial support and, of course, equipment. While some computers are loaned out for employees to learn on, the machines that are to be committed to experimental operations must be allocated in some fashion. A reward system might be established, including discounts toward the purchase of computers and related equipment.

This approach has several important advantages. First, it builds upon employee enthusiasm and interest, rather than attempting to overcome inertia. Second, it builds from the ground up, based upon employee perceptions of what applications may work, rather than from the top down, based upon expert and outsider perceptions of what may work. Third, there are minimal losses associated with failure, since a variety of efforts are attempted, and it is expected that many will not succeed.

Expansion

The final stage in the incremental approach entails the enlargement and integration of the collection of computers into a system. A fully developed system might work much like an automated office system, as described in Chapter 5. It would include a local and an external communications network, a central processor with secondary memory, and specialized peripherals. The work stations are the microcomputers already purchased and in operation. Most of the processing is still done within the microcomputer work stations, while the central processor largely handles communications coordination and shared files.

The addition of equipment to develop an office network allows each work station to share access to files with other stations, use electronic interoffice and external mail, and conveniently use specialized peripherals.

A CLOSING OBSERVATION

The comprehensive and incremental strategies represent two radically different ways to introduce a computer into an organization or work process. Regardless of approach, there are nevertheless some important skills and understandings that a manager should have to be an effective leader or participant in the implementation of a computer system.

Probably the most important role of the manager is in the analysis, explanation, and development of the work process itself. The computer professional—whether an organization employee, outside consultant, or local store sales representative—can help in the selection and development of equipment and software. The manager, however, is the only one who really understands the job that the computer is to perform. For example, if the computer cannot help an employee to do a task correctly and completely, it is not useful. The role of the manager as one who establishes priorities becomes critical when a task is important to several units within an organization, but different aspects of the task are valued. If the task is not fully understood, the computer may complete only the portion of the task that is important to one unit and perform inadequately for the others.

The critical issue for the manager, then, is to bring a full understanding of the work process to bear on the computer planning and implementation process. In the end, the computer specialist will he held responsible for the successful operation of the computer and software. The manager will he held responsible for the ongoing completion of the work process in an efficient and productive manner.

CHAPTER 12
CRIME, SECURITY, AND COMPUTERS

Our employees really appreciated the introduction of automated office systems to our consulting firm. Production of reports was simplified, and our work quality improved. Our only negative experience occurred when we terminated an employee who had been consistently absent from or late to work. He was upset and angry that I dismissed him and apparently decided to strike back. He understood how valuable our computer system had become in the development of reports and projects. He also understood that a magnet, when passed over a diskette, can erase or disorganize the information stored on it. On his last day of work, he was filing diskettes, some of which went into our project file, some into our archives file, and some into our programs and systems file. In each case, he waved a magnet across many diskettes, destroying their contents. It was a disaster for the firm, and yet it was also difficult to prove his intentional role in the vandalism, since he alleged that he did not understand and was never trained about the effect of a magnet on a diskette.

The expanding use of computers is not limited to legitimate business and personal applications. The criminal use of computers is also on the increase, because of the growing demand for equipment and the increasingly sensitive and important applications. A criminal with minimal skills and experience can steal and resell a terminal, microcomputer, or printer. A criminal with skills in computer programming can sabotage central operations of a business or drain off its funds.

Security is a major ongoing focus of administrative attention in the management of large computer systems. Broadly defined, security is the absence of risk or danger. Basic operational procedures to promote computer security have been developed over the last 25 years, in response to the following types of incidents.

Computer equipment has been stolen and resold. Initially, much equipment had little value on the stolen goods market because it was easy to identify and there were few legitimate dealers. With the proliferation of retailers of new and used equipment, the resale of stolen equipment has become simpler and more lucrative.

Computer programs are pirated to be sold to end-users without payment of royalties to copyright owners. Programs are also stolen to aid in the development of embezzlement schemes and other illegal activities.

Programmers (both consultants and regular employees) have manipulated computer programs to permit embezzlement of funds. The programs are changed so that exception reports are not issued when a particular account is grossly overdrawn, or computational procedures are manipulated. For example, in rounding down financial calculations, fractions of pennies may be accrued to a special account. In a small business this technique can produce only small change. In a business with many accounts and a large cash flow, the pennies can add up quickly.

Computers can be targets for sabotage and vandalism because of the sensitivity of both the equipment and the applications performed. Simple vandalism might involve arson or explosives. A technically proficient vandal could cause a computer to erase its files or to produce deceptively inaccurate output.

This chapter examines some of the vulnerabilities of traditional large computer systems and the operational procedures that have been developed to reduce risk. The similarities and differences in the vulnerabilities of large and small systems will be examined, and the differences in approaches to risk reduction will be presented.

Generally, there are four areas of vulnerability for computers, whether they are large systems, enhanced terminals to large systems, small business systems, or personal computers. The four areas are: environmental risk, organizational and procedural risk, hardware and software risk, and legal risk. While all systems share exposure to all of these risks, a basic distinction can be drawn between specialized and common risk.

Specialized risk is more prevalent in large and complex systems, and it relates to manipulation of programs for embezzlement, theft of secret information stored in the computer, and sabotage. This type of risk results from the unique characteristics of large-scale computer systems and the work that they do.

Common risk is more prevalent for terminals and work stations of large systems, and for small business and personal computers. It is the same type of risk as exists for an electric typewriter or any other expensive and marketable piece of office equipment. For example, it can be stolen, or coffee can be spilled on sensitive components.

A manager should be aware of the spectrum of risk exposure associated with computers. Overattention to common risk can lead to losses from specialized theft. On the other hand, a small business owner should be primarily concerned about common risks for a computer used as a word processor only. As the owner expands the use of computers in the operations of the business, he or she gradually increases exposure to specialized risk. Therefore, the spectrum of risk will be examined for each type of vulnerability.

ENVIRONMENTAL RISK

Environmental risk focuses upon the location of the computer, rather than upon the computer itself and its operations. Losses occur as a result of failures in the environment: power losses, air conditioning breakdowns, unauthorized entries, and general disasters.

Supply and Support Breakdown

The specifications of most computers include a section usually entitled "environment," which describes the necessary characteristics for a physical environment to support the operation of the computer. At a minimum, the section describes the power requirements of the system and the temperature ranges within which the system functions. An inadequately planned environment can permit a breakdown in minimum operating conditions. A power outage can cause damage to disks as well as result in the loss of information in the primary memory of the computer. Operation of the computer when the environment is too hot can lead to costly damage to electronic components.

The vulnerability of supply and support systems can be due to external problems, such as a break in a power line. Malicious breakdowns are also significant risks, which increase as an organization becomes better known and is subject to greater public controversy. An irate employee or citizen, aware of the location and function of an important computer system, can disable electric power without access to the building that houses the computer itself. Most larger computer systems have backup electrical generators or battery packs that turn on when power goes down. Small businesses may overlook this requirement because it was initially unnecessary.

As a computer becomes more central to the operation of a business, other precautions are also desirable. Secondary systems to monitor temperatures in the critical areas might be installed. Secondary monitoring (even if it is only a thermometer) is very desirable, since thermostats only tell the temperature at their exact locations and since computers can give off amounts of heat not considered in the original planning of the heating, ventilation, and air conditioning system of the facility.

Other aspects of the physical environment should be considered as well, such as the structural capacity of the floor and building housing the system. As a computer system grows, there is an increase in the weight of processors, telecommunications devices, disks, printers, supplies, furnishings, and the numbers of operators as well. A room designed for light office functions may be strained to its limits.

Consideration of natural and man-made disasters may seem a bit extreme, but some sites have greater probabilities of certain disasters than others. As a computer system becomes more central to the operation of a business, some assessment and contingency planning should be considered. At the simplest level, there should be contingency plans for days when employee commuting is restricted because of snow or other weather conditions. At a more complex level, the location of the computer system of a major organization should reflect consideration of site-related risks. Some businesses even make arrangements for backup sites for their computer operations in case their system should cease to function. They coordinate with another company using the same equipment or arrange coverage with a company that specializes in providing backup.

For a small business computer or office work station, supply and support risks are easier to identify and manage. Generally, loss of air conditioning and power do not create the amount of damage that would occur in a large system. Loss of primary memory or loss of material stored on disk can be mitigated by carefully backing up programs and records from time to time. The general environmental demands are usually less stringent as well.

Small battery packs can be acquired to support microcomputer systems, and devices are marketed that will provide for emergency power for limited periods of time. One other precaution is sometimes overlooked. It is prudent to mark on the circuit breaker which circuits support a computer. Sometimes a person working with the electrical system of the building may flip the switches of a circuit breaker to determine which areas are associated with particular circuits. While this would have little effect on most office equipment, it would destroy information in a computer and perhaps damage the equipment as well.

Physical Theft

For both large and small computer systems, theft is a significant risk. There are several factors that serve to increase this risk. Equipment that is highly unusual is a less satisfactory target for theft than equipment that is common and often bought and sold on the used market. As small computers and peripheral devices become more common, they will become more lucrative targets for thieves. Theft of peripheral equipment, especially printers, will become more prevalent as individual computers become common, because the same printer that can be driven by a large computer system can be driven by a small system. In the past, a thief would have difficulty selling a stolen printer because of the limited market and the procedural safeguards in organizational purchasing processes. When many individuals are in the market for used printers, unloading stolen ones is much easier.

The decentralization of computing eliminates one protection against theft of equipment— the connection of equipment to a main computer. Although many terminals are off-line much of the time, while they are on line, there are a variety of safeguards against their unauthorized use or removal. Furthermore, many criminals are not sufficiently informed about computers to know whether a terminal is on or off line.

The protection of an enterprise against theft could be the subject of a book by itself and therefore cannot be treated thoroughly here. However, there are several basic ideas to consider:

Identify the assets to be protected, and locate them in one or more places that can be physically secured.

Physical security can be provided architecturally, such as by a locked door to a secure room, or by such other means such as a locked cabinet. Any valuable equipment should be kept in a locked office at night, not left out in a corridor or open area.

Limit access to the secured areas to only those with a need to be there. Informal access control is afforded by locating the equipment in a place that is not subject to routine public access and observation. While this does not eliminate unauthorized access completely, it does reduce exposure.

Provide for surveillance, either through direct observation by employees or through such indirect means as intrusion detection devices or closed-circuit television.

Render the equipment difficult and time-consuming to steal—for instance, by bolting terminals to desks.

All of these procedures can be done in such a way as to make minimal changes in the atmosphere of the work environment. For a small business computer or enhanced terminal, reducing the risk of theft requires the same types of measures.

Sabotage

When an individual or organization desires to strike out and harm an organization, perhaps as a result of a grievance or as a political statement, a computer is an obvious target because of its central role in the organization, its ease of identification, and because it is easy to damage.

Common sabotage involves direct physical damage to the computer, its peripherals, or related supplies, such as disks. The risk of this type of sabotage is not generally higher than it would otherwise be for related types of office equipment, such as copying machines and typewriters. The cost of damages may be somewhat higher, though, because computer equipment is often more expensive and complex. A computer may be a somewhat more desirable target for sabotage because it may symbolize what the saboteur hates about the organization or because the damage is perceived to be more expensive. However, when the motivation is general and the skill of the saboteur is limited to physical destruction, probably most objects of perceived value will be targets.

Specialized sabotage is accomplished by someone who knows how the target computer works. Rather than simple physical destruction, specialized sabotage usually involves changes in programs, which creates operational destruction instead. The following are some examples of what can be done.

A bug, or error, can be introduced into one or more programs to cause a malfunction. A "time bomb" is a bug that occurs long after the process has been set in motion, so that it is very difficult to discover where the error is, or the extent of damage. Other types of changes can cause the computer to fail to issue exception reports, so that errors persist after they should have been picked up and corrected. In one case, programmers telephoned a program revision to a computer that caused a continuous error in reading tapes and disks. This was done during a strike against the company.

Specialized sabotage is very difficult to prevent when it is done by an insider or someone with access to the internal operations of the computer. Some basic protections are discussed later, in the section on organizational and procedural risk. Protecting against specialized sabotage from outside is somewhat easier to accomplish. It requires restriction of physical and operational access to the computer by unauthorized persons, as well as some procedural safeguards (discussed in the next section) to ensure that copies of programs are compared to their originals from time to time.

For the small business computer or enhanced terminal, the risks of common sabotage are much greater than the risks of specialized sabotage, unless the computer is being used in a highly controversial project or function. This would create a motivation that might make the computer a symbolic target.

We have thus far reviewed the environmental risks of supply and support breakdowns, theft, and sabotage. These risks are inherently greater for larger computers than for smaller ones, because the large systems are more dependent upon specific environmental conditions. Smaller computers offer environmental risks, but they are much more comparable to the risks associated with an electric typewriter (damage, theft, and sabotage) than to the more complex risks associated with large systems.

ORGANIZATIONAL AND PROCEDURAL RISK

Losses due to organizational and procedural malfunctions result from how an organization uses a computer. Poor personnel management and lack of organizational structure and control can lead to losses in many areas, and computer operations are not immune.

There is a mystique about computers that leads many inexperienced and untrained persons to suspend critical judgment. A manager who would carefully select account clerks, and carefully structure their work, might allow the employment and supervision of computer operators to be more informal, on the assumption that internal mechanisms within the computer program would audit and cross-check work. While this is to some extent true, an experienced programmer or computer operator, working with the system day to day, can find bugs and loopholes to be exploited if the opportunity is presented. As a result, organizational and procedural aspects of computer systems become critically important in reducing risk.

Personnel

Probably the greatest area of loss exposure for a computer operation lies with personnel, especially those cleared for access to central computer operations. If all computer administrators, operators, programmers, and users were always loyal and honest, then many of the remaining organizational controls would not be needed. The best that can be done in the real world is to strive to select, motivate, and retain the most competent, honest, and loyal people.

Although there are textbooks and manuals on good personnel management practices, there are several procedures that should be stressed in the selection of workers to program or operate a computer system. Background investigations of employees should be undertaken commensurate with the level of responsibility to which they are to be assigned. This should also apply to present employees who are to be promoted beyond their current level of responsibility. As a computer system becomes larger and more complex, it may be desirable to set up a security clearance system, so that a structured process is established to assign employees greater levels of responsibility and access. Adequate compensation and positive management practices can help in attracting and retaining good employees, and can promote attitudes that are not destructive.

For a small business computer, or for an enhanced remote terminal or work station, the problems of employee security have less to do with the computer than with the overall functional responsibilities of the employee. For example, anyone processing checks by computer should a similar background to someone processing checks by hand.

A separate risk for the small business operator is the use of consultants. As substitutes for specialized employees, computer programming consultants can be very effective. However, when the business owner and core staff cannot program the computer and when the software is not a user-friendly adaptive package, then the business is somewhat at the mercy of the consultant.

Organizational and Procedural Controls

Assuming that employees are as honest and loyal as possible, another dimension of security can be provided through proper operational and procedural controls. These provide checks and balances that help reduce the opportunity for misconduct and assure its early detection. There are six general principles that should be followed.

1. *Documentation of programs and procedures* is a necessity. Program documentation allows a person or organization to examine and work on a program written by another, providing a backup programming capacity and a secondary check on work performed. Documentation of procedures provides for accountability of those working with the computer, increasing the standardization and reliability of work performed and providing an additional protection against unusual misconduct.

2. *Inventory controls* provide for accountability of supplies and equipment, as well as programs and source documents. Loss

of disks and other storage media, computer forms, original source documentation, and input data not only represent the loss of the value of the asset. Lack of controls over such materials provide easy ways for programs to be modified off site, and for source, input, and output documents to be modified. Information storage media, such as disks and tapes, are a special concern. When a tape or disk is "erased," in many computer systems what is actually changed is only the directory—the place on the disk or tape that indicates where the information is located. Because there is no longer a record of the erased file, the next time the disk or tape is used, the computer may write over the old file. However, a trained and experienced person could retrieve the erased information by examining what was written onto the disk or tape directly. Completely effective erasure requires that new information be written onto the tape or that a magnet scramble the information. Implementing a structured inventory procedure reduces risk and makes criminal access to the computer system more difficult.

3.   Separation of functions is a basic procedure in manual accounting processes, which is sometimes overlooked in computer-based procedures when work is combined to be accomplished by one person. Several types of separation of function are desirable. One is *separation of functions in programming.* The process of writing a program should be separate from the process of testing it, and those functions should be separate from the process of routinely running or operating the program. For a large computing operation, this is relatively easy to set up. For a one-person operation or small system, such separation is usually provided through the purchase of programs from external sources. This separates the development of the program from testing and operation. The separation of testing and operation usually occurs naturally, since management may be responsible for initial setup and implementation, whereas line employees run the program from day to day.

4.   Another dimension is *separation of functions in routine operations* of a computer system. Users, operators, programmers, and maintenance staff should each be separate persons or organi-

zations, each with a basic incentive to assure the appropriate performance of the others. Again, in a large system this can be accomplished relatively effectively. Some organizations have gone so far as to provide separate building entrances, parking lots, work areas, and cafeterias for these employees. For a small organization, separation can be provided through the use of separate vendors for the different functions and by splitting computer work between several employees.

5. *Audit procedures* are critical to the assurance of the quality and accuracy of work performed with the aid of a computer. Some computer programs are self-auditing to a limited extent, in that computational results can be compared when they have been developed from various sources and methods. The only reliable and valid audit, however, begins with the original source documentation—the paperwork that was originally used as the source for the information put into the computer, or computer-generated paperwork independently verified. Then people uninvolved in the original work recompute and verify a randomly selected sample of transactions to determine whether the computer is performing as required.

6. *Backup procedures* provide for copies of important files and programs separate from those routinely used. This assures that a major breakdown will not result in information loss and program damage of anything prior to the most recent backup. Usually a backup schedule is established, such as once per day, once every hour, or, on some highly sensitive functions, on a practically simultaneous basis. Some systems provide for some of the backup material to be stored off site, so that even the total destruction of the computer and the site would not damage the off-site material. Backup material can also be used to compare current programs and files with originals, to determine that only authorized changes and differences have been made.

Each of these principles can be implemented for a small computer system, or even for a personal computer, although the methods of implementation become simpler and some reliance on outside vendors and consultants may become necessary.

HARDWARE AND SOFTWARE RISK

Computer equipment and software can be designed and developed so as to contribute to security. There are basically three features of an internally secure system: general reliability, access security, and communications security.

General Reliability

General reliability is the opposite of frequent breakdown and repair. An unreliable program or computer exposes the user to loss of work production, detected and undetected error, and exposure to risk in the repair process, especially if the machine has to be moved and if work has to be done elsewhere during the repair period. A computer should be a highly reliable device, unless the environment is inadequate or the work to be done is improperly matched to the capacities of the computer, software, and peripherals.

Access Security

Only authorized persons should be able to operate a computer system. In a large system, elaborate procedures not only limit access to authorized persons but also limit the types of activities each user can undertake. Similar capabilities are available for small or personal computer systems, and they ought to be employed if the computer's application is sensitive.

Access security in large systems is generally provided primarily through the use of passwords. Each user is given a password that is associated, within the operating system of the computer, with access to certain types of functions. People authorized to operate the machine would be permitted to do so, while people employed to enter data would be permitted only to perform that function. Thus, the password system can reinforce other functional separations discussed above.

Many excellent password systems exist. The greatest weakness, however, is not with the system, but rather with the users. For convenience, users will construct passwords that are obvious, such as their office or home phone number, or they will leave them around in obvious places, such as in their top desk drawer or under the pad on their desktop. Thus, unauthorized access to large computer systems is sometimes obtained by getting discarded printouts from wastebaskets in areas frequented by users, determining who the user is by the nature of the printout, and figuring out the password by trial and error. Sometimes access is even easier when a user leaves a full program deck, including cards with account numbers and passwords, in a location where the key information can be observed.

After unauthorized access occurs, there are a variety of strategies employed to sabotage or steal from computer systems. Many of the ways depend greatly upon the specific nature of the computer system, but the following is a summary of common strategies.

Probably the most common approach is for a person with authorized access to a system to use it on unauthorized activities, or to sell use to others. Another common approach is to obtain someone else's account number and password and use them on an unauthorized basis or sell them to another.

When a system produces exception reports when something is unusual or out of order, a clever programmer could cause the computer to fail to report something (such as an overdrawn account). Then the programmer could make withdrawals from that account without the system reporting the unusual condition. This technique is often applied to inactive accounts that are not subject to frequent inspection. Such a strategy would apply primarily to financial systems, but the technique is equally applicable to a variety of other situations.

Manipulation of calculation processes is a more complex technique and is applicable to fewer situations. A good example is the deposit of "round down" amounts into a separate account. Rounding down to the nearest penny does not generate a great deal of money unless the number of transactions is great. However, when rounding down is to the nearest dollar, amounts can be greater. Changing records directly is another frequent technique, which is sometimes easier and more effective using computers because there are no erasure marks or other signs of the change.

One alternative method of access security that is receiving more frequent use, especially in highly sensitive systems, is called *biometrics*. Voiceprints, fingerprints, and other unique characteristics of people are used in place of passwords. This assures that the user is actually the person intended. The problem with such systems is that they are more expensive and somewhat less convenient than password systems.

For a small computer system, access control through software is more difficult to achieve, because a motivated user could obtain a disk from another computer that is not controlled and use that disk to operate the target computer. Some computers come equipped with locks and keys that work reasonably well for the unsophisticated user, but they be circumvented by a motivated and experienced person.

Communications Security

A breakdown in access security would permit an unauthorized person to use the computer system in a normal manner. A breakdown in communications security would allow a broader range of intervention in the computer system. Generally, there are two types of unauthorized interventions:

1. Someone could tap a communications line and simply listen, with a computer, to the information and messages transmitted.
2. Someone could tap a communications line and modify a transmission. The modification could be merely destructive, such as inserting meaningless noise, or it could fulfill a criminal purpose.

There are several techniques to overcome the potential for a breakdown in communications security. The most common approach is to employ code words and expressions in highly sensitive communications so that the underlying message is not understandable to unauthorized persons. This approach works for very simple and infrequent messages, but it breaks down for routine communication of larger volumes of information.

Another common approach is to scramble the information according to a prearranged format that is unintelligible unless the receiver understands how to unscramble the message. The key to the scrambling is usually changed frequently. A problem with this technique is that computers are becoming more and more powerful in their ability to decipher scrambled messages. If there is some underlying order to a message, unless the scrambling code is very complex, a computer can be programmed to attempt many possible combinations and coding techniques to identify those that produce the most orderly result. For the typical business user, there is little risk of such an intervention. However, if the information could be of great value to someone or to some organization, simple scrambling systems may not be adequate.

For small computer systems that rely heavily upon communications, systems have been developed that provide some measure of protection. The basic vulnerability of many such systems is that they are sold commercially and are therefore available to those who might desire to intervene in transmissions as well. For most purposes they are very adequate, but not entirely reliable.

LEGAL RISK

A manager could take extensive precautions to prevent losses due to physical and operational security breaches, only to experience a substantial loss due to legal liability and risk. While this is a somewhat intangible aspect of computer security, it is no less important. There are three basic types of risk to be considered: ordinary business liability, software copyright liability, and information privacy and security liability.

Ordinary Business Liability

In any business transaction there is risk. It is possible, for example, that a contract providing for lease of a piece of equipment does not adequately specify performance or does not adequately specify the conditions under which the contract may be terminated. This creates a dimension of risk that is significant, but not unique or unusual to computer equipment or projects. However, because computers are relatively expensive and complex, the amount and complexity of the risk increases proportionately.

The appropriate remedy is twofold: smart management, and good insurance. This is also true for the operations of a business or organization in general, and the subject need not be further elaborated here.

Software Copyright Liability

The use of computer programs under a license from the owner establishes legal obligations on the part of the user that often include penalties for failure to comply. These penalties can apply not only to the organization but to individual employees as well. Generally, software is protected by the owner in several ways:

It is usually packaged in a "dressy" format that is difficult to copy, so that a software pirate would have to go to considerable trouble to create a convincing imitation of the software to sell to a business as the real thing. Thus, most pirated software is obtained by a user who knows it is pirated.

The program and any accompanying manuals are usually copyrighted, so that unauthorized distribution and use is a violation of copyright law.

Usually, any employees involved in the original creation of the package have signed antidisclosure agreements, which establish penalties for them if they take the program and distribute it or develop a comparable one.

Despite these legal protections, there is a great deal of software piracy, primarily because it is very difficult and expensive to take legal action against a pirate, and because the practice is so pervasive. Thus, generally only the most extreme cases are subject to legal action.

It is wise for a business or governmental organization to avoid the unauthorized use of software. Most people do not condone the theft of property from other persons or businesses. Furthermore, the minimal initial savings involved would not be worth the risk associated with the possible subsequent outcomes. For instance, while an individual owner-user can keep his or her own secrets, in an organization, a disgruntled employee or one with moral objections to software piracy could turn in the business and provide the necessary evidence to make a strong legal case. In addition, the business does not have the opportunity to take advantage of technical assistance through the developer of the software, in the form of newsletters, updates, and problem alerts.

Information Privacy and Security

A final type of legal risk in the use of computers is associated with the misuse of information. As a general matter, the following rule might be applied. If you would not disclose a piece of information if it were not stored in a computer, you should not disclose it when it is in a computer. This rule seems simple enough, but the nature of computer and general information systems make this a bit complicated to implement. Computer systems sometimes provide ready access to information to which one might otherwise not have access, such as criminal or credit histories. This is compounded by the fact that computers are intentionally designed so that it is relatively easy to get information out. As a result, an unauthorized person (for example a sales employee with access to a corporate computer for sales functions) could, with a bit of experimentation, gain access to personnel records also maintained on the computer. Precautions must be taken just as precautions are taken with manual records that are private.

FINAL OBSERVATIONS

The problems of security for small and large computer systems are very different. The large systems face some relatively unique problems associated with their extensive use throughout the organizations they serve and the vulnerabilities of their technologies. The small systems face more conventional risks, similar to the risks associated with the equipment value of a typewriter and the sabotage and privacy importance of a key filing cabinet. Both types of risk are very important and deserve thorough management attention.

BIBLIOGRAPHY

Allison, Graham T. *Essence of Decision: Explaining the Cuban Missile Crisis.* Boston: Little-Brown, 1971.

Anthony, Robert N. *Planning and Control Systems, A Framework for Analysis.* Cambridge, Mass.: Harvard University Press, 1965.

Barnard, Chester I. *The Functions of the Executive.* Cambridge, Mass.: Harvard University Press, 1966.

Brandon, Dick H. *Management Planning for Data Processing.* Princeton: Brandon/Systems Press, 1970.

Chorafas, Dimitris N. *Office Automation, The Productivity Challenge.* Englewood Cliffs, N.J.: Prentice-Hall, 1982.

Drucker, Peter *Technology, Management and Society.* New York: Harper & Row, 1970.

Garrity, John T. "Top Management and Computer Profits," *Harvard Business Review,* 1963, 41, No.4.

Gold, Bela *Productivity, Technology and Capital.* Lexington, Mass.: Lexington Books, 1979.

Gruenberger, Fred *Information Systems for Management.* Englewood Cliffs, N.J.: Prentice-Hall, 1972.

Hackman, J.R. et al. "A New Strategy for Job Enrichment," *California Management Review,* 1975, 17: 57–71.

Harold, Frederick G. *Handbook for Orienting the Manager to the Computer.* Princeton: Auerbach Publishers, 1971.

Karloff, Robert J., and Lee, Leonard S. *Productivity and Records Automation.* Englewood Cliffs, N.J.: Prentice-Hall, 1981.

Knox, Frank M. *Managing Paperwork, A Key To Productivity.* New York: Thurmond Press, 1980.

Long, Larry E. *Design and Strategy for Corporate Information Services.* Englewood Cliffs, N.J.: Prentice-Hall, 1982.

Myers, Charles A., Ed. *The Impact of Computers on Management.* Cambridge, Mass.: MIT Press, 1967.

Orlicky, Joseph. *The Successful Computer System.* New York: McGraw-Hill, 1969.

Perry, William E. *So You Think You Need Your Own Business Computer.* New York: John Wiley, 1982.

Stewart, Rosemary *How Computers Affect Management.* Cambridge, Mass.: MIT Press, 1971.

Stokes, Paul M. *A Total Systems Approach to Management Control.* New York: American Management Association, 1968.

Toan, Arthur B. *Using Information to Manage.* New York: The Ronald Press, 1968.

Washnis, George J. Ed. *Productivity Improvement Handbook for State and Local Government.* New York: Wiley, 1980.

Whistler, Thomas L. *The Impact of Computers on Organizations.* New York: Praeger, 1970.

INDEX

Accounts payable and receivable, 103, 143

Acid test, 104

Acquisition, in implementation 236–238

Air conditioning, 131

ALGOL, 46

Architecture, 131–134, 250–253

ASCII, American Standard Code for Information Interchange, 39

Assessment, in implementation 234–235

Authority, 17

Automation, *see* Office automation

BASIC 46–47, 49, 51–52, 60, 72, 140

Baud, 39–40

Benchmark, 159

Biometrics, 261

Bit, 31

Byte, 31

CAD/CAM, 53

Cash management, 142–143

Central data processing organizational structure, 196–198

Centralization, 17

Charge-coupled devices, 34

Classification model, 78–84

Closed-routine tasks, 211

COBOL, 46, 51–52

Communication, 12, 115–120, 185

Comparison model, 66, 78–79

Competence, 5, 7–16

Comprehensive approach to implementation, 233–242

Compuserve, 109

Conflict, 8, 15, 90, 163, 185, 207

Control:

central, 196–198

impact of computers, 207–209

by management, 148

Copier, 7, 111, 124–125

Copyright, 263–264

CP/M, Control Program for Microcomputers, 49–50

CPM, Critical Path Method, 86, 169, 235

Crime, 192, 247–264

Current, *see* Power supply

Cursor, 126

Customer satisfaction, 145–146

Daisy wheel printer, 44

Data base management system, 92, 101–103, 148, 151, 156, 164

small scale, 106

Decentralization, 17, 252

Decision tree model, 66, 71–74

Dehumanization 129–130

Deletion, in word processing, 126
Descriptors, 168
Desktop computers, 4, 14, 158, 161, 166, 214
Discretion, 130, 218–219
Disk, 257
  hard, 35, 37–38
  shared, 24–25
Diskettes, 35–37, 114, 257
Documentation, 146–147, 163, 256
Document search, *see* Search
Dot matrix printing, 43–44

EAROM, 34
Econometric model, 66, 69–71
Electronic mail, 117–118
Employee satisfaction, 220–228
EPROM, 34
Estimation of costs, 148–149
Evaluation, 11, 147, 163
Expansion, in implementation, 245–246
Experiment, in implementation, 245

Fiber-optics, 117
Field:
  in a record structure, 93–95, 161, 179, 258
  sort, 97
Financial statement model, 66–69
Flextime, 166, 226
Flow model, 71–74
Formatting, in word processing, 126
Fortran, 46, 51–52
Furniture, 133–135, 225–226

GPSS, (General Purpose Simulation Software), 72
Graphics, 46, 53–54, 171

Hard disk, *see* Disk
Heat, 131–132
Home computeritis, 216

Implementation, 230–246
Incentives, 165, 227
Incremental approach to implementation, 233–246
Information:
  entry and display, 41–46
  processing, 21, 30–33
  transmission, 38–41, 50–51
Ink jet printing, 44
Insertion, in word processing, 126
Installation, 239–240
Instruction sets, 30–31
Introducing computers, in implementation, 243–245
Inventory, 3, 57, 67, 143–144, 148–149, 187, 256–257
  model, 87–89
Investment, 57–104
Iteration, 72

Job enrichment, 15, 220–228

Lap computer, 23
Liability, 262–264
Light, 133
Linear model, 66, 84–85

Mail, *see* Electronic mail
Mailing lists, 106
Maintenance, 158
Management style, 190–192
Market strategy model, 66, 83–84, 149
Measurement, 153–157, 166
Megacomputer, 196
Memory:
  bubble, 34, 38
  primary, 21, 33–34
  secondary storage, 34–38
Middle management, 217–219
Mini-central organizational structure, 200
Minicomputer 26–27, 99
Modem, 40–41, 117–118
Morale, 15, 109, 145, 186, 212–213, 230

Motivation, 8, 15, 145, 165, 261
Multi-user systems, 23–26, 29, 49
Multi-vendor organizational structure, 201–203

NAPLPS, North American Presentation-Level-Protocol Syntax, 52–53
Networks, 6–7, 169–170, 245–246

Office automation, 14, 110–136, 151, 215, 225
Open routine tasks, 211
Operating systems, 47, 49–50
Organizational structure, 10–11, 14, 165, 195–212, 255–259

Parallel communication, 39
PASCAL, 46, 51–52
Passwords, 259–260
PERT, Program Evaluation and Review Technique 86–235
Piracy, 263–264
Planning effects, 206–207, 235
PLATO, Control Data Corporation, 170
Power supply, 132, 176, 250–252
Prediction, 67–78
Printers, 42–46, 135
Privacy, 264
Process control, 107–109
Productivity, 4, 7, 152–171, 176, 187, 212, 227
PROM, programmable read-only memory, 34

Quality, 145–146, 157, 201

RAM (random access memory), 33–34, 38
Records:
    organization, 146–147
    random and sequential access, 93–94
    storage, 7
Resource management, 105–106

Retrieval, 4, 99–100
Risk, 17, 248–264
ROM, read-only memory, 34
RS-232-C, 39–41, 108

Sabotage, 248, 253–254
Sampling model, 66, 79–80
Scanner, optical, 96, 124
Scheduling, 66, 85–87, 121
Search:
    for documents, 167–168
    in records management, 99–100
    in word processing, 126
Secretary, 120–123, 129–130, 140–141, 223–224
Security, 247–264
Selection model, 84–89
Semiconductor technology, 5, 32–33
Serial communication, 38–41
Single-vendor organizational structure, 200–201
Software, 6, 8, 21–22, 46–53, 159–161, 236, 239
    applications, 13
    crime, 254, 257–258
    executive support, 127–128
    failure, 15, 176, 180–184, 186–187, 189–193
    languages, 51–52
    packages, 63–65
    piracy or theft, 263–264
    records management, 103–107
    spreadsheet, 47, 61–63, 67–89
    user-friendly, 161, 228–229
    word processing, 125–127
Sort, 96–98
Source, The, 169
Specification, 8, 176, 237
Spreadsheet, 47, 61–63, 67–89
Statistical:
    analysis, 63–64, 80, 164
    Analysis System (SAS), 64
    Package for the Social Sciences (SPSS), 64

Supervision, impact of computers on,
    209

Tape, 35–36, 257
Task analysis, 166–167
Telecommunication, 7, 29, 39–41, 50–
    51, 115–120, 132–133, 185, 196, 261–
    262
Telephone, 40–41, 117–118, 123, 132–
    133, 180
Terminal:
    dumb, 6, 42
    video display, 42–43
Theft, 252–253
Time-sharing, 169–170, 184
    organizational structure, 198–200
T-Maker, 61, 156

Training, 3, 8, 170–171, 226–227
Transition:
    in implementation, 240–241
    preparation in implementation, 238–
    239

User-friendly, 161, 228
Users' groups 228

Vandalism, 248
Visicalc, 61, 156
Voice recognition, 96

Word processing, 3, 51, 114, 125–127,
    140–142
Work station, 4, 116, 120–124, 126–128,
    134–135